Sister Kenny

The woman who invented herself

Allan Hildon

ISBN:978-1-5272-5885-3

for

Steven Pryke
and
Josephine McKinnon

CONTENTS

Bibliography 159

About the Author 162

FOREWORD

When I commenced a masters degree in public health at the University of Sydney in 1995 my mother gave me a copy of Victor Cohn's biography of Kenny – *Sister Elizabeth Kenny; The Woman Who Challenged The Doctors*. She thought it would appeal to my new found interest in scholastic pursuits. I was astonished that as a qualified nurse and an early beneficiary of Jonas Salk's vaccine I had no knowledge of Kenny or the polemic she attracted. And, in no small way, embarrassed at how little I knew about the history of the polio epidemics which swept Australia and America in the early twentieth century. I was also seduced by Cohn's eloquent portrayal of a troubled and enigmatic woman. I decided to use her story as the subject of an assignment on the history of public health. My take on the Kenny in 1995 reflected the received wisdom that she had fallen foul of the medical profession's intolerance of threats to its dominance of health care occupations. The essay earned a distinction and I was delighted. Job done, my attention then switched to the next assessment deadline in my course.

As I pursued my new career in public health I occasionally reflected on the disappearance of Elizabeth Kenny from the collective consciousness in Australia. Slowly my thoughts turned to the plausibility of a story which may just have been too good to be true. Had I fallen into the trap of approaching the Kenny saga as a black box, a mystery so complex it was best taken at face value? Should I let sleeping dogs lie? Eventually, my decision to explore the Kenny treatment controversy in more detail was driven as much by curiosity about her as a person as my professional interest in the social history of epidemic diseases. At the time I could not imagine that I would devote the next two decades of my life to investigating the source and meaning of the Kenny treatment discovery legend.

The academic journey which led to the production of this book has not followed a conventional course. I emigrated to the United Kingdom in 1999, reversing the journey my father made in the early 1950s. In 2003 I was excited to obtain an academic appointment at the University of Essex – a job that I only imagined in my dreams. After six years of teaching and nurturing the academic development of NHS healthcare managers and public health students I craved for a project that would satisfy my own intellectual curiosity. My initial intention was to write a biography of

Kenny's life, but I lacked the confidence to undertake historical research and held idiosyncratic views about the purpose of biography. I couldn't see the point of a writing a biography which simply filled in the gaps. I held the view, expressed so well by Jamie James, that a biography which is a compendium of facts, dates, and dalliances, leaves the subject *'as dead at the end of the book as he was when the reader picked it up'*. I valued biographies that dared to speculate, challenge preconceptions, and reveal a dialogue between the biographer and their subject, deceased or living. The problem was, I knew a lot about epidemiology and clinical governance, but not much about biographical research. As I was fond of saying to my students, the solution to the impasse would be found by starting with something I knew.

In 2009 I secured a small research grant which enabled me to visit the Minnesota History Center in St Paul, Minnesota, home of the world's largest archive of Kenny records and documents. I naively assumed that the documents would reveal their own story to me even though I had no clear plan for exploring the contents of nine large archive boxes. Visiting the Minnesota History Center Library was a transformative experience. No-one forgets their first encounter with original historical documents – the primary sources as historians nobly entitle them. I barely noticed the monastic discomfort of the reading room as I delved through letters, reports, photographs, and press cuttings, many in parlous physical condition. I returned to UK dazzled by the potential for a new appraisal of Sister Kenny and set to work drafting two essays and a paper which I presented at the Australia and New Zealand Society for the History of Medicine conference in Brisbane in 2011. After this burst of enthusiasm I lost momentum as I lacked a clear sense of direction and a structure for my research.

Rescue came in a chance conversation with Professor Mike Roper, a fellow member of academic staff at the University of Essex and an *expat Aussie*. Mike's suggestion that I pursue my research as a PhD project was to be the best advice I could receive. Whilst a PhD project would place restrictions on the scope of the project and the style of my writing, it provided a framework for developing my academic skills and processing the findings of my enquiries. I firmly believe that the thesis which provides the foundation for this book would not have been possible without Mike's patient and inspiring supervision.

I would also like to acknowledge the support and generosity of the many people I have encountered who held a shared interest in the Kenny legend or found joy in helping others in their research endeavors. I am grateful for the encouragement of Naomi Rogers who helped to guide my early reading, and Wade Alexander for sharing the unabridged first draft of his biography of Kenny. I am indebted to Sue Hoyte at the Sister Kenny Institute in Minneapolis for introducing me to Margaret Ernest in 2009. Margaret was

Kenny's personal secretary from 1940 to 1945. Meeting Margaret was a great privilege. And, how could I not mention the lunch with Phyllis Beetsch where she shared hilarious anecdotes about her father, Victor Cohn. *'It's only life'* still brings a smile to my lips. I must include my gratitude to local historians in the Clifton district – Joy King, Shirley Murray, and volunteers at the Clifton Museum – for sharing their knowledge of Kenny's life in Clifton, and to the staff of the Gale Family Library for their expert guidance on navigating the extensive archive of Elizabeth Kenny papers. Lastly, I owe a special thanks to my fellow *Kenny tragics*, notably Graeme Tessier and Lachlan Madsen, for their encouragement and critical feedback over the past decade.

It is often said that all biography is autobiography. I would broaden that claim to say all research is autobiographical. I have no issue with recognising and representing the I in history or biography, but I accept that embracing subjectivity in biographical writing can be fraught with challenges. This book, and the research which led to its production, is an expression of my evolving sense of Elizabeth Kenny as a person. Whilst it is, to the best of my knowledge, factually accurate, there is an inevitable bias in the choice of material to include and exclude, and a bias which arises from my interpretation of the surviving record of her life. History is not what we know, it's what we think about what we know.

This book sets out an explanation in my own voice for the single most neglected aspect of the polio treatment controversy which engulfed the industrialized nations in the mid twentieth century: why does our understanding of the aetiology of a disputed therapy for a viral disease, for which there is no pharmacological cure, rest on a story which Elizabeth Kenny told in the last decade of her life? The exploration of this beguiling conundrum provides an opportunity to examine the processes underpinning the development of scientific knowledge, and, in the words of Albert Hunter and John Brewer, to demonstrate the ability of individuals to *'rise above their social and historical conditions and, by exercising will, to alter the course of their own lives, the course of events, and ultimately the course of history.'*

INTRODUCTION

Imagine a world in which epidemics of an incurable, painful, and debilitating viral disease are sweeping unpredictably and uncontrollably through the richest and most scientifically advanced nations. Would a fearful public expect health authorities to condemn an apparently effective treatment because its discoverer can't explain why their therapy is more effective than conventional medical care which, by the way, is ineffective and cruel? And, if the individuals most affected by this disease are children, would their parents be comforted by reassurances from medical practitioners and researchers that they were abiding by the time-honored maxim *first do no harm* as they diligently tested and evaluated emerging therapies? Or, would those parents prefer doctors to abide by the equally time-honored maxim *for God's sake, do something!*

As it happens, little imagination is required to consider these questions – one need go no further than the controversy which accompanied the treatment of poliomyelitis before the advent of mass immunization. For more than twenty years medical practitioners in Australia, the United States, and the United Kingdom contested the efficacy of a therapy for poliomyelitis which was promoted by a retired Australian army nurse who called herself Sister Kenny. Kenny's opposition to conventional medical practices, especially the prolonged use of plaster casts and metal splints, won her few supporters in Australia and the United Kingdom. Those medical practitioners who were prepared to overlook her ignorance of the pathology of the disease and give her the benefit of the doubt were often discouraged by her acerbic tongue and intolerance of criticism. Nonetheless, her dogged determination, talent for self-promotion, and her astute cultivation of political support eventually resulted in a grudging acceptance of her therapeutic techniques in her home State of Queensland. Most medical practitioners outside of Queensland dismissed her as a quack or a plagiarist.

The advent of the Second World War proved to be a turning point in her career. Spurred on by a generous grant from the Queensland Government, and her exasperation with the Australian medical establishment, Kenny took her campaign to America where her ideas were received with more enthusiasm. Her unstinting commitment to polio rehabilitation earned her fame and respect from the American public.

Today, Kenny is still fondly remembered in Minneapolis and acknowledged as a pioneer in the field of rehabilitation medicine. In Australia, she is largely forgotten except among a small number of nurse historians and the dwindling ranks of polio survivors.

Whilst the rancor and controversy associated with the treatment of polio in the pre-vaccine era has faded from living memory, the story of Elizabeth Kenny's twenty years campaign to convince a doubting medical establishment of the superiority of her method for treating polio remains one of the great medical legends of the twentieth century. In the legend, Kenny is depicted as a lone maverick who confronts a belligerent medical establishment, and in doing so demonstrates that truth will, in the long run, always prevail over professional self-interest. The story of Kenny's first encounter with polio in the Australian outback lies at the core of the legend. The essence of the story is captured in a newspaper article published in 2009 in the Australian city of Brisbane.

> *In 1909, a young Darling Downs lass called Elizabeth Kenny, aged just 23, made what appeared to be a remarkable breakthrough. The unqualified bush nurse, the daughter of an Irish vet who migrated to NSW, was handed an infant girl in agony from twisted limbs. She was at a loss about the mysterious ailment the girl's father called cow disease. Kenny saddled up and rode to the nearest telegraph station where she cabled a doctor friend, who diagnosed infantile paralysis and informed her nothing could be done. Undeterred, she applied warm, moist strips of cloth. The next morning the girl's limbs were better. Authorities tried to debunk the method, but after it was endorsed by US experts, her fame took off.[1]*

The story also remains alive in the collective memory of the citizens of Minneapolis in America. In 2004, Adam Wirtzfeld, an illustrator and visual storyteller, created a comic book biography of Kenny for the annual Lutefisk Sushi Exhibition. Wirtzfeld based his comic on Kenny's memoir and Victor Cohn's biography.

The story has a naive charm, which may account for its longevity, but, in the parlance of the antiques trade, it suffers from a dodgy provenance. Whilst there is evidence that Kenny treated children with longstanding paralysis during the 1920s, there is only the flimsiest evidence that she treated polio patients prior to the 1930s. Furthermore, there is no record of the story prior to its publication in American in 1940. Despite the absence of corroboration to the claims Kenny made in America in the 1940s almost every historical analysis of the Kenny polio treatment controversy starts with the assumption that Kenny discovered or developed her concepts for treating polio whilst working alone in rural Australia prior to the WW1. Kerry Highley, an Australian researcher, is the sole dissenting voice. Highley suggests that Kenny probably developed her therapeutic approach while treating paralysis patients in the 1920s, but she does not explore the relevance of her observation to claims which Kenny made about the development of her therapeutic techniques.[2]

Sister Kenny treating children with infantile paralysis. Adam Wirtzfeld.

The historical study of the acrimony which Kenny encountered in her transnational campaign to change the treatment of polio has justifiably focused on the clinical efficacy of her therapeutic techniques and the social significance of her challenge to medical authority. But, for reasons which I will explore later in this book, it is the story of Kenny's discovery which has taunted my curiosity and preoccupied my scholarship for the past two decades. Despite my initial uncritical acceptance of the Kenny legend, the more I investigated the constituents of Kenny's treatment discovery story the more I grew to question its veracity and its authenticity.

The mystery surrounding the origins of Kenny's treatment discovery story deepened as a result of the launch in 2008 of Trove, an online digital archive developed by the National Library of Australia. The archive of Australian newspapers which may be accessed through Trove allows researchers unprecedented access to the public discourse within Australia in the first half of the twentieth century. My exploration of the Trove database revealed evidence that the treatment discovery story is probably recycled from an earlier story associated with Kenny's life which is entirely unconnected with the treatment of children with poliomyelitis. The significance of the implications of this narrative anachronism on our understanding of one of the great medical polemics of the twentieth century cannot be overstated.

Polio – the arrow that flieth in the dark

To understand the Kenny story one first needs to understand polio. Polio is an abbreviation of *anterior poliomyelitis*, so named because the disease affects the anterior section of the spinal cord. Polio is a viral infection which is thought to have been silently endemic throughout the world for thousands of years. The distortion to limbs which may occur in an acute case is so characteristic it is thought that a case is depicted in an ancient Egyptian funereal stele. The first clinical description of the symptoms of polio in a medical text did not occur until 1789. The disease has also been known as infantile paralysis as it most often occurs in children, or as Heine-Medin disease in honor of Jakob Heine and Karl Oskar Medin who are credited as the first physicians to comprehensively describe the disease.[3] Small, localized, and apparently random outbreaks of the disease were recorded in Western Europe and in the United States throughout the second half of the nineteenth century. In the early decades of the twentieth century these localized outbreaks were replaced by epidemics of increasing size and intensity in the United States, Canada, and Australia, and to a lesser extent the United Kingdom. Paradoxically, healthy and well-nourished children appeared to be most at risk of acquiring the infection. Most cases occur in children, and most cases are limited to a short episode of fever, but in its acute form the disease can cause death or result in severe disability.

Ironically, some might say cruelly, polio only emerged as a public health menace as improved sanitation impeded the acquisition of natural immunity through childhood exposure. The paradox of polio being more prevalent in populations with low rates of infectious diseases and low rates of infant mortality is illustrated in Figure 1.[4] This paradox baffled medical scientists for decades. The impact of natural immunity on the epidemiologic profile of polio was not understood in the nineteenth century. In 1908 Ivan Wickman, a Swedish medical practitioner, realized the epidemic character of outbreaks was triggered by a reduction in natural immunity due to improved sanitation. Wickman had the insight to realize that many children would experience a mild infection which would leave them with an acquired immunity. Children who did not acquire a natural immunity would be left more vulnerable to a more serious infection in later life. Polio epidemics were occurring because improved sanitation was reducing the likelihood of children acquiring a natural immunity. Regrettably, Wickman died soon after publishing his findings in a Swedish medical journal. It would be nearly thirty years before his ideas were appreciated in English speaking countries.

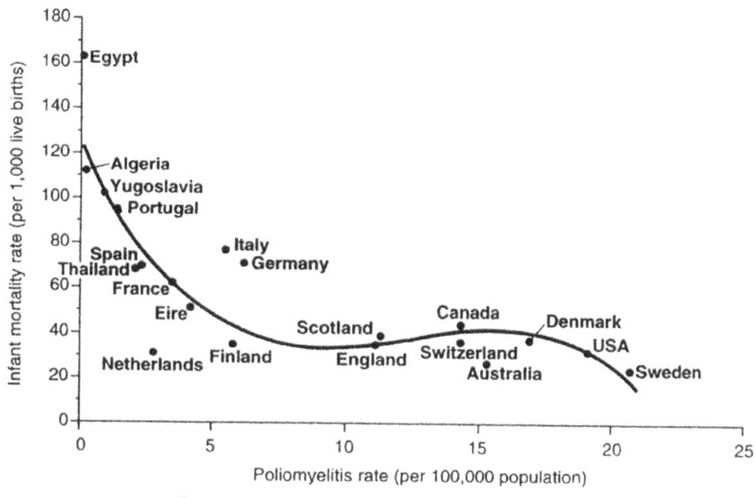

Fig. 1 Global expansion of poliomyelitis 1921-1955

The so-called polio paradox still attracts conjecture in the current era. Richard Bruno, a specialist in psychophysiology, offers a superficial analysis of the epidemics in New York in 1916 and Amsterdam in 1943 as evidence that the polio paradox does not exist, but his conclusion is not supported by experts in the study of epidemic disease. The emergence of the twentieth century polio pandemic fundamentally challenged beliefs about sanitation and disease prevention and befuddled the best efforts of scientists to develop a cure or an effective therapy for its debilitating after-effects.[5]

It is difficult to assess the true scale of the devastation caused by poliomyelitis as the quality and extent of public health surveillance varied enormously in the countries where the prevalence of the disease was thought to be highest. The epidemiologic profile of polio in Australia is relatively well documented as the routine surveillance of infectious diseases commenced early in the twentieth century. Major outbreaks in Australia in 1905 and America in 1916 were followed by outbreaks of varying size and frequency between 1917 and 1965. Most cases occurred in children under five years of age, and there was a slightly higher prevalence in males and in urban areas.[6]

Surveillance records indicate that despite Australia's small population at least 26,000 people were diagnosed with the most severe paralytic form of polio between 1917 and 1960. This may very likely be an underestimate of the real number of cases. The proportion left with residual paralysis is unknown. In 1958 American researchers estimated that approximately 300,000-350,000 people in the United States were stricken with the paralytic form of the disease between 1947 and 1956, leaving around 50,000 with severe residual crippling.[7] The number of cases in America since the first major outbreak in New York in 1916 could easily be in the millions. It is not surprising that the Pulitzer Prize winning author, David Oshinsky, claims that, from an American perspective, polio was one of the most feared diseases of the twentieth century.[8]

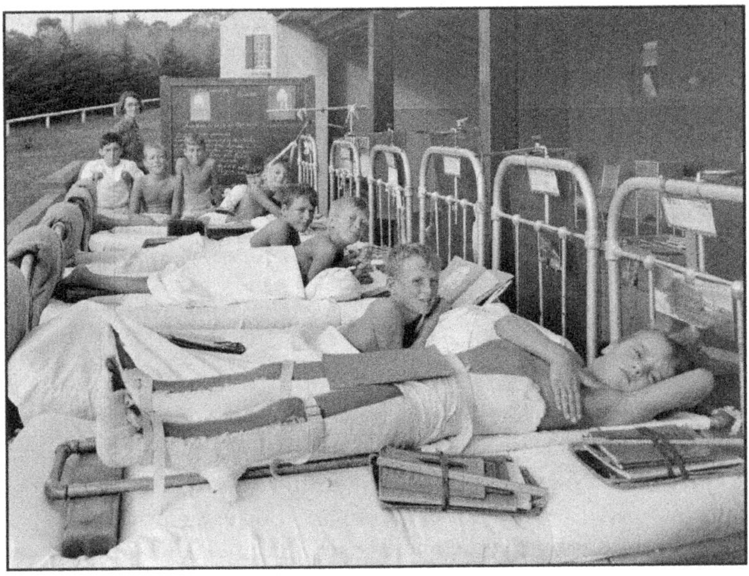

Polio ward, Frankston Children's Hospital, 1936. State Library of Victoria.

The therapeutic regime which Elizabeth Kenny developed in the mid-1930s attracted widespread and heated opposition from the medical establishment in Australia, but this opposition was an edifice built on feeble foundations. Prior to Kenny's campaign medical science had endorsed the use of electrotherapy, blistering, ice baths, injections of urotropin, nasal sprays, encasement in plaster casts, and the injection of human convalescent serum to treat or prevent polio. All these remedies were useless, some were plainly barbaric, and most were the scientific equivalent of witchcraft. The long term immobilisation of paralyzed limbs in metal splints and plaster casts, was emblematic of the orthodox medical concept of the disease and its treatment. The noted American historian and polio researcher, John Paul, claimed that by the 1940s the prolonged use of immobilisation had acquired the status of a medical fetish.

Despite the potential for residual crippling, most people in the current era, even students of public health, may find it difficult to appreciate why polio was such a feared disease – it was, after all, a relatively uncommon infectious disease with a low death rate. In most years between 1905 and 1955 there were around 200 cases per year in Australia. The largest outbreak in Australia occurred in 1938, with 2698 cases of polio notified for the whole country. In the same year there were 8,831 cases of diphtheria, 5,932 cases of scarlet fever, and 3,572 cases of pulmonary tuberculosis.[9] All these diseases had a higher death rate than polio and all were associated with serious residual debilities. Polio generated fear because it was:

Unpredictable – in the early decades of the twentieth century there was insufficient knowledge of the transmission of the polio virus to understand why a disease which was usually diagnosed in a small number of scattered cases would suddenly erupt into a large outbreak. As an example – in the Australian State of Victoria there were a total of 1564 reported cases between 1917 and 1937, representing an average of 20 cases per year. In 1938 there were 1369 cases. Health authorities had no idea why this occurred. Public anxiety was also fueled by the unpredictable outcome of polio infection – some children died within a few days, most recovered fully, and some were left with crippling deformities.

Uncontrollable – public confidence in medical science had been built on the success of public sanitation in eradicating or controlling many bacterial and microbial infectious diseases, but this confidence was undermined by the inability of sanitation and quarantine to control outbreaks of polio. Polio also contributed to a decline in public confidence in scientific medicine as early hubris among medical researchers was replaced by dismay at the lack of progress in the development of a cure or a vaccine. Simon Flexner, the celebrated American virologist, claimed in 1911 '*the achievement of a cure, I may conservatively say, is not now far distant*'.[10] Flexner spoke in haste and would be dead for decade before the long-awaited vaccine would be ready for use.

Indiscriminate – one of the most disturbing features of polio was the apparent indiscriminate way it appeared to *choose* its victims. Many diseases have traditionally been associated with social or personal characteristics, but polio affected rich and poor alike. Polio was thought to be indiscriminate because, contrary to accepted wisdom, the healthy and well-nourished children from *good* families and communities appeared to be more susceptible than children who lived in dirty, impoverished, and *undesirable* communities. As Naomi Rogers, Professor of History at Yale University, deftly observes '*The notion that dirt could protect a child from disease was thoroughly alien to all conventional etiological explanations of the working of disease*'.[11]

Irrational – the unpredictable, uncontrollable, and indiscriminate nature of polio created a perfect existential storm which positioned polio as the embodiment of the absurdity of random and meaningless disease. The horror of the absurdity and irrationality of polio is eloquently described by Charles Mee, a polio survivor who contracted polio in 1952 at the age of fourteen:

> *If there is no rational cause for what befalls us, if luck can begin and change and end our lives, then nothing lies beneath our feet but an abyss of complete meaninglessness: no pattern, no design, no logic, no coherence, nothing to count on, nothing to understand and master, no program to get with, no hope to share our destinies. If this is true, then we are all absolutely vulnerable – and to accept that is horrifying* [12]

Making sense of the incomprehensible

The aphorism *nature abhors a vacuum* may be used to explain why, in the absence of a scientific explanation, individuals search for alternative explanations of the human experience of disease. For millennia the most common explanations for disease drew inspiration from theological or supernatural beliefs. The discovery of disease-causing microorganisms and pathogens in the nineteenth century introduced the era of scientific medicine and the framing of health as an absence of disease. In the current era, where infectious diseases are rare, individuals are increasingly likely to understand their experience of illness through narrative concepts. In a later chapter I will explore the role of metaphor and narrative in communicating, explaining, and shaping the personal experience and scientific investigation of disease, but for now it is enough to explore the importance of metaphor in portraying the public and the scientific understanding of polio in the pre-vaccine era.

Every aspect of the polio pandemic was understood through metaphor. Doctors engaged in a battle to defeat polio. People who campaigned for improved treatment of polio victims were crusaders. Scientists raced to develop a vaccine, and the vaccines, when they were finally available, were hailed as a miracle. Many of the metaphors associated with polio are not unique to the disease, but two groups of metaphors are deserving of closer examination due to their prominence in the polio corpus. These are the metaphors of *illness is a being* and *medicine is war*.

The *illness is a being* metaphor assigns human or animal attributes – such as stealth, heartlessness or maliciousness – to the disease. The prominence of the *illness is a being* metaphor in the polio literature relies as much on the historical context of the epidemics as the unpredictable behavior of the disease. The discovery in the nineteenth century of the link between infectious disease and microorganisms undermined centuries old beliefs that epidemics of diseases were attributable to divine intervention or other supernatural forces. Prior to the advent of scientific medicine epidemic disease had been attributed to '*comets, earthquakes, storms, and other absurd causes, and even to the poisoning of wells by Jews'.*[13] The success of medical science in the late nineteenth century in revealing the biological causes of many epidemic diseases created an opportunity to produce metaphors which could explain the transmission of diseases which were bacterial in origin. When new viral diseases emerged, which did not conform to the expected behavior of bacterial diseases, further refinement of the metaphors of disease were required to explain these new threats.

In 1947 the National Foundation for Infantile Paralysis (NFIP) produced a short film, *In Daily Battle*, which portrays polio as a shadowy demonic entity which hovers over communities seeking out its victims. The portrayal of polio as a supernatural being with the figurative form of a shadow was more than a clever cinematic visual effect, it was an example of a powerful non-literary metaphor with historical foundations which had political and cultural resonance in the mid twentieth century. The use of shadow as a metaphor for death or for the soul of the deceased has its origins in ancient Greek culture. In the twentieth century shadow was frequently used as a metaphor for the menace presented by the Nazis during the WW2, and by the Soviet Union during the Cold War era. The *illness is a being* metaphor was ideally suited to polio because it helped to explain the irregular pattern of outbreaks and the unpredictable outcomes of infection. Polio, like humans, could be capricious.

The pervasiveness of the *illness is a being* metaphor in polio narratives may also represent the reawakening of a narrative understanding of health and illness in the industrialized nations which were most affected by polio. Jack Coulehan, a medical practitioner who worked with a Navajo community in northern Arizona, argues that a scientific view of illness as a purely physiological process fails to appreciate that people see themselves as characters in a life story and understand their illnesses in a narrative way.[14] If physicians ignore or devalue that narrative, then health care is bound to suffer, and medicine is dehumanized. The corollary to this proposition is that using benign rather than malign metaphors for illness may serve an empowering purpose by placing emphasis on the relationship between the individual and illness which enables illness to be understood in human terms even if the characteristics are not necessarily benevolent. This personalized approach to illness is exemplified by the current trend for people to consider illness as a personal experience rather than seeing disease as an invader.

The most prominent conceptual metaphor in the polio corpus is the *medicine is war* metaphor. The *medicine is war* metaphor frames the disease as an enemy which must be defeated through battle. The ubiquity of war metaphors in the polio corpus arises from several interconnecting factors. First, the polio corpus overwhelmingly portrays an American experience of the disease and reflects narratives which are embedded in American culture.

Few non-American voices are represented in the sizeable body of survivor memoirs or the academic appraisal of the cultural response to polio in the twentieth century. *A Summer Plague*, by Tony Gould, is a rare example of a memoir written by a polio survivor who is not American. Gould contracted polio as a young man while serving in the British Army in Malaya. Daniel Wilson, an American polio, draws on the testimony of 150 polio survivors to argue that the unique epidemiologic profile of polio meant that middle class American families were the most susceptible to the disease. Wilson observes that polio challenged public faith in the ability of science to eradicate disease, and undermined public confidence that the American dream of peace, progress, and prosperity was within the grasp of ordinary families.[15] By adopting a rhetoric of war in the face of this existential threat Americans could show the world that they would not submit passively to the tyranny of a virus.

War metaphors are also prominent in the polio corpus due to the enormous influence of polio's most recognized victim; Franklin D. Roosevelt, President of the United States of America from 1933 to 1945. Roosevelt employed the rhetoric of war against polio throughout his political career for the benefit of fundraising and his presidential campaigning. Ironically, the recent retrospective analysis of Roosevelt's medical records suggests that his paralysis was probably not caused by polio. In 1944 Roosevelt published an open letter which unmistakably frames the eradication of polio as a war.

> *Not until we have removed the shadow of the Crippler from the future of every child can we furl the flags of battle and still the trumpets of attack. The fight against infantile paralysis is a fight to the finish, and the terms are unconditional surrender.*[16]

These words were skillfully crafted by Roosevelt to exploit growing public confidence that victory was within reach in Europe and the Pacific due to America's intervention in the WW2. Roosevelt's words were unambiguous; if America could win the war against fascism, it could win the war against polio.

The final critical element in the pervasiveness of war metaphors is the role of the NFIP in framing the American response to the care of polio patients and the development of the polio vaccines. The NFIP was established by Roosevelt and his former law partner, Basil O'Connor, in 1938. O'Connor's plan was straightforward; emphasize the threat of polio to innocent children, collect small donations from a lot of people, and fund medical research to find a cure. O'Connor's plan proved to be pure genius; the NFIP became the largest single philanthropic charity that has ever existed. Oshinsky observes that O'Connor's framing of polio as *'uniquely dangerous on the one hand, eminently beatable on the other'* made the defeat of polio

'America's greatest medical crusade'.[17]

Whilst there is widespread agreement that fundraising and the dissemination of public health propaganda in the United States was assisted by the exploitation of metaphors of war their use was not universally beneficial to the lived experience of polio patients. Gary Reisfield and George Wilson observe that war metaphors resonate with many patients and physicians, but also observe that they are *'inherently masculine, power-based, paternalistic, and violent'* and are of little value to patients who do not cope with illness or adversity through confrontation.[18] The negative implications of the cultural framing of patients as victims or casualties, and the medical profession as generals or heroic warriors, has been discussed in a number of polio memoirs. Recently it has been argued that using military metaphors to frame patient experiences of diseases which are degenerative or incurable may be counterproductive as the war will inevitably be lost. This observation is especially salient to polio given the absence of a cure, and the emergence of post-polio syndrome for the long-term survivors of polio.

A new approach from an unlikely source

The current conventional treatment for the debilitating effects of all stages of poliomyelitis is a refinement of techniques promoted by Elizabeth Kenny during the 1930s and 1940s.[19] Whilst Kenny's approach to physical therapy is conventional in the current era, in the 1930s many Australian medical practitioners considered it to be ineffective and potentially harmful. Three official government inquiries in Australia between 1934 and 1938 concluded her methods were no better than conventional medical care and unjustifiably expensive. In part, opposition to Kenny's approach to the treatment of paralysis derived from its unlikely provenance.

Elizabeth Kenny was born in Warialda, New South Wales, in 1880. She had very little formal education, and no recognized nurse qualifications. As a young woman she occasionally worked as a bush nurse in the Darling Downs region of Queensland, and despite having no nurse training she opened her own private hospital in the town of Clifton in 1912. During WW1 she served with the Australian Army Nursing Service (AANS), earning the rank of Sister. Kenny was unable to work as a Registered Nurse after the war as she lacked the qualifications required for nurse registration, but she retained the title Sister for the rest of her life.

In 1922 she found employment as a private nurse for Daphne Cregan, a child who suffered from a crippling form of cerebral palsy. For three years Kenny treated Cregan's muscle paralysis with a regime of hot sulphur baths, massage, exercise, and nocturnal immobilisation with bark splints.[20] The extent of Cregan's apparent recovery earned Kenny a reputation within her local community as a healer of crippled children. Nonetheless, despite episodic involvement in the care of a small number of crippled children during the 1920s, she showed no interest in sharing her concept of the treatment of paralysis or developing a career in the rehabilitation of disabled children.

The Elizabeth Kenny Clinic, George Street, Brisbane, 1935. Trove NLA.

Kenny's first opportunity to demonstrate her rehabilitation methods to a wider audience came in 1932 when Queensland experienced the largest outbreak of infantile paralysis since records began. The owner of the Queen's Hotel in Townsville allowed Kenny to conduct a clinic in the hotel for children with various forms of paralysis. Although Kenny had not treated acute cases of polio, her apparent success in treating children with long term paralysis offered a glimmer of hope to parents who were growing impatient at the lack of progress in the development of treatments for the disease. The therapy was laborious but required little specialised equipment. Her techniques quickly gained public approval and political support in Queensland, but prominent members of the Australian medical establishment disputed the aetiology and clinical effectiveness of her techniques even though they were not especially radical. Her opposition to the prolonged use of immobilisation was the feature which set her therapy apart from conventional practice and garnered disapprobation from medical practitioners. An official evaluation of the Townsville clinic in 1934 concluded her techniques produced results no better than conventional methods.[21]

The gradual evolution of her techniques, and the language she used to describe her concept of the disease, did little to assuage entrenched medical scepticism in Australia. The report of the Queensland Royal Commission on Modern Methods for the Treatment of Infantile Paralysis, published in 1938, was harshly critical of her techniques. Despite the lack of medical endorsement, Kenny received substantial political patronage in her home

State of Queensland. By the end of the 1930s, government sponsored clinics utilising Kenny's methods were established in most State capital cities. These so-called *Kenny Clinics* received broad public support and have been claimed to represent the most significant, albeit short-lived, challenge to medical dominance of health care in Australia during the twentieth century.

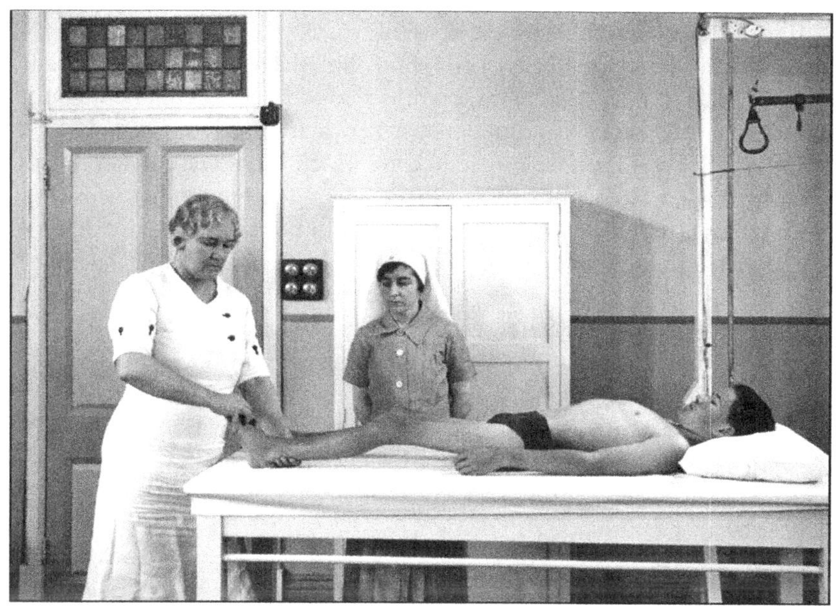

Elizabeth Kenny examining a patient. Sydney, 1939. Trove NLA.

Sister Kenny was a household name in Australia in the late 1930s. During the devastating outbreak in the summer of 1937/38 Kenny was quoted or cited in several thousand news articles published in Australian newspapers, but the rapid decline in cases after the 1937/38 outbreaks, and the advent of the WW2 in 1939, diverted public and political attention from Kenny and her clinics. In 1940 the Queensland Minister for Health and Home affairs encouraged the Queensland Premier to provide funds which would allow Kenny to take her campaign to the United States in the hope of finding a more receptive response from American medical practitioners. Their altruism was underpinned by a desire to rid themselves of a quarrelsome champion of a therapy which was expensive to administer and deeply resented by the medical establishment.

Kenny's journey to America proved to be her salvation. Within months of arriving in Minneapolis her approach to treatment was endorsed by respected medical practitioners, and her work was being sponsored by the NFIP, America's most influential polio charity. In 1941 the NFIP officially endorsed the Kenny method as the most effective system for the treatment of polio. Kenny's techniques for treating paralysis, and her concept of the pathology of the disease, were not universally accepted by the American medical profession, but she is recognized as having made a profound impact on the treatment of paralytic polio and the rehabilitation of patients with paralysis. John Paul claimed Kenny was pivotal in producing an *'about-face in the aftercare of paralytic poliomyelitis'*.[22]

It is difficult to overstate the esteem in which she was held by the American public. Kenny was visited by the American Consul on her death bed in Toowoomba in 1952. His accent is said to have cheered her. Upon learning she was gravely ill admirers in America arranged for her to be administered trypsin, an experimental drug which was so rare it had to be flown from New York to Brisbane before being delivered to her bedside under police escort. The drug arrived too late to be of benefit. Her death was reported on the front page of The New York Times on 30 November 1952.

The global polio pandemic was eventually brought under control through the introduction of mass vaccination in the late-1950s. Notwithstanding the success of global polio eradication campaigns, the disease is still present in countries with ineffective vaccination programs. As the wild polio virus survives in the human population, and there is still no pharmacological cure for the disease, vaccination remains the frontline defense against future polio epidemics.

A neglected legacy

Elizabeth Kenny has been dead for more than half a century, yet the polemic associated with her contribution to the treatment of polio continues to be relevant in the twenty first century. In the early days of her polio career health care professionals were quick to dismiss her ideas and practices because her techniques lacked an empirical evidence base and her ideas were expressed in a language they did not recognize. Subsequent analyses have interpreted the response of the medical profession to Kenny and the Kenny Clinics as a case study of the medical profession's organized response to the perceived challenge to its dominance of health care professions. Little has changed in the last sixty years. When UK health authorities proposed in 2000 to allow Registered Nurses to prescribe drugs, medical leaders warned of the dire consequences of allowing nurses to perform a task which historically had been the exclusive privilege of medical practitioners. Nurses, according to the BMA, could not be trusted to prescribe drugs as they lacked the extensive training of a doctor. The BMA's warnings proved to be unfounded. Research sponsored by the Cochrane Collaboration has demonstrated that nurses are capable of the same quality of care as doctors in the primary care setting, and non-medical prescribing is now widespread in primary care settings in the UK. The objection of the medical profession to the introduction of non-medical prescribing in the United Kingdom is a contemporary example of the profession's continuing readiness to claim authority and sovereignty over other health professions even where there is no evidence to support such claims.

Polio is now largely unknown in most industrialized countries because of the success of mass vaccination programs, but it remains a disease of major public health and cultural significance. Polio has not been conquered; it has been contained through prophylaxis. Social and medical historians have documented the public euphoria which accompanied the discovery of a safe and effective vaccine in the mid-1950s, but this euphoria was based on an inflated confidence in the science which had created the vaccine, and a mistaken expectation that the philanthropy which financed the development of the vaccines could be replicated in the battle against other health scourges. Marc Shell claims there is a *conceptual misprision of polio* which conceals the inadequacies of the public health response to the disease in the post-vaccine era and discourages societal recognition of the cultural impact of the disease. [23]

For two decades Elizabeth Kenny was synonymous with the international battle against one of the most feared diseases of the twentieth century, yet she was never recommended for official honors in Australia and was denied recognition in the Polio Hall of Fame, the most important polio memorial in the United States. In the current era she is an obscure figure little known outside Queensland in Australia and Minnesota in the United States. Admittedly, Kenny's fame in the mid twentieth century was closely associated with a disease which has largely disappeared from public consciousness. Nonetheless, few Australians have achieved the level of international acclaim which Kenny attracted throughout the 1940s, so her relegation to the status of an arcane historical curiosity deserves further examination.

Unanswered Questions

Throughout her career, Kenny was unwavering in her insistence that her method of treating infantile paralysis was original and differed substantially from the broad range of therapies she collectively labelled as orthodox methods. The extent to which this view was disputed was drolly summarized in 1937 by Max Herz, an Australian orthopedic surgeon; *'the principles set down are good and new; only the good ones are not new and the new ones are not good'*. The historical and research literature shows that during the period she worked in Australia the primary focus of public and medical attention was her insistence on abandoning the excessive use of immobilisation. The origins of her method of treating polio cases was not examined by any of the official inquiries conducted during the 1930s. On the rare occasions she was asked in Australia to explain how she had developed her techniques she would state she had developed them while nursing meningitis patients on transport ships returning to Australia during WW1. An article published in The Auckland Star in 1935 reported '*she built up a method of treatment of her own, differing essentially from the orthodox treatment, and after the war she applied it with remarkable success to cases of infantile paralysis*'.[24] An article published two years later in the Australian Women's Weekly states '*From her exceptional success nursing these meningitis cases [on troop ships] germinated the idea for the method she is now using for infantile paralysis*'.[25]

Soon after arriving in the United States Kenny presented an entirely new explanation, claiming she had developed her techniques while treating children with the disease in the outback of Australia before she had any knowledge of the disease or conventional approaches to its treatment. Whilst Kenny is known to have embellished the evidence supporting the superiority of her method, the authenticity of her account of the discovery of her method has rarely been questioned. Virtually all the conjecture surrounding her claims to have discovered a new method for treating polio focuses on the issue of whether it was superior to conventional practice. The debate focusing on the origins of her method is preoccupied with the question of whether she copied her techniques and ignores the significance of the meaning or purpose of the discovery story she presented to the American public in the 1940s. The only record of a bush nurse's chance encounter with a baffling new disease is Kenny's personal testimony. There are no known witnesses, and there are no contemporaneous records which corroborate her description of this important event. Consequently, our understanding of the origins of the treatment for a viral disease for which there is no pharmacological cure rests on a story which Kenny told in the last decade of her life.

The scarcity of analysis of the origin of her method is matched by the scarcity of analysis of the rationale underpinning one of its defining features. The most distinguishing and vehemently opposed feature of the Kenny system for treating poliomyelitis was the general avoidance of the use of immobilisation, but there has been little scrutiny of why she dispensed with a therapeutic tool which she is known to have used in the treatment of paralysis cases in the 1920s. Kenny's abandonment of splinting has universally been examined from the perspective of whether it was potentially damaging to the patient. This pre-occupation with the clinical significance of immobilisation has distracted our attention from the social significance of immobilisation and our understanding of the factors which motivated her to adopt such a radical and controversial change in her techniques at such a late stage of her life – she was, after all, in her early fifties when she first took an interest in the treatment of polio.

Perhaps the most intriguing aspect of the controversy surrounding the treatment of polio is the extent to which opposition to the method was conflated with a deep and profound hostility directed towards her as a person. Kenny was a complex and confrontational person who lived in an era where women were rarely praised for self-promotion or displaying antagonism towards male hegemony. Past examinations of her life have partially acknowledged the contribution of gender bias in the response of the medical profession to Kenny's campaign, but these examinations have positioned her as an actor in a depersonalized examination of the social significance of the treatment controversy. Kenny possessed a reputation for brusqueness and appears to have had little appreciation of the wisdom of the expression *you will catch more flies with honey than vinegar*, but she was also extremely adept at exploiting the print media for the purpose of self-promotion. This conundrum suggests that something more than her antagonistic manner was underpinning the hostility which so many medical professionals directed towards her.

Through much of her adult life Kenny carefully nurtured a public identity as a woman who eschewed married life for a life of service to her community. In private she made little attempt to conceal her contempt for men and her revulsion at the prospect of marriage, but there is little evidence of her possessing any interest in the social, political, or sexual emancipation of women. Kenny was twenty-five years of age when women's suffrage was enacted in Queensland in 1905, but she does not acknowledge this historic milestone in women's civil rights in her memoir. Her adoption of a nine years old girl in 1926, when Kenny was forty six years old is sometimes seen as an indication of her interest in a conventional family life, but the adoption was primarily arranged to provide companionship for Kenny's mother while Kenny pursued her new career as the inventor of an ambulance stretcher. In the final decade of her life she abruptly retreated from her longstanding outspoken opinions on marriage when she adopted ludicrous and deceptive tactics to explain her spinsterhood and her personal sacrifice to a curious American audience.

Kerry Highley concludes her appraisal of Kenny's role in the Australian polio treatment controversy with the claim '*During her lifetime, Kenny managed to conceal everything she wished to conceal, and allowed her own history to begin with her enlistment in the First World War but, following her death, not all her secrets remained secrets*'.[26] Despite Kenny's gender role nonconformity, no published analysis of her life or work has questioned whether one of those secrets was related to her sexuality, or whether homophobia or heterosexism contributed to the opposition she encountered or influenced the conceptualization of her therapeutic techniques. In fact, there is evidence that scholars have avoided the analysis of her ambiguous sexuality and undisguised misandry, or her relationships with women known to be lesbian. Anne Finger, a cultural historian of polio, appears to be a lone voice questioning whether Kenny may have been a lesbian. Finger does not explore the issue of Kenny's sexuality directly, but her suggestion that it should be examined by the historian, Naomi Rogers, indicates that Finger believed there was credibility to the proposition.[27]

During the early 1940s Kenny had a close friendship with Mary McCarthy, the original screenwriter for the Sister Kenny film released by the RKO studio in 1946. Kenny abruptly terminated her acquaintance with McCarthy when McCarthy had a breakdown following her separation from her lesbian partner, Elizabeth '*Dickie*' Dickenson.[28] The research notes of Kenny's biographers, Victor Cohn and Wade Alexander, indicate they were aware of the closeness of Kenny's friendship with McCarthy and Dickenson, but they portray the abrupt severance of the friendship as being the result of a dispute over film credits.

Kenny's behavior throughout her adult life was paradoxical, redolent with contradictions and conundrums, and, occasionally, farcical. She also played a central role in the international quest to overcome one of the most significant threats to public health in the twentieth century. The portrayal of Kenny as an idiosyncratic footnote in the grand history of polio in the twentieth century disguises the social and historical significance of her contribution to rehabilitation medicine. This superficiality must be challenged if we are to fully appreciate whether the evolution of her approach to treating polio was an addendum to, or an artefact of, her remarkable life.

Scope and approach

A vacuum lies at the core of the Kenny treatment controversy – if she did not discover an alternative therapy for poliomyelitis whilst working as a bush nurse in rural Queensland, what was the origin and purpose of a story which has survived unchallenged for decades, and why has this story outlived the memory of the events upon which it is based? This book untangles the threads which constitute the fabric of the Kenny polio treatment discovery story to produce an alternative understanding of the story's purpose and meaning, and its contribution to the development of the Kenny system of treating paralytic poliomyelitis. The book also considers whether the professional response to the adoption of her therapeutic techniques was influenced by a covert stigmatization associated with presumed discredited personal characteristics.

The exploration of these themes is guided by the hypothesis that the development of the Elizabeth Kenny system for treating poliomyelitis is the product of her existential quest to discover meaning and fulfilment in her life. This hypothesis is grounded in three propositions. First, Kenny's nurse identity should be understood as the means to her gaining social acceptance, and a defense against social approbation, rather than a career choice based on her interest in the health and wellbeing of children. Further, the substantial body of life writing which she published in the 1940s through press releases, interviews, and her memoir, should be considered as narrative accounts of her evolving personal identity rather than the factual reporting of experiential events. And finally, her evolving concept of the treatment of polio should be understood as being grounded in her metaphorical understanding of the disease rather than being the product of empirical evidence drawn from clinical practice. These propositions will be explored in detail in following chapters.

This book breaks from convention in its approach to the analysis of historical events which possess social and scientific significance. First, I have chosen to use biographical techniques to explain, not just describe, the polemic which surrounded the treatment of polio in the mid-twentieth century. In doing so I have jettisoned many of the conventional rules of historical research which continue to dictate that the primary role of biography is to reveal the factual legacy of an individual life without assigning anachronistic or subjective interpretation to the meaning or purpose of the individual's life choices. My approach to biography unapologetically incorporates the twin heresies of subjectivity and anachronism. I wholeheartedly support the sentiment expressed by Jamie James, an author of two biographies, who claims '*If a biographer cannot find himself in his subject, then the result is a compendium of names and dates, people met and places visited—useful information, perhaps, but the subject is just as dead at the end of the book as he was when the reader picked it up*'.[29] Whilst I recognize the risks in attempting to step outside my own cultural and historical context, I believe it is possible to recognize aspects of identity and behavior which transcend time and social structures. To achieve this goal, I explicitly acknowledge the idiosyncratic beliefs and experiences I believe are shared with my subject due to my Anglo-Australian cultural heritage and my own transgressive sexual identity.[30]

As I'm happy to live by the motto, *I'd rather be skinned as a wolf than a sheep*, I'm happy to add anachronism, '*the worst of all sins, the sin that cannot be forgiven*',[31] to my list of academic misdemeanors. Anachronism is the depiction of past phenomena in terms of values, assumptions, or interpretative categories of the present day. Unlike natural and applied scientists, social scientists usually hesitate in using contemporary theoretical concepts to explain historical behavior or events, but I believe it is more useful to consider anachronism to be like a drug – *the dose makes the poison*. This maxim, attributed to the 16th century physician Paracelsus, is one of the guiding principles of modern-day toxicology. Paracelsus argued that all substances become harmful when consumed in high enough quantities. Hence, it is possible to consider there is a potential for the modest application of anachronism to provide a beneficial effect.

It is right to consider the anachronism of facts – the claim that antibiotics were prescribed during WW1 – to be the product of poor scholarship, but the anachronism of language is difficult to avoid as the development of language is an iterative process and discourse abhors a vacuum. The anachronism of perspective – the use of contemporary interpretive frameworks to explain the past – is more difficult to resolve.[32] Nonetheless, it is virtually impossible to attempt to interpret the significance of Elizabeth Kenny's social and sexual identity without introducing contemporary language and notions of sexual categories. I believe the risks associated with anachronism may be ameliorated by explicitly acknowledging the rationale for using contemporary concepts and language to interpret the meaning of historical behavior and events, thereby allowing the reader to draw their own conclusions.

Finally, many readers of this book may not recognize it as a biography because it does not attempt to describe the whole life of the protagonist. My defense to this allegation: others have already done this sufficiently well. My interest lies in the stories told by and about Elizabeth Kenny, who produced the stories, where they were produced and reproduced, what purpose were they intended to serve, who were their audiences, and how they became narratives with a life of their own. I am interested in the stories told by and about Elizabeth Kenny not simply because her stories are compelling and have achieved the status of folklore, but because they are concerned with personal experiences which have become part of a public narrative about the production of medical knowledge and the challenge to scientific orthodoxy. This book is as much a biography of a story as it is a biography of a person.

The approach I have taken to the analysis of historical, biographical, and narrative evidence will be applauded by some and condemned by many. I'm sure Harry S. Truman was speaking wisely when he quipped '*If you can't stand the heat, get out of the kitchen!*', but I would rather heed the advice of the American lyricist, Tom Lehrer: '*Don't be nervous, don't be flustered, don't be scared. Be prepared!*'.

Synopsis of the chapters

The structure of the book proceeds as follows:

Chapter one introduces the reader to the *textbook* Kenny – the historical figure which has been portrayed and defined by the biographies, hagiographies, trade publications and academic literature published over the past seventy years. In this chapter I argue that the received wisdom on Elizabeth Kenny's journey to international fame as a polio therapist has been overwhelmingly shaped by two publications – the biography produced by Victor Cohn in 1975, and the memoir co-authored by Elizabeth Kenny and Martha Ostenso in 1943. I will also show that the historical portrayal of Kenny is biased towards an American perspective of the global polio pandemic. This bias has fostered the uncritical acceptance of the public narrative she cultivated in America during the 1940s and contributed to a neglect of important formative events and experiences in Australia during her youth and middle age.

Chapter two explores the development of Elizabeth Kenny's identity as a nurse over a twenty-year period. Whilst Kenny claimed that she had lived in obscurity while devoting years of her life to developing her method of healing crippled children, I will show that she inhabited multiple identities which were mostly a response to circumstance and her burning desire for a more fulfilling life than was available to her in rural Queensland. This chapter reveals that prior to emerging as a polio therapist in the early 1930s Kenny had devoted twenty years of her life to crafting the personas of a hospital nurse, a war nurse, and an inventor to secure personal and financial independence, whilst showing little interest in the care of children. My analysis of these key episodes in Kenny's life shows she was prepared to dissemble and deceive, and take substantial risks, to achieve personal ambitions which were often myopic and illconceived, but in doing so she forged an empowered personal identity.

Chapter three examines the extent to which the stigma associated with heterosexism and homophobia shaped the life and work of Elizabeth Kenny. In this chapter I present the argument that Kenny's gender nonconformity and open contempt for men may have been interpreted as a sign of her homosexuality, thus providing a focus for covert homophobic prejudice. I believe that Kenny was aware of the disapproval which she risked attracting and attempted to project the impression of adhering to the social norms of her era to avoid being labelled as a discredited individual. I conclude that Kenny's primary defense against social disapprobation was to seek refuge in her nurse identity and the sanctuary of the *clinic* – a refuge where her otherwise discredited attributes were normalised, and her quest for social acceptance was enabled.

Chapter four examines the origins of the story which lies at the heart of the Kenny legend. My analysis of disease surveillance records and local newspaper news reports shows it is highly unlikely that Kenny treated any children with recent or paralytic polio infection prior to the early 1930s. Australian newspaper reports and several government enquiries confirm that prior to 1940 Kenny attributed her knowledge of rehabilitation to her war time nursing experience. All the documentary evidence suggests that Kenny contrived her discovery story when she worked in America in the early 1940s. This chapter also reveals evidence from recently digitised Australian newspaper reports that Kenny drew inspiration for her treatment discovery story from the public narratives she employed to promote the sale of an ambulance stretcher she invented in the mid-1920s.

Chapter five provides a detailed analysis of the content and emplotment of the Sylvia Stretcher invention story and the polio treatment discovery story. My analysis of these hitherto unconnected stories shows that both are crucial to the creation of Kenny's personal identity myth and her public identity as a polio therapist. Crucially, my analysis shows that the discovery story should not be understood as a record of an historical event, rather, it should be considered as a problem-resolution personal experience narrative which embodies Kenny's metaphorical understanding of polio and its treatment, and illuminates her self-identity towards the end of her life.

Chapter six appraises the broader purpose of the polio treatment discovery story and the reasons for its longevity. In this chapter I will show that the story has endured long after Kenny's death because it forms a narrative glue which provides continuity to the disconnected phases of her life and her episodic habitation of the personae of a nurse. This chapter also considers how the credibility of the story has been bolstered by its conformity with popular tropes and the portrayal of idealized characters within a romanticized setting. Further, I will discuss how the story which Kenny contrived was a two-edge sword as its widespread acceptance as a factual representation of her discovery may ultimately have undermined the scientific credibility of the method, thereby easing the incorporation of her techniques into conventional medical practice. Finally, I conclude that the development of Elizabeth Kenny's therapeutic system was inextricably linked to her struggle to achieve an authentic personal identity and a socially sanctioned public identity, and that the narratives through which we identify ourselves with others are inextricably linked to the production of public achievements. Elizabeth Kenny should be remembered as a woman who invented an identity for herself, and in doing so produced a paradigm shift in the treatment of one of the most feared diseases of the twentieth century.

---

[1]   Brendan O'Malley, The Courier Mail, 3 April 2009.

[2]   Kerry Highley, *Dancing in my dreams* (Melbourne: Monash University Publishing, 2015), p. 79.

[3]   A comprehensive account of the history of polio may be found in: John Paul, *History of Poliomyelitis* (New Haven: Yale University Press, 1971).

[4]   Matthew Smallman-Raynor and Andrew D. Cliff, *Poliomyelitis: A World Geography: Emergence to Eradication.* (Oxford: Oxford University Press, 2006).

[5]   An insightful analysis of the impact of polio on the public understanding of infectious disease is provided by Naomi Rogers, *Dirt and Disease: polio before FDR* (New Brunswick: Rutgers University Press, 1992).

[6]   John Howard Lidgett Cumpston, "Anterior poliomyelitis" in *Health and disease in Australia: a history*, ed. Milton Lewis, (Canberra: AGPS, 1989), pp. 326-328.

[7] K. S. Landauer and G. Stickle "An analysis of residual disabilities (paralysis and crippling) among 100,000 poliomyelitis patients: with special reference to the rehabilitation of postpoliomyelitis patients", *Archives of physical medicine and rehabilitation,* vol. 39 (1958) pp. 145-151.

[8] David Oshinsky, *Polio: An American story* (New York: Oxford University Press, 2005), p 5.

[9] Australian Government, Department of Health, *National Notifiable Diseases Surveillance System tables (dis_aus19_91).* https://www.health.gov.au/internet/main/publishing.nsf.

[10] Oshinsky, *Polio,* p. 18.

[11] Rogers, *Dirt and Disease,* p. 13.

[12] Charles Mee, *A nearly normal life* (Boston: Little, Brown and Company, 1999). p. 77.

[13] Paul, *History,* p17

[14] Jack Coulehan, "Metaphor and Medicine: Narrative in Clinical Practice", *Yale Journal of Biology and Medicine* vol. 76, (2003), pp. 87-95.

[15] Daniel J. Wilson, *Living with Polio: The epidemic and its survivors* (Chicago: University of Chicago Press, 2007), p. 17.

[16] Roosevelt's words are quoted in Paul, *History,* p. 319.

[17] Oshinsky, *Polio,* p. 53.

[18] Gary M. Reisfield and George R. Wilson, "Use of metaphor in the discourse on cancer: When the tumor is not the target", *Journal of Clinical Oncology* vol. 22 no. 19, (2004) pp. 4024-4027.

[19] Frederick C. Robbins and Thomas M Daniel, "A history of poliomyelitis" in *Polio,* (ed.) Thomas M. Daniel and Frederick C. Robbins (Rochester: University of Rochester Press, 1997), pp. 5-22.

[20] The methods Kenny used to treat Daphne's paralysis are described in a letter to Victor Cohn dictated by Daphne in 1956. Daphne Cregan to Victor Cohn, letter, 18 May 1956, 146.K.8.6F Elizabeth Kenny Papers – Minnesota Historical Society (henceforth EKP-MHS).

[21] Raphael Cilento, "Report on the muscle re-education clinic, Townsville (Sister E Kenny) and its work", (1934), Box 13 Elizabeth Kenny Collection, Fryer Library, University of Queensland.

[22] Paul, *History,* p. 340.

[23] Marc Shell, *Polio and its aftermath* (Cambridge: Harvard University Press, 2005), p. 2.

[24] "New Treatment", *The Auckland Star,* 9 March 1935, p.4.

[25] "Sister Kenny's Treatment for Infantile Paralysis", Australian Women's Weekly, 27 November 1937, p. 3.

[26] Highley, *Dancing in my dreams,* p. 176.

[27] Anne Finger, *Elegy for a disease: A personal and cultural history of polio* (New York: St Martin's Press, 2006), p. 178.

[28] Margaret Ernest, Kenny's secretary 1941-1945, personal communication to the author, 9 September 2009.

[29] Jamie James, *Biography, Autobiography, Fiction* (2016). https://fsgworkinprogress.com/2016/07/29/biography-autobiography-fiction.

30   I am not being deliberately evasive in using the word transgressive to describe my sexual identity. As I age, I feel less inclined to describe myself as *gay* as it implies a community attachment which I no longer experience, and Gore Vidal's *homosexualist* is simply too arch. Whilst *queer* probably best captures my self-identity in the contemporary discourse, it is a word with too much baggage for a man of my generation. Transgressive feels like the least bad alternative.

31   The French historian, Lucien Febvre, described anachronism thus in *The Problem of Unbelief in the Sixteenth Century. Le problème de l'incroyance au 16e siècle: la religion de Rabelais.*

32   These categories of anachronism are drawn from Georgi Verbeek, "Anachronism and the rewriting of history: The South Africa case", *The Journal for Transdisciplinary Research in Southern Africa* vol. 2, no. 1, (2006), pp. 181-200. doi.org/10.4102/td.v2i1.314.

1. THE TEXTBOOK KENNY

The historical figure who is remembered in reference books, academic journals, trade publications and films is a character constructed by the scholarship of historians and sociologists, and the reportage of journalists, lay chroniclers of polio epidemics, and *polios* – the self-assigned identifier used by many people who live with the legacy of polio infection. Among the myriad of people who have given testimony to the controversy which surrounded Kenny and her method of treating polio, she is probably more responsible than anyone other individual in creating the caricature of a selfless nurse who dedicated her life to the care of children and fought the prejudice of a belligerent medical establishment.

I have included this chapter for two reasons: first, to provide the reader with an appraisal of Kenny's involvement in the international polio treatment controversy which have been examined by other authors and scholars; and second, to provide background information which could assist the reader to draw their own conclusions about the relevance and validity of the arguments set out in this book.

Deferential commemorations

Two comprehensive biographies have been published since Kenny's death in 1952. The first, published in 1975, was written by Victor Cohn, an American journalist who worked as the science and medical reporter for the Minneapolis Star Tribune during the years Kenny was based in Minneapolis.[33] Cohn established a rapport with Kenny which provided him with a personal insight which few journalists enjoyed. Following her death in 1952 he wrote a series of biographical articles titled *Angry Angel*. He also persuaded the Star Tribune to sponsor his visit to Australia in 1953 to collect material for an extended biography. A first draft, which was more than a decade in the making, was rejected for reasons which are not known, but a second draft was eventually accepted and published in 1975 by the University of Minnesota Press.[34] Cohn's biography is based on extensive research in America and Australia, and is written in a journalistic style which for the most part is deferential and unchallenging. Cohn's daughter believes his view of Kenny changed over time, and he toned down his comments because Kenny's sister, Julia Farquarson, had threatened legal action for Cohn's misrepresentation of her sister in *Angry Angel*.[35] There are no surviving drafts or working documents for Cohn's original manuscript but extracts of interviews with friends and colleagues are held in the Elizabeth Kenny Papers in the Minnesota History Center, Minneapolis. The only record of his personal opinion of her character is an undated two page document titled *Some of my own Sister Kenny memories and impressions*.[36]

A second substantive biography, published in 2003, was written by Wade Alexander, an American who, as a child, was treated for polio by his mother using the Kenny method.[37] In 1994 Alexander used his attendance at the Fourth World Congress of Teachers of the Alexander Technique in Sydney, Australia, as an opportunity to learn more about the woman who had indirectly changed the course of his life. Alexander was surprised to discover that no-one at the congress knew of Kenny's contribution to polio care, and that there was little public awareness of her personal history. Undaunted, he obtained a copy of Kenny's memoir from the University's medical library and returned to America determined to write her biography. Alexander spent nine years researching Kenny's life, obtaining new insights into her family history. Alexander sets the tone for his biography in the Introduction by stating that he did not intend to analyze his observations about Kenny's behavior because his biography *'is not a psychobiography'*.[38] Nonetheless, it still offers a valuable contribution to Kenny scholarship as it introduced new information about her early life.

Cohn's biography may be considered as serving the purpose of a public commemoration of a woman who he observed to be heroic and troubled. Alexander's biography is probably best described as a labor of love which recognizes the impact on his own life of two significant women; Elizabeth Kenny, and his mother nursed him when he contracted polio as a child.[39] Although written nearly half a century apart I believe the two biographies share two important characteristics. Both primarily focus their attention on reporting Kenny's struggle to achieve recognition in America during the 1940s, and both demur in their comments on her personal relationships. Cohn and Alexander are also united in misunderstanding the meaning and significance of important evidence they independently acquired about her life in Australia.

Cohn and Alexander knew that Kenny was born in 1880 and was living with her parents in Headington Hill when she was treated by Aeneas McDonnell for a broken wrist in 1898, but neither challenges her claim in her autobiography that she was a young girl when this event occurred despite knowing the meeting was an important milestone in her life. Cohn and Alexander also record that Kenny cited at least five dates for the discovery of her method whilst working as a bush nurse in the Clifton district, yet neither seriously questions the significance of her imprecision in providing a date for this life changing event despite their knowledge that she was a renowned pedant when it came to the reporting of the facts pertaining to her work. Additionally, neither author discusses why there are no known patients in a small geographical region who were treated for polio by Kenny prior to 1930.

Both biographers are uncritical of Kenny's portrayal of her early life, her nursing experience prior to WW1, and her army nursing service. Crucially, both fail to adequately examine her obfuscation about her personal relationships. These are significant oversights, but the most important biographical misdemeanor they commit is the anachronistic interpretation of her motives for embarking on several dramatic career changes during her adult life. Cohn and Alexander uncritically accept Kenny's account of the adoption of her nursing identity, and the development of her method. This may be partially explained by the paucity of first-hand accounts of her early adult life, and the assiduous efforts of her family to protect her reputation after her death. Nonetheless, both biographers had access to reliable evidence which discredited her claim to have eschewed a conventional life to dedicate her life to public service and the care of children stricken with polio.

Putting aside these flaws, contemporary researchers still owe an enormous debt to Cohn and Alexander as without their interest in Kenny, and without their scholarship, almost all traces of Elizabeth Kenny might have disappeared. The importance of the legacy of Cohn's meticulous research in Australia is inestimable. There would be precious little for Kenny scholars to analyze if it were not for Cohn's journalistic eye for a lead when investigating a story. But therein lies a hidden danger, as researchers have too often overlooked the fact that Cohn was investigating a story, and the protagonist in that story was known to be an unreliable informant.

Academic literature

The academic literature examining Kenny's life has been produced sporadically over a forty years period by a relatively small number of authors. The corpus is based on a wide range of interdisciplinary approaches and may be grouped into six broad themes: her contribution to nursing theory and practice; the medical dominance of health care occupations; the social construction of knowledge; her contribution to polio treatment; the cultural significance of polio; and forgetting.

Contribution to nursing theory and practice

Kenny's use of the title Sister for thirty years after her discharge from the AANS at the end of WW1 is probably the single most important factor which underpins her public recognition as a nurse, but there is substantial evidence that many of her professional antagonists in Australia did not believe she was entitled to use the title because it implied she was a registered nurse. Doubts about her nursing qualifications and her conspicuous absence of employment in health care institutions prompted many nurses, massage therapists, and medical practitioners to refer to her as Miss Kenny even though she was unwavering in her use of the title Sister Kenny. The records of the Australian Physiotherapy Association show that in 1934 the Queensland Branch of the Australian Massage Association decided that Kenny should only be described as Miss Kenny as she had no formal nursing qualifications.[40] Putting aside the question of whether or not Kenny was a *bona fide* nurse practitioner, there is a body of literature which examines Kenny's contribution to nursing theory and practice.

In 1971 the eminent virologist and polio historian John Paul wrote:

> *If the spectacle of a physician, supposedly dedicated to the healing art, is apt to become tarnished when he shows himself publicity and power minded and engages too heavily in medical polemics, how much more tarnished is the image of a nurse who, forsaking her natural duties, becomes similarly embroiled.[41]*

Paul's comments are sexist, even by the standards of his own era, but his statement indicates that he did view Kenny as a nurse; albeit one who had strayed from her natural duties. These duties include tending to the daily work of a hospital ward while caring for and rehabilitating her patients, presumably under the instruction of the male doctor. Nurses, in Paul's world view, did not think independently, question doctors' orders, or campaign for access to humane treatment for a crippling disease. Nurses should be seen but not heard.

John Wilson, an Australian academic with an interest in nursing history, has made the most significant contribution to the literature from a nursing perspective. Wilson acknowledges that Australian nurses appeared to have little interest in Kenny or her story. Reflecting on his early nursing research, Wilson laments that his article on Kenny published in the Australian Journal of Advanced Nursing in 1986 was '*the first publication about Sister Kenny's experiences in Australian nursing literature in sixty years*'.[42] Wilson is correct in observing the paucity of Australian or international nursing literature examining Kenny's work in the mid-twentieth century, but he overlooked the seminal article written by Edith Hall in 1981.[43]

Hall is alone in the literature in reflecting on Kenny's nursing credentials from the perspective of being a nurse and polio patient. Recalling the pain and loneliness she endured during her hospitalisation with polio in Australia in the late 1930s, Hall vividly describes the stark contrast between the conventional nursing care she received, and the treatment which children received in the adjacent Kenny Ward.

> *The main Kenny treatment was heat application and sandbags to keep limbs in position.*
> *At this stage, I was wearing plaster casts on both legs and arms, a boned*

corset, Resting Steel on Bradford Steel frame with neck band padlock (to prevent escape) and was trussed in a full Thomas Splint - all pieces held together by an assortment of bandages and leather straps. The only movement possible was eyes and tongue. [44]

Hall argues that the partnership established between the nurse and patient during the muscle re-education process employed in the Kenny method was in sharp contrast to the imposed passivity inherent in the immobilisation therapy recommended in conventional therapy. Hall's observation of Kenny's methods implies she believed Kenny was forging a new, more patient-centered, model of nursing practice.

Wilson's early publications focus primarily on the organized response of the medical profession in Australia to a perceived threat to their control of health care resources and the authority of medical knowledge.[45] In the 1986 article *The Sister Kenny Clinics: what endures?* Wilson claims Kenny demonstrated two nursing attributes: the capacity to apply nursing knowledge to the independent diagnosis, prescription and care of patients; and the potential to respond to public health needs in new ways as an alternative to medical practice. These may appear to be unexceptional claims in the current era, but Wilson argues that these attributes may not have been considered appropriate or desirable for nurses in her lifetime and may not have been widely embraced as positive nursing attributes by her nursing contemporaries.[46]

In 1992 Wilson shifted his attention to the tactics which the Australian medical establishment employed to undermine public support for the growing number of Kenny Clinics. *Sister Elizabeth Kenny's Trial by Royal Commission* presents the argument that the medical establishment conspired to denigrate Kenny's methods, only to be thwarted by the growing public interest in the work carried out in her clinics. Wilson claims that Kenny failed to convince medical practitioners of the value of her ideas because she had difficulty in communicating '*the essential principles of her clinical nursing skills*' as she lacked formal hospital-based education.[47]

In the introduction to *Through Kenny's Eyes*, the 1995 publication based on his doctoral thesis, Wilson reaffirms his dismay that the small number of Australian academics who were interested in Kenny relied on myth, folklore, and the observations of a handful of North American authors. He may have been even more dismayed if he had realized that most of the academic literature had been written by physiotherapists. In *Through Kenny's Eyes* Wilson explores Kenny's behavior as a nurse to elicit her understanding of the concepts of health, person, environment, and nursing. Wilson's research explores many of the enigmas and contradictions associated with Kenny: she used the title Sister but she rarely wore a nurse's uniform or allowed herself to be photographed in a nurse's uniform; she lacked formal nursing qualifications but insisted that the technicians who administered her treatment be trained for two years before practicing independently; she positioned herself in the role of a matron in her hospital clinics but preferred that her technicians were not nurses; and she emphasized the mystic nature of the intensely personal interaction between therapist and patient, but claimed she had discovered a new scientific concept of the disease. With this is mind, it is ironic that he is ambivalent in his engagement with the central question of whether the woman who called herself Sister Kenny should be considered a nurse in her own or the present era.

The rarity of peer reviewed academic papers since the publication of Wilson's thesis suggests that nurses have not heeded Wilson's call for more nursing research on Kenny and her contribution to nursing practice. Sonda Oppewal's paper published in 1997 is an historical case study which sets out to analyze the strategies Kenny used to obtain medical endorsement for her method of treating poliomyelitis.[48] Oppewal describes the strategies which Kenny used to overcome the disadvantage she experienced as a woman and as a nurse in a male dominated society. These strategies are not categorized as being inherently attributable to nursing theory or practice, nor are they proposed as strategies which nurses could adopt to improve their professional status or practice.

Kimberly Carter, a nurse academic, brings the discussion of Kenny's contribution to nursing down to earth with a thud. Carter argues that the dissemination of Kenny's method in the United States during the 1940s did little to change the subordinate role of nurses. Carter also notes that despite the investment by the NFIP in the training of nurses and Kenny technicians, their role was purely operational, and the nursing profession was not represented in any of the five international polio conferences held between 1949 and 1961. Nonetheless, Carter acknowledges that Kenny's success in fund raising in the United States did demonstrate that nurses had the ability to secure resources which they could independently use for nursing research in an era when '*Nursing [as a profession] was young, nursing education was disorganized, and nursing research was essentially non-existent*'.[49]

The most recent publication to feature an appraisal of Kenny's contribution to nursing practice is a paper written by Janet Golden and Naomi Rogers.[50] Their paper discusses how a nurse, Irene Shea, was introduced to the Kenny method in 1942, and offers a rare insight into the experience of a nurse who wrestles with her conflicted response to learning new but contested nursing skills. Ultimately, Golden and Rogers present Kenny as an actor in a historical melodrama and offer few conclusions about the contribution she made to nursing practice in her era or to subsequent generations of nurse practitioners. Nonetheless, they imply Kenny's '*gritty determination*' as a nurse and educator, and her refusal to show deference to medical practitioners, are positive attributes for a nurse.

Medical dominance of health care occupations

The opposition of medical practitioners to Kenny's concept of polio, and her method of treating the after-effects of the disease, are recurring narratives in the literature. These narratives frequently portray Kenny as a lone maverick facing united opposition from *medical men*. Kenny was unabashed in claiming her medical opponents were suspicious, envious, mean spirited, self-interested, stubborn, short-sighted, ignorant, and uncaring. In case her point had been missed, she also claimed they were affronted by the prospect of being instructed by a nurse and outraged that patients might be treated in a manner which was not endorsed by their medical colleagues. This portrayal of medical practitioners acting collectively to protect their self-interest is better understood through an exploration of the concept of medical dominance.

The medical dominance of health care occupations is a topic which has received considerable attention in the medical sociology literature, and it is a recurring but often muddled theme in the literature associated with the polio treatment controversy. The muddle arises from the intersection of the analysis of the role of gender bias within health care occupations, the power of the medical profession within health care occupations, and the wider topic of the medicalization of health and illness during the twentieth century. An earlier quote from John Paul illustrates the entrenched beliefs which applied to the social organization of health care during Kenny's lifetime – doctors were men, nurses were women; doctors diagnosed and gave instructions, nurses cared and fulfilled orders. The legitimacy of this natural order was rarely questioned prior to the 1970s.

The discussion of the medical opposition to the Kenny method was minimal until Claudia Thame completed her PhD thesis in 1974.[51] Thame only allocates a few pages within the appendices of her unpublished thesis to the discussion of Kenny, but those pages have been widely cited. Whilst the debate over the comparative merits of Kenny's and orthodox methods of polio treatment was prominent in the print media throughout the 1930s, Thame argues that too much attention has been placed on the technical reasons for medical practitioners objecting to her techniques. Thame proposes that the prospect of resources being placed under the control of someone outside the profession was of more concern to medical practitioners in Australia than the professional identity of their competitor. The Australian branches of the BMA had shown its intolerance of competition from Lodge Doctors in the 1920s,[52] and it did not welcome the advent of State funded Kenny Clinics in the 1930s. Thame states that the medical profession eventually won the battle for control of polio treatment in Australia through '*a judicious and unacknowledged*' incorporation of her techniques into conventional medical practice, thereby ensuring they would continue to control access to patients and resources.[53]

Evan Willis develops this theme in his analysis of the impact of the Kenny Clinics on the occupational division of labor within health care in Australia.[54] Willis describes the occupational division of labor as arising from the efforts of a professional group to claim a monopoly over services, and assert authority to direct and evaluate the work of others without being subject to reciprocal direction or evaluation. By occupying the dominant position in a hierarchy of health occupations, medicine has been able to control the production and application of knowledge within its own ranks and in competing occupational groups such as nursing and professions allied to medicine.[55] Willis claims Kenny challenged medicine's dominance of the health division of labor in two ways. Firstly, Kenny introduced a new body of knowledge which was beyond the interpretation and regulation by the dominant group. The second and perhaps more significant challenge came from the threatened disruption to the medical monopoly of the health market by a competing occupational group. The Kenny method represented an entirely new product in the health market of the 1930s, possessing the potential for rendering redundant a range of therapeutic interventions traditionally administered and regulated by doctors. Further, the Australian Kenny clinics were initially established as independent rehabilitation centers administered by nurses and health bureaucrats instead of medical practitioners.

Willis claims that the nurse-dominated Kenny clinics challenged the market domination by doctors as health service providers and threatened their position at the apex of the occupational hierarchy. Willis argues that whilst the medical profession in Australia and the United States initially responded to the introduction of the Kenny method by questioning her legitimacy as a practitioner and disputing the scientific validity of her concept, the ultimate triumph of medicine was guaranteed by the profession exerting political influence to ensure treatment services were confined to hospitals rather than nurse run clinics, thereby maintaining their control over entrenched occupational relationships.

Social construction of knowledge
The President's Birthday Magazine 1938, published by the NFIP, contains an article with the title *What Science Is Doing*.[56] The lengthy article informs the reader that *scientific men* are working around the clock to develop a cure or vaccine for the dreaded disease. There are pictures of monkeys in cages and scientists looking through microscopes; pictures of science in action. The careful placement of an advertisement for household appliances reminds the reader of the power of science to solve problems like polio. In less than 40 years, we are told, scientists and engineers have enabled millions of ordinary American families to have bathtubs, telephones, and automobiles. The message is clear – if scientists can put a bathtub in every home, they can also beat polio. The hubris of the message is misplaced as

an effective vaccine would not be available for another twenty years. In the real world, the NFIP was promoting the use of woolen bandages soaked in boiling water as an essential component of the most effective treatment for the after-effects of polio infection. As Naomi Rogers observes '*Crippled children and hot packs were not as exciting or modern-sounding as the promise of a polio vaccine*'.[57] In the real world, scientists were red faced with embarrassment, not anger, as their promised panacea failed to materialise.

The literature associated with the polio treatment polemic frames Kenny's concepts and methods as '*born outside a medical or scientific community*'[58], and a product of '*virtuoso ignorance*'[59]. In other words, she struggled to explain what she was doing and why her techniques worked. John Wilson asserts that medical practitioners could not understand Kenny's attempts to explain her techniques because these explanations contradicted their interpretation of evidence which had a pathological origin. In other words, her *a posteriori* knowledge was derived from empirical observation, whereas medical practitioners' *a priori* knowledge was derived from their reasoning on the action of the virus. The conventional view of science in the polio years was that the diligent application of scientific methods, including experimentation and testing, would inevitably lead to the truth of a theory being revealed. Whilst this approach undeniably expanded scientific knowledge throughout the twentieth century it is equally true that medical knowledge has often been extended through reckless trial and error. Nonetheless the absence of testing was, and continues to be, a key criticism of the Kenny method. Those critics of the Kenny method who argue that only a randomized control trial (RCT) could prove the superiority of her method overlook the fact that RCTs were not widely used in Kenny's lifetime, and if they had it would have been impossible to ensure patients and clinicians were blind to the therapy being applied.

Rogers, writing in 2008, continues her exploration of the politicization of the assessment of the scientific validity of Kenny's techniques in her paper *Silence has its own stories: Elizabeth Kenny, Polio and the culture of medicine*.[60] Rogers observes that professional stakeholders were quick to voice their belief that Kenny's method lacked scientific credibility because it had not been subjected to scientific confirmation. Citing a quote from a neurologist who is alleged to have considered her theories '*physiological nonsense*', Rogers concludes Kenny's work may have seemed distant from '*the ideals of a precise, rational and unemotional medical science*' because the '*messiness*' of clinical practice precluded it from being considered scientific. This is a tenuous argument as there is not a clear dichotomy between pure scientific medicine and medicine which is practiced at the bedside. The question of whether Kenny's method was a discovery or an invention will be examined in a later chapter.

Contribution to polio treatment

The reporting of Kenny's contribution to the polio treatment has until recently been exceptionally polarized. Kenny was adamant that her conceptualization of the disease was so different from the standard medical view that she had discovered a new disease. There are two key principles which separate Kenny's concept of polio from the standard medical view. First, she believed the virus attacked muscle cells, whereas the standard medical view was that it attacked nerve cells. Second, she believed the contractures which are characteristic of paralytic polio were caused by spasm in affected muscles rather than paralysis. Her contemporaries be they nurses, doctors, or massage therapists, aligned into two distinct camps – the converts and the disbelievers.

Kenny's techniques were subjected to sustained and intensive examination in Australia throughout the 1930s. It is note-worthy that the medical practitioners who engaged in the interrogation of her techniques did not publish their objections through the academic literature, preferring to voice their disapproval through the conduit of quasi-judicial reviews. In 1933 Raphael Cilento was appointed to investigate the operation of the first Kenny clinic in Townsville. Cilento's preliminary report was cautiously supportive, claiming improvement in long standing paralysis cases.[61] The final report completed a year later was less enthusiastic, claiming Kenny had not fulfilled her requirement to train nurses to carry out her techniques, and concluding the results of her therapy were no better than that which would be achieved through routine practices. A subsequent Royal Commission of Inquiry, which included a Commissioner who was openly hostile towards Kenny,[62] and Parliamentary Reports in NSW and Victoria in 1937 also dismissed Kenny's therapy as achieving results which were no better than those obtained from conventional medical practice.[63] A sole dissenting voice among Australian medical practitioners, reporting improved outcomes from Kenny's treatment,[64] was dismissed as being biased as the author had observed Kenny's methods in the Townsville Clinic.[65]

The recent publication of research undertaken by Kerry Highley provides a long overdue analysis of the mixed response of medical experts in Australia, America, and the United Kingdom to Kenny's concept of the disease and its treatment. Highley reaffirms the received view that opposition to Kenny rested more on her status as a nurse and lack of finesse in communicating with medical and massage practitioners than the evidence for the efficacy of her therapeutic approach. Highley concedes that prominent medical authorities did support Kenny throughout the period she worked in Australia, and usefully extends past analyses of medical opposition to include a thoughtful analysis of the role of Jean Macnamara and the Australian branch of the British Medical Association.[66] Drawing attention to Macnamara's covert influence, Highley discredits the view that the medical profession acted collectively to undermine public confidence in Kenny's methods. Echoing Thame's conclusion, Highley also points out that the clearest proof of the value of Kenny's concept of treatment is that it eventually merged with conventional medical methods *'in a synergistic relationship instead of being locked in a battle for power'*.[67]

Whilst the Australian medical establishment preferred to covertly attack Kenny through the vehicle of public enquiries, medical practitioners in the United States voiced their support or opposition to Kenny's methods through the more public platform of academic journals. As has been previously reported, the American medical profession was more collectively welcoming of Kenny's techniques, but remained dubious with respect to her theory about the site of attack of the virus. Her most prominent critic was Bruce Gill, a former Professor of Orthopedic Surgery. In 1943 Gill wrote a long densely worded letter to the Journal of Bone and Joint Surgery criticizing every aspect of Kenny's methods and concepts, and her publicity seeking self-promotion.[68]

Fortunately for Kenny, she attracted more supporters than opponents in America. Within one year of the first demonstration of her technique, orthopaedic specialists wrote in the prestigious Journal of the American Medical Association:

> *Miss Kenny has presented ideas which are new in the symptamology and treatment of infantile paralysis. Results have been obtained in the cases of acute involvement which seem superior to those secured with therapeutic procedures previously generally accepted.*[69]

By 1942 Kenny's method was accepted as the treatment of choice for patients presenting in the acute stages of polio,[70] possessing such advantages over previously recognised methods that the training of American physicians in the method was urged as an imperative.[71]

The debate over Kenny's contribution to the polio treatment knowledge base continued after her death. In 1955 Mylan Knapp published a complementary summary of the contribution of Kenny to the treatment of polio. From this point on the medical literature is virtually silent on her contribution to polio care, but Kenny's work remained a point of contention within the physiotherapy profession for years to come. Philippa Martyr's appraisal in 1997 of the sources of opposition to the Kenny system of rehabilitation presents a balanced and detailed account of the intersection of three opposing forces whilst assiduously avoiding comment on the superiority or otherwise of Kenny's methods.[72] Whilst it isn't clear why she waited three years to respond, Margaret Denton, an Australian historian of physiotherapy, robustly disputed Martyr's appraisal of the organized efforts of the Australian Massage Association to undermine support for the government sponsored Kenny Clinics.[73] Denton reiterated

Florence Kendall's lifelong assertion that Kenny's techniques had not been adequately evaluated and had produced results no better than conventional therapy.[74] A paper on the history of splinting, written by Elaine Fess in 2002, restated the assertions that Kenny's method had not been properly evaluated and *'had no effect on residual paralysis'*[75]. Whilst Denton and Fess possessed knowledge of splinting which was endorsed by their academic peers, I believe they were flogging an academic and rhetorical dead horse in their accusation that the efficacy of Kenny's techniques had not been proven because they had not been properly evaluated.

Perhaps the final and lasting test of the value of Kenny's contribution to the polio treatment knowledge base is whether, in this era of commitment to evidence-based practice, it has made an enduring contribution to clinical practice. The Queensland Department of Health publishes guidelines for General Practitioners on the management of the late effects of polio. This guidance acknowledges the work of Sister Kenny in setting *'the hallmark for the treatment of paralytic polio'*.[76] The acknowledgement is consistent with the views of John Paul who stated in 1971:

> *In retrospect there is no denying that Sister Kenny's ideas and techniques marked a turning point, even an about-face, in the aftercare of paralytic poliomyelitis. By determination and sheer will power she helped to raise the treatment of paralyzed patients out of the slough into which it had sunk in the 1930s.*[77]

In 1985 Sir Frank Macfarlane Burnett, Nobel Prize winning Australian scientist, and the discoverer of multiple strains of polio virus, stated in an interview that Kenny's ideas about the pathology of polio were *'rubbish'*. Nonetheless, he was unequivocal in his support for her therapy – *'I very definitely got the impression that if a child of mine got polio I'd ring for Sister Kenny'*.[78]

Cultural significance of polio

The analysis of the cultural significance of polio by Naomi Rogers leaves few topics unexplored and few questions unanswered for future researchers. Over a period of twenty five years Rogers has examined the community responses to polio quarantine measures, the scapegoating of European migrant communities in the early American epidemics, public health practitioners' fixation with pest control and public sanitation, the loss of public confidence in the authority of science and medicine, and the involvement of antivivisectionists in the debate over polio vaccine development.[79] There is barely a scholarly article or book chapter which omits Rogers as a citation in the exploration of the cultural significance of polio and Kenny's work in America in the 1940s.

The cultural significance of polio has been addressed by many historians, but Rogers is unique in addressing the significance of the representations of Kenny through the medium of film. Kenny produced or contributed to several films depicting her work and life. Rogers proposes that Kenny recognised early in her polio career that film could do more than simply disseminate her ideas; it could legitimise them with a public and a scientific audience.[80] Rogers has also used Kenny as a case study to demonstrate the capacity of film to be a teaching instrument, a vehicle for self-promotion, and a propaganda tool for her campaign to increase her influence over public health policy in the United States.[81]

In the decade spanning the new millennium the location of the analysis of the cultural significance of polio shifted to literature written by authors who had contracted polio as children. These accounts represent a quantum shift in the analysis of polio, introducing a synchronicity of interdisciplinary research with biography and autobiography. The most widely cited publications in this genre are *Polio and its aftermath* by March Shell;[82] *A summer plague* by Tony Gould;[83] and *Elegy for a disease* by Anne Finger.[84] The subjectivity which these authors apply to their analysis of historical records prompts them to explore issues and ask questions which have been ignored in the research literature. Gould is virtually unique in questioning, albeit obliquely, Kenny's description of her first attempt to ease the discomfort of a child who had been stricken with polio: *'part of the potency of the Kenny myth derives from the fact that she convinced herself of its validity before she set about persuading others'*.[85]

The questioning of Kenny's account of her discovery places Gould in the company of an extremely small band of scholars.[86] Shell proposes that the cultural significance of polio *'was overplayed in the first half of the century and then underplayed in the second half'*.[87] Shell uses the autobiographical accounts of polios to illustrate the impact of polio on cinema, art, literature, notions of childhood, public health, and the cultural portrayal of disability. Finger eloquently weaves a personal narrative with her social analysis of the dehumanising effects of the polio experience in the historical portrayal of the disease. Most notably, Finger explores the desexualising of male and female polios in the polio discourse and is alone in the literature in questioning why there has been so little conjecture on the sexual identity of Elizabeth Kenny.[88]

Forgetting

Almost every chapter, journal article, conference paper, or media article ever written about Elizabeth Kenny since her death in 1952 acknowledges that her international fame diminished rapidly throughout the 1950s, and that she was effectively forgotten by the 1970s. Stark evidence of this phenomenon can be found in two articles published in 1955 in the newly established Australian Journal of Physiotherapy. The articles, written by prominent Australian physiotherapists, Marjorie Farnbach and Elma Casely, report the importance of physiotherapy in the treatment of polio and paralysis.[89] Both papers acknowledge the work of Australian doctors and scientists in the battle to defeat polio, and the extent to which polio epidemics had raised public awareness of the therapeutic value of physiotherapy, but neither author acknowledges Kenny's existence let alone her contribution to patient care. I believe Farnbach's and Casely's denial of Kenny's contribution to the treatment of polio was not an accidental lapse of memory, it was almost certainly a deliberate act of forgetting. As Rogers observes *'Forgetting is sometimes seen as a passive process rather than an active one, but both remembering and forgetting are responses to the present'*.[90] The present, for Farnbach and Casely, was almost certainly a long-awaited opportunity to promote physiotherapy as a profession unimpeded by the limelight-hogging Elizabeth Kenny.

Rogers offers several explanations for the speed with which Kenny was forgotten. In a paper delivered in 2010 she observes *'In the history of polio, memorializing has always been politically and socially fraught'*.[91] In this paper Rogers claims Kenny was forgotten partly because polio shifted from being a story about medicine and patient care to a story of the triumph of science over polio, and partly because she amassed more political opponents than political allies during her career. Rogers returns to the subject of forgetting in *Polio Wars*, but adds, with little critical reflection, that polio is now an old person's disease in North America, and therefore is a disease with little news worthiness or interest for modern health care practitioners.[92] I am not convinced by this argument as it is widely recognised that advocacy groups representing the health care needs of people living with Alzheimer's disease and dementia have given these diseases a much higher public profile in recent decades.

In the opening pages of *Elegy for a Disease* Anne Finger observes that *'I should not be surprised that when a doctor writes the history, doctors and scientists are given center stage'*.[93] Her remark is well founded – John Paul devotes eleven of the 469 pages of *History of Poliomyelitis* to the development of the iron lung, and four pages to the work of Elizabeth Kenny. Nonetheless, Finger should also include historians as being equally myopic in their view of the disease – David Oshinsky allocates only five pages of his Pulitzer prize winning *Polio an American Story* to Kenny's work. Finger paints an awkward portrait of Kenny in two substantial sections of her autobiography: a saint-like figure for some former patients; for others, a woman whose treatment regime bordered on abuse. Kenny defied gender conformity and was exceptional in her lifetime in earning international fame as an independent woman rather than as a movie star or as the wife of a prominent man.[94] Nonetheless, Finger concludes, like many others, that Kenny *'faded out of our collective memories, becoming a footnote to a disease that had itself become a footnote'*.[95]

Marc Shell demands that a far more radical response is required if we are to move beyond eulogising the development of the Salk and Sabin vaccines as the key features of the global polio pandemic. Whilst Shell does not directly comment on Kenny's work, he is emphatic that the notion that polio has been conquered is a sham which needs to be exposed. Shell notes that the lifespan of polio epidemics in the industrialised nations of the twentieth century approximates to the life span of a human, giving rise to the misleading notion that the history of polio has a beginning, middle and end.[96] Shell argues that the perception that we live in a world which is post-polio is glaringly contradicted by the fact that there are still approximately 1.6 million polios living in the United States, and that in the United States polio is second only to stroke as the cause of paralysis.[97] A similar proportion of survivors can be found in Australia, where thousands of people struggle to achieve recognition of the health impact of post-polio syndrome. For Shell, the treatment of polio is a footnote to a disease which itself has become a footnote to the triumph of science over a disease.

Hagiography

A notable feature of the Kenny literary corpus is the presence of biographies which should be categorised as hagiography. Whilst a hagiography is rarely written in an academic style or based upon critical analysis of biographical data, I believe this genre of writing has played a substantial role in shaping the academic discourse on the polio treatment controversy. Technically, a hagiography is a biography of a saint or a venerated person, but the term is often used in a pejorative sense to describe biographical writing which is uncritical or excessively deferential to its subject. Hagiography should not be automatically dismissed as lacking worth as it has the potential to reveal the social context and implied meaning of events which may be perceived to represent heroic acts or moments of divine intervention in the world.

There are three hagiographical monographs which I believe are worth noting. Each is written by an American author and published in the USA, but they differ in their proximity to Kenny and their reliance on primary sources of data. *I knew Sister Kenny: A story of a great lady and little people* was written by Herbert J. Levine, a medical practitioner who knew Kenny from 1946 until her death in 1952.[98] Levine's book chronicles the formation and subsequent demise of the Centralia Clinic in Centralia, Illinois, the first Kenny clinic to be established outside Minneapolis.[99] The book's title and subtitle unambiguously tells the reader that Kenny is set apart from ordinary people. Levine describes how a *great lady* uses her influence to bring salvation to Centralia in the form of a polio clinic. For researchers and biographers, the book also provides a first-hand account of the impact her failing health had on her loss of control of the Elizabeth Kenny Institute. As useful as the book is in terms of its portrayal of the emotional and cultural significance of polio to the citizens of Centralia, Levine shows no sign of recognising the role Kenny played in the closure of the clinic. Minnesota health officials wanted the clinic to provide a range of therapies, but Kenny insisted that only technicians which she had trained could deliver the unadulterated treatment which she approved. Her insistence was at odds with the small number of technicians who she had trained. Faced with her implacable stance State officials withdrew funding and the clinic closed. The citizens of Centralia believed that they lost their clinic due to the heavy hand of bureaucracy. In Levine's eyes Kenny was a heroic figure who placed the welfare of crippled children above her own.

Sister Elizabeth Kenny, by Henry Thomas, is an entirely different form of hagiography.[100] If imitation is the sincerest form of flattery, Henry Thomas must surely be Elizabeth Kenny's most sincere admirer. Thomas' book is so plagiarised from Kenny's 1943 memoir it is surprising Kenny's publishers didn't sue. The dustcover introduces Kenny as *'one of the major pioneers in the battle against infantile paralysis'*, and its publication in 1958 appears to be an attempt to capitalise on the fame of Jonas Salk, the scientist who lead the development of the first polio vaccine. The book imputes Kenny's sanctity unambiguously. In the chapter titled *Elizabeth Kenny — Doctor of Humanity* Thomas cites the former Chancellor of the New York University as claiming: *'In her native Queensland, little children start their morning devotions with a prayer to Sister Kenny'*.[101] Not surprisingly there is no speculation on the possibility of Basil O'Connor, President of the NFIP, starting his day giving thanks for the death of the bane of his existence.

The most recent hagiographical appraisal of Kenny is *Healing Warrior: A story about Sister Elizabeth Kenny*.[102] The book was written by Emily Crofford with the assistance of grants from the Minnesota State Arts Board and the National Endowment for the Arts. The content is almost entirely drawn from Kenny's memoir and Victor Cohn's biography. *Healing Warrior* was judged to be outstanding by the National Council for the Social Studies and the National Science Teachers Association in the United States.[103] Despite its accolades, *Healing Warrior* is most notable for the complete absence of cross examination of the facts presented by Kenny in her memoir. Indeed, Crofford explains to her youthful readers that Kenny had no choice but to lie about her qualifications because American doctors would not believe her claims about her polio therapy if they knew she was unqualified. Truthfulness, it seems, is not a mandatory weapon in a healing warrior's arsenal.

Conclusion

This chapter appraises a representative but not exhaustive selection of the literature relating to Elizabeth Kenny and poliomyelitis which I have consumed over a period of twenty-five years. The portrayal of Kenny in the published literature is understandably shaped by the nature of the publication. Academic journals and thesis-based publications generally address Kenny as a case study, or as an actor in a sociological drama because that approach is required by publishers who target an academic audience. In these publications the accuracy of citations and the originality of sources are valued more than the subjective interpretation of the facts for a modern audience. Biographies and trade publications intended for a non-academic audience tend to focus on the chronological ordering of events and the framing of Kenny as an actor in an existential drama, and whilst subjectivity is more evident in these publications, best practice dictates that the author maintains a neutral stance in the telling of *the* story rather than the telling of *their* story.

Whilst the conclusions I reach may differ from those held by some of the authors I have cited in this chapter, I acknowledge the value of the facts, observations, and analyses they present. My main concern with much of the available literature is that it frequently falls into the trap of populating the many gaps in her life story with the accounts she presented to the world in the final decade of her life. As Victor Cohn discovered in the 1950s, the best documented episode in her life before 1934 was the three years she was attached to the Sea Transport Service during WW1, and these sparse service records are full of inconsistencies and omissions. In contrast, the Minnesota History Center holds nine large archive boxes of documents which record the ten years she worked in America. This imbalance has, in my opinion, fatally compromised a great deal of the received wisdom which applies to our understanding of the polio treatment controversy and Kenny's personal history.

The remainder of this book presents a deliberately sceptical appraisal of the claims which Kenny made about her experiences as a nurse and as a therapist. Too much of the received wisdom with respect to Kenny's discovery of a treatment for polio is a black box which has remained sealed for decades. My intention is to unlock the box to reveal the basis of Kenny's discovery narrative. My analysis of the narratives which she created will be driven by questioning whether the story is consistent with the facts rather than questioning whether the facts are consistent with the story.

---

[33] Victor Cohn, *Sister Kenny The Woman Who Challenged The Doctors*. (Minneapolis: The University of Minneapolis Press, 1975)

[34] Phyllis Beetsch, Cohn's daughter, to author, personal communication, September 2009. Family members interviewed in Washington D.C. and Minneapolis confirm there is no surviving copy of the original manuscript.

[35] The Elizabeth Kenny Papers in Minneapolis contain a letter from Farquarson to Cohn which complains about his portrayal of Kenny in the *Angry Angel* articles. Julia Farquarson to Victor Cohn, letter, 10 October 1954, 146.K.8.6F

EKP-MHS.

[36] Victor Cohn, "Some of my own Sister Kenny memories and impressions:", 146.K.8.6F EKP-MHS.

[37] Wade Alexander, *Sister Elizabeth Kenny* (Rockhampton: Central Queensland University Press, 2003).

[38] Alexander, *Sister Kenny*, p. vi. Alexander's approach to interpreting the data he collects suggests that he conjoins the concepts of analysis, criticism, and judgement.

[39] These categorisations draw on the typology presented by Thomas Söderqvist in Thomas Söderqvist, "What is the use of writing lives of recent scientists?" in *The historiography of contemporary science, technology, and medicine*, (ed.) Ronald E. Doel and Thomas Söderqvist, (London: Routledge, 2006), pp. 101-127.

[40] Source: Philippa Martyr, "A small price to pay for peace: The Elizabeth Kenny controversy re-examined", *Australian Historical Studies* vol. 108, (1997), pp. 47-65.

[41] Paul, *History*, p. 344.

[42] Wilson, *Kenny's eyes*, p. 6.

[43] This omission is probably due to online indexed databases not being available in the 1980s and early 1990s when Wilson was conducting his research.

[44] Edith M. Hall, "In the Ward Next Door to Sister Kenny", *The Australian Nurses' Journal* vol. 10, no. 10, (1981), pp. 57-58.

[45] John Wilson, "The Sister Kenny Clinics: what endures?" *The Australian Journal of Advanced Nursing* vol. 3, no. 2, (1986), pp. 13-21; and John Wilson, "Sister Kenny's Trial by Royal Commission", *History of Nursing Journal* vol. 4, no. 2, (1992), pp. 91-99.

[46] Wilson states that the two prominent medical and nursing journals in Australia effectively disenfranchised Kenny by excluding her from reports on polio care from 1940 to 1953. Wilson, *Sister Kenny Clinics*, p. 14.

[47] Wilson, *Trial*, p. 99.

[48] Sonda Riedesel Opperwal, "Sister Elizabeth Kenny, an Australian Nurse, and Treatment of Poliomyelitis Victims, *Journal of Nursing Scholarship* vol. 29, no. 1, (1997), pp:83-87.

[49] Kimberly F. Carter, "Trumpets of Attack: Collaborative efforts between nursing and philanthropies to care for the child crippled with polio 1930 to 1959", *Public Health Nursing* vol. 18, no. 4, (2001), pp. 253-261.

[50] Janet Golden and Naomi Rogers, "Nurse Irene Shea studies the 'Kenny Method' of treatment of infantile paralysis 1942-43", *Nursing History Review* no. 18, (2010), pp. 189-203.

[51] The thesis is embargoed for publication until 2033, but a bound copy is available at the Fisher Library, University of Sydney.

[52] Lodge Doctors were medical practitioners employed by benevolent societies. Their services were available to the members of these societies at a discount rate. The BMA waged a successful battle to undermine public confidence in these doctors, accusing them of providing inferior care to private medical practitioners.

[53] Kenny unwittingly contributed to the assimilation of her techniques in Australia

by insisting that her patients always be under the care of medical practitioners. Jean Macnamara, Australia's foremost expert on poliomyelitis and prominent opponent of Kenny's techniques, agreed to a Kenny Clinic being established under her control during the 1937 epidemic in Victoria. Ann G. Smith, "Macnamara, Dame Annie Jean (1899–1968)", *Australian Dictionary of Biography* (National Centre of Biography, Australian National University, 2009). http://adb.anu.edu.au/biography/macnamara-dame-annie-jean-7427/text12927.

54 Willis, *Sister Elizabeth Kenny*, pp. 30-38.

55 In Kenny's lifetime these were restricted to nurses and massage therapists. In the current era these include nurses, physiotherapists, and occupational therapists.

56 The President's Birthday Magazine was public relations vehicle used by President Roosevelt. de Kruiff P, "What Science Is Doing", *The President's Birthday Magazine*, (National Foundation for Infantile Paralysis, 1938). Pamphlet, 61.143.7.2.5B EKP-MHS.

57 Naomi Rogers, "Sister Kenny Goes To Washington", in (ed.) Robert D. Johnston, *The Politics of Healing* (New York: Routledge, 2004).

58 Betty Ligon uses this phrase to reiterate statements made by in papers by Martyr (1997) and Rogers (1993). Betty L. Ligon, "Sister Elizabeth Kenny: A controversial participant in the war against polio", *Seminars in Pediatric Infectious Disease* vol. 2, no. 4, (2000), pp. 287-291.

59 Mark Swaim uses this expression to describe the process of discovery unimpeded by pre-existing knowledge of a phenomenon. Mark W. Swaim, "A dogma upended from down under: Sister Elizabeth Kenny's polio treatment", *North Carolina Medical Journal* 59(4): (1998), pp. 256-260.

60 Naomi Rogers, "Silence has its own stories: Elizabeth Kenny, Polio and the culture of medicine", *Social History of Medicine* vol. 21, no. 1, (2008), pp. 146-161.

61 Raphael Cilento, "Report on Sister E. Kenny's after-treatment of cases of paralysis following poliomyelitis", (1933), Fryer Library, University of Queensland, Box 18 UQFL44.

62 Dr. James V. Duhig was appointed to the 1936 Royal Commission of Inquiry in Queensland. In a letter to Victor Cohn, Duhig described Kenny as a liar and impostor *'with a curious and occasional criminal obsession about her ability to cure poliomyelitis in all stages'*. James Duhig to Victor Cohn, letter, 16 Nov 1955. 146.K.8.6F EKP-MHS.

63 Willis, *Sister Elizabeth Kenny*, p. 33.

64 F.H. Mills, "Treatment of acute poliomyelitis: An analysis of Sister Kenny's methods", *The British Medical Journal* vol. 1, no. 4020, (1938), pp. 168-170.

65 M. Forrester-Brown, "Treatment of anterior poliomyelitis", *The British Medical Journal* vol. 1, no. 4021, pp. 252-3.

66 See chapter five of Highley, *Dancing in my Dreams*.

67 Highley, *Dancing in my Dreams*, p. 109.

68 A. Bruce Gill, "Kenny concepts and treatment of poliomyelitis", *Journal of Bone and Joint Surgery* no. 26, (1944), pp. 87-98.

69 Wallace H. Cole and Miland E. Knapp, "The Kenny Treatment of Infantile

Paralysis: a preliminary report", *Journal of the American Medical Association* vol. 116, no. 23, (1941), pp. 2577-2580.

[70] Although there were semantic changes in the description of her techniques the core components of her method remained consistent between 1937 and 1942. Morris Fishbein, President of the American Medical Association, did not personally approve of Kenny but agreed to allow a favourable paper to be published in the JAMA in 1942. Mary Daly, Jerome Greenbaum, Edward Reilly, Alvah Weiss, Philip Stimson, "The Early Treatment of Poliomyelitis: with an evaluation of the Sister Kenny treatment", *Journal of the American Medical Association* vol. 118, no. 17, (1942), pp. 1433-1443.

[71] John F. Pohl, "The Kenny Treatment of Anterior Poliomyelitis: report of the first cases treated in America", *Journal of the American Medical Association* vol. 118, no. 17, (1942), 1428-1433.

[72] Martyr, *Price for Peace*, pp. 47-65.

[73] Denton, *Further Comments*, p. 152. Whilst Denton's paper was emphatic in its response to Martyr, it was not published until three years after the publication of Martyr's paper.

[74] In a lecture published shortly before her death Florence Kendall, who worked as a polio therapist with her husband in the United States during the 1940s and 1950s, confirmed her belief that the Kenny method had not been adequately evaluated and had not produced the results which Kenny claimed. Florence Kendall, "Sister Elizabeth Kenny Revisited", *Archives of Physical Medicine and Rehabilitation* no. 79, (1998), pp. 361-365.

[75] Elaine E. Fess, "A history of splinting: To understand the present, view the past", *Journal of Hand Therapy* vol. 15, no. 2, (2002), pp. 97-132.

[76] Queensland Health, The late effects of polio: Information for General Practitioners, (2001).

[77] Paul, *History*, p. 344.

[78] Macfarlane Burnett interview by Christopher Sexton, audio recording, (1985), Australian Science and Technology Heritage Centre, Inventory Identifier 18/003, Box Number 1, Series 18.

[79] Rogers addresses all these topics in *Dirt and Disease: Polio before FDR* and revisits these themes in journal articles and book chapters published throughout the 1990s and 2000s.

[80] Rogers' examines the symbolism of the portrayal of Kenny in the 1946 RKO film Sister Kenny in: Naomi Rogers, "Sister Kenny", *ISIS* vol. 84, no. 4, (1993) pp. 772-774.

[81] Naomi Rogers, "American Medicine and the Politics of Filmmaking: Sister Kenny (RKO, 1946)" in *Medicine's Moving Pictures*, (ed.) Leslie J. Reagan, Nancy Tomes, and Paula A. Treichler, (Rochester: University of Rochester Press, 2007), pp. 199-238.

[82] Shell, *Polio.*

[83] Gould, *Plague.*

[84] Finger, *Elegy.*

[85] Gould, *Plague*, p. 87.

[86] Anne Finger observes that the portrayal of the discovery of the method in the

film "Sister Kenny" is inconsistent with the development of her techniques throughout the 1930s, Finger, *Elegy*, p. 96, but like Kerry Highley and Tony Gould she does not explore the significance of the implications of this observation.

[87] Shell, *Polio*, p. 10.

[88] Finger, *Elegy*, p. 178.

[89] Marjorie Farnbach, "Physiotherapy for poliomyelitis patients", *Australian Journal of Physiotherapy* vol. 1, no. 4, (1955), pp. 182-187; and Elma Casely, "Physiotherapy in South Australia", *Australian Journal of Physiotherapy* vol. 1, no. 4, (1955), pp. 164-169.

[90] Naomi Rogers, *Polio Wars* (New York: Oxford University Press, 2014) p. 425.

[91] Naomi Rogers, "Gender, history and the process of forgetting: The case of Sister Kenny", Paper presented at SUNY Stony Brook University, (2010).

[92] Rogers, *Polio Wars*, p. 426.

[93] Finger, *Elegy*, p. 11.

[94] Finger's comment is a reference to Kenny's friendship with Rosalind Russel and Eleanor Roosevelt. Nonetheless, Finger observes that almost all the women who were deemed influential in the Gallop polls were married to famous men or had inherited family fortunes.

[95] Finger, *Elegy*, p. 92.

[96] Shell, *Polio*, p. 6.

[97] Shell, *Polio*, p. 205.

[98] Herbert J. Levine, *I knew Sister Kenny: A story of a great lady and little people* (Boston: The Christopher Publishing House, 1954).

[99] The Centralia Clinic opened in August 1947 and closed in March 1949.

[100] Henry Thomas, *Sister Elizabeth Kenny* (New York: G.P. Putnam's Sons, 1958).

[101] Thomas, *Kenny*, p. 121.

[102] Emily Crofford, *Healing warrior: A story about Sister Elizabeth Kenny* (Minneapolis: Carolrhoda Books, 1989).

[103] The NCSS website states books are notable if they *'emphasize human relations, represent a diversity of groups and are sensitive to a broad range of cultural experiences, present an original theme or a fresh slant on a traditional topic, are easily readable and of high literary quality, and have a pleasing format and, when appropriate, illustrations that enrich the text'*. http://www.socialstudies.org/resources/notable.

2. FORGING A NURSE IDENTITY

Ordinary beginnings

Elizabeth Kenny was born in 1880 in Warialda, a small town in the region of New South Wales known as the Northern Tablelands. Her mother, Mary Moore was an Australian born descendant of a Protestant Irish convict. Her father, Michael Kenny, was a Roman Catholic Irish free settler who migrated to New South Wales in 1862. Mary and Michael were married in a manse by a Presbyterian minister. In this deeply sectarian era, Michael's marriage to Mary was not welcomed by her family, and it was not recognized by the Catholic Church. Despite these obstacles, they remained married until his death in 1913, and had nine children, seven of whom survived to adulthood. Elizabeth was their fifth child. Michael Kenny can best be described as an itinerant farm laborer, pursuing employment wherever it became available in the north east of New South Wales and the south east of Queensland.

The Kenny family moved frequently as Michael sought employment in a period of economic instability. The gold rush of the 1860s and the growth of exports in commodities such as wheat and wool fueled a sustained period of economic growth throughout the 1880s, but a sudden decline in commodity prices resulted in a major depression which lasted throughout the 1890s. In 1893 the Kenny family moved to the region of Queensland known as the Darling Downs. Here she is believed to have attended school for a short time before the family moved to a property near Clifton called Headington Hill. In 1899 Michael Kenny purchased a small farm near the town of Nobby. This town, which was too small to be reported in the 1901 Queensland census, would be the epicenter of Elizabeth Kenny's world for the next fifty years.

Peer accounts reveal that Kenny had an active social life as a young woman and was pursued by several suitors, but she showed no interest in their courtship. Kenny's sister, Julia, commented that when her mother would ask Elizabeth why she didn't '*settle down and have a family like your sisters*', Elizabeth would snort '*The very thought of it*'.[104] Kenny's overt disinterest in, or distaste for, marriage may not seem remarkable to an observer in the twenty-first century, but it set her apart from many of her peers. The Australian census of 1901 shows that two thirds of the women aged between twenty-five and thirty in Queensland were married or had already been widowed.[105] Elizabeth Kenny was emphatic in declaring that she had no appetite for an ordinary life, and no interest in living *on a farm like all the rest*,[106] but she also lacked the resources which could enable her to maintain an independent existence.

As a young adult with little formal education, no trade, no qualifications, a renowned objection to domestic work, and an even fiercer hostility towards marriage, Kenny had few choices in life other than to live with her relatives and assist her mother in the provision of home nursing services, or bush nursing as it was commonly called in rural locations. In the region of Queensland where Kenny lived as a young adult most medical practitioners and trained nurses worked in towns and cities. This provided an employment opportunity for women without nursing qualifications to provide midwifery and nursing services for people who lived in remote locations or were unable to afford the services of a qualified medical practitioner. Bush nursing was not a reliable source of income as clients would often *pay in kind*, but, importantly, it afforded some respectability to women who had, in Kenny's words, failed to *get married like the rest to justify my existence*.[107]

The seemingly inauspicious start to Kenny's life may not appear to have offered her a firm foundation upon which she could build a fulfilling life, but in the context of the expectations held for young women of her social and economic status her rural upbringing was enough to prepare her for marriage and the limited employment opportunities which were available in rural Queensland. There were substantial differences in the employment opportunities for women and men in the Federation era. The participation rate of men in paid employment in Queensland was four times that of women, and there were equally significant variations in the gender distribution within occupational categories. Although men made up a slightly higher proportion of the population in rural areas, the participation rate of men in primary production was five times that of women. Those women who participated in paid employment were mainly employed in domestic service. Notwithstanding the substantial overall difference in participation in paid employment, it is noteworthy that the participation rate for women and men in industrial occupations was almost equal, and women made up a third of the professional workforce.[108]

Variations in participation rates and employment categories demonstrate that work was not allocated on a purely gender basis. Despite its vast size and small population Australia was, paradoxically, one of the most urbanized societies in the world in the first decade of the twentieth century. In 1901 Australia had a population density of less than one person per square mile, whereas the United States of America had a population density of twenty people per square mile. Despite this low overall population density, a third of the Australian population lived in the capital cities, whereas only 7% of the population of France lived in Paris and 21% of the population of England lived in London.[109] This incongruity between population density and urbanism is reflected in major differences in the social and demographic profile of town and city dwellers. In 1901 nearly half the Queensland population of half a million people lived in six cities, yet agriculture and mining produced most the State's domestic product and income.[110] This polarization of the population and the economy meant that women living in rural areas were severely restricted in their employment opportunities as jobs in factories, commerce, and domestic service were concentrated in urban areas.[111] As a young adult, Kenny found herself in an iniquitous situation. Even though there were few opportunities for her to engage in industrial or domestic service occupations, there was little prospect of her earning an independent living through employment in primary production as this type of employment was considered improper for women.

The dawn of the twentieth century heralded momentous changes in Kenny's world. In the space of a few years Kenny attained the legal status of an adult, Queensland became a State in the newly federated Commonwealth of Australia, and women were granted the franchise to vote. These events provided women with an unprecedented degree of emancipation, but we have no knowledge of how Kenny viewed the impact of these changes on her own life or the social status of women as they are completely ignored in her memoirs. Beverley Kingston argues that whilst the social status of women was improving, the myth that Australian women were better off than women elsewhere in the world is predicated on a convenient conjunction of nostalgic stories of courageous pioneering women and mid-nineteenth century male values which positioned women in the role of home making, child rearing, and nation building. Women's work, Kingston argues, was defined by what men thought proper for women. Kingston concludes that women with no training or capital effectively had two options – *marry well* to escape the necessity for employment or rely on their domestic skills to secure employment in domestic services.[112]

According to Kenny's relatives she was not work shy, but the work which was on offer within her limited horizon was not to her liking. Years later she is said to have claimed *'It was a terrible calamity when I went out to make my own living'*.[113] The calamity to which she was referring was, in fact, a turning point in her life. In 1907 she travelled to Guyra in New South Wales to visit her recently widowed grandmother. Guyra was renowned as a major potato growing district, supplying potatoes to Queensland, New South Wales and Victoria. Outbreaks of potato blight in Queensland and Tasmania during 1909 severely disrupted the distribution of this staple crop within Australian markets.[114] Kenny revealed her nascent business acumen by organizing the sale of potatoes to markets in Brisbane. In doing so she apparently won the esteem of the local producers while earning a substantial income for herself.[115] This was a laudable accomplishment for an impoverished and uneducated woman to achieve in an era where women had limited opportunities to acquire independent capital.

Notwithstanding the pride she expresses in her achievement, her success appears to have come at a personal cost as she also claims to have earned the approbation of the '*young people of the village*' for daring to:

> *do a thing no woman would think of doing. I was not refined, I was not nice. A girl who knew her place looked to her male relatives to dispose of the crude details of business. It was vulgar to be healthy, ladylike to be delicate.*[116]

Kenny wrote these words in the early 1940s. The approbation which Kenny professes to have suffered does seem disproportionate to the seemingly innocuous misdemeanor of trading potatoes, and it is worth noting that her cousin, with whom she was living, appears to have escaped public scorn even though she gained her livelihood by working in a shop with her husband.[117] The hand written manuscript which forms the basis of a memoir published in 1943 places more emphasis on her peers' rejection being founded on her disdain for the prospect of '*whiling away the time with a piece of embroidery and waiting for the knight errant to appear on the scene*',[118] than the impropriety of a single woman undertaking men's work. Kenny's words suggest she perceived that her moral integrity was being questioned because at the ripe old age of twenty-nine she was rejecting marriage while showing no signs of embracing a socially acceptable spinsterhood. Whatever the cause of her indignation, the rejection rankled for many years. The episode is additionally noteworthy as it is a rare first-hand portrayal of her self-image at a key point in her life.

The description of Kenny's first attempt to earn her independence through commerce offers a glimpse of her talent for ingenuity and opportunism when faced with a challenge. The episode also suggests there was an emerging conflict between her yearning for independence and her desire for social acceptance. This small step towards independence had given her confidence in her ability to do work traditionally reserved for men and provided her with capital which she could use as she wished, but it also left her wary of the social stigma that could accompany behavior which transgressed the norms of the cloistered rural society in which she lived. Poised to capitalize on her business acumen Kenny abruptly abandoned her venture as a produce trader, and her ties with Guyra, and set out on a journey which ultimately would define the rest of her life.

Inventing Nurse Kenny

The date of Kenny's departure from Guyra is unclear. Minnie and James Bell told Victor Cohn that Kenny left Guyra after living with them for two to three years. Kenny's cousin, Alicent Woodward (nee Moore), claimed Kenny left Guyra in early 1911 to assist her with the birth of her son, Wilfred, in Walcha in January 1911.[119] There is no extant record of where she resided between January and November 1911. Whilst there is uncertainty in the timing of Kenny's departure from Guyra and her immediate destination, there is reliable evidence that she was carrying items in her luggage which would be instrumental in the creation of a new identity. Shortly before leaving Guyra Kenny purchased a red silk cape, black cloak, white pinafore, black velvet cap and some starched white collars from a local tailor.[120] In essence, Kenny had purchased the traditional uniform of a trained nurse. Upon her eventual arrival in Nobby in late 1911 the unqualified, but suitably attired, Elizabeth Kenny was ready to offer her services to the citizens of the Clifton Shire as Nurse Kenny, Medical and Surgical Nurse.[121]

The question of whether Kenny could legitimately claim to be a qualified nurse has been debated at length. In 1943 Kenny claimed that after leaving Guyra she had '*entered a private hospital and began my training*',[122] but omitted to state when or where this occurred, or the length of the course. As formal nurse training in the era consisted of a three years residential course conducted by a recognized State approved hospital there was insufficient time between her departure from Guyra and her arrival in Nobby in 1911 for her to undertake training which could lead to a recognized qualification. Recent research by Kerry Highley raises the possibility that Kenny may have enrolled on a nursery nursing course at the Sydney Norland Institute in 1911. It is likely that Kenny knew of The Norland course as it was advertised in The Guyra Argos during 1910 and 1911, promising an applicant an annual income of £40-50 upon graduation. The advertised cost of the Norland course is consistent with claims Kenny made about the cost of her nurse training,[123] and the twelve months course included three month's midwifery and surgical experience. Whilst Highley's hypothesis is compelling it is unlikely that Kenny undertook the Norland course as there was insufficient time for her to complete the course in Sydney and return to Nobby by October 1911 as she was still resident in Walcha in February 1911 where she had assisted her cousin in the birth of her son.

When Kenny left Guyra she left behind a reliable source of income and a reputation as a competent produce trader. She also left behind the domestic independence she experienced living with her married cousin which she would not have enjoyed while living with her parents or grandmother. Leaving Guyra for an uncertain future as a nurse may seem reckless, but her preparation for the undertaking suggests it was based on at least some measure of rational assessment. The questions which therefore beg to be answered are – how and why, at around the age of thirty, did Kenny adopt the personae of a trained nurse; what benefits could she have hoped to acquire through her ruse; and what did her actions reveal about her personality?

From a contemporary viewpoint Elizabeth Kenny appears to have performed a conceit in assuming the role of a trained nurse despite her lack of formal training, but her actions should be understood in terms of the broader social context and status of nursing in this period. Nursing was still in its infancy as a recognized professional role for women in the Federation era. The job was not well paid, and the conditions of employment were poor even by contemporary standards – in 1910 trainee nurses worked longer hours and received less pay than domestic servants, and it was not uncommon for nurses working in the community to be paid in *kind* rather than cash for their labor.[124] Adding insult to injury, women who worked as nurses were still subject to lingering prejudices which questioned their morality and sobriety.[125] Reformers, such as Lucy Osborne in Australia, had acted to counter these prejudices by requiring trainee nurses to live in hospital dormitories to shield them from the temptations and dangers of ordinary life. This strategy also had the added benefit to employers of ensuring the nursing workforce could work long hours in erratic shift patterns long after similar work practices were abandoned in other industries.

Despite the many undesirable characteristics of the job, demand for nurse training grew steadily in the early decades of the twentieth century. The status of the job was increasing due to the State regulation of health care professions, improvements in nursing education, and the recognition of the contribution of nursing services to troop morale in military campaigns such as the Crimean and Boer wars.[126] All these changes had an impact at an individual level as well as a collective level. The combined effect of technological changes in the practice of medicine in the early decades of the twentieth century and the reorganization of hospital services which occurred during the First World War meant that institutions became the primary location of nurses' work rather than the home or the community. This relocation of the role to institutional settings contributed to the growing professional status of nurses, but it also limited the capacity of nurses to individually negotiate a fee for their services with their private patients. Ironically, the forces which were shaping the professionalization of nursing would also lock nurses into a cage of professional subservience which arguably still exists over a century later.

Kenny's perception of nursing as an occupation would have been shaped by her observations of the work of nurses, and the public discourse which accompanied the evolution of the role. In rural Queensland nursing and midwifery services were often delivered by mature women working with clients in their own homes, or in small privately-owned hospitals or *lying-in* homes. Several small private hospitals, owned and managed by nurses, operated in the nearby town of Clifton between 1906 and 1926. These establishments could call upon the services of the town's doctor and pharmacist. Interviews with Kenny's relatives in the 1950s confirm that as a young woman Kenny had assisted her mother with home nursing and the delivery of babies in the community. Her relatives claimed that prior to her venture as a produce trader she supplemented her income in Guyra by providing home nursing services, mostly assisting with home births under instruction from the town's doctor.[127] She is also known to have worked for a brief period as a domestic servant in a private hospital called Scotia in the town of Guyra.[128] While she was not employed as a nurse at Scotia, she was most likely able to observe the organization of the hospital and the manner in which nursing care was delivered in an institutional setting. These experiences may have provided an insight into the organization and delivery of nursing care.

Throughout her life Kenny was recognized as being a quick study, but insight and attentiveness alone could not be a substitute for the years of formal training and examination which was required before a woman could claim the privilege of the title Trained Nurse. Nonetheless, in the context of her personal experience it is possible that she concluded her knowledge of nursing practice within the home and institutional settings was enough to embolden her to assume the public identity of a trained nurse. It is also important to note that in 1910 it was neither illegal nor uncommon for untrained nurses to use the title of Nurse to describe their occupation as the use of the title was not subject to legal control in Queensland until the establishment of a Nurses' Registration Board in 1911.

A further reference point for understanding Kenny's perception of the role of nurses can be found in the public discourse which reflected and shaped the evolving role of nurses during this period. The role and status of traditional forms of home nursing or bush nursing was widely debated topic in the first decade of the century. District nursing services, modelled on services established in the United Kingdom, were steadily growing in the larger urban areas in which most of the population lived. In September 1909 Lady Dudley, wife of the newly appointed Governor-General of Australia, made a public address in which she called for the extension of district nursing services to pastoral and agricultural populations. The address precipitated a vigorous public debate within the nation's newspapers which idealized the contribution of trained nurses to rural health care.

> *Unquestionably no other additions to a bush population would be more welcome than a sensible trained nurse, who could minister to the sick. Only those who have lived among the pioneer settlers far removed from medical or skilled assistance can appreciate the boon which the residence of a trained nurse in their midst would confer.*[129]

Such was the enthusiasm of the public discourse on the merits of bush nurses that a medical practitioner in Maitland, NSW, claimed in a letter to his local newspaper *'(trained) bush nurses will be missionaries of health, of sanitation, of cleanliness and of comfort all over Australia'*.[130] These lofty claims provide evidence of the extent of the changes in the public image of nursing in Australia, and the speed with which these changes were occurring.

The campaign for improving nursing services to rural population did not result in the creation of a national scheme as advocates had hoped, but the campaign was effective in promoting public awareness of the need for better organized nursing services in rural areas, and the raising of public confidence in the authority and legitimacy of trained nurses to provide services beyond midwifery and palliative care. Kenny would almost certainly have been exposed to this debate as there are numerous records of articles reporting the campaign in newspapers which served the Guyra district, and it is likely her perception of the scope of a nurse's role was informed by this public discourse.

Kenny's new identity as a trained nurse may have appeared to be an ideal solution to her predicament, but did she fully understand the risks associated with her actions? Her new life may have appeared to offer substantial benefits, such as a reliable source of income and increased social status and independence. Nonetheless, the manner and haste in which she enacted her transformation presented her with risks which she may not have fully appreciated. The immediate risk associated with assuming the role of a trained nurse was the potential for incurring public humiliation should her lack of formal training be revealed. Kenny may have looked the part, but she possessed neither a certificate or record of training, nor a badge designating where she had trained.[131] Paper records can be forged or lost, so her inability to produce a certificate of training would not have automatically resulted in prosecution, but it could have aroused suspicion among her nursing colleagues. On the other hand, a badge, whilst not a legal requirement until 1911, was a visible symbol of a nurse's credentials which most trained nurses displayed with great pride.[132] The practice of training institutions presenting their graduate nurses with a badge originated in the United Kingdom in the late 1800s and was widely adopted in Australia.

Notwithstanding the importance of avoiding public disgrace, the foremost risk associated with assuming the guise of a trained nurse may not have been evident to Kenny when she was preparing for her new career.

Growing discontent among medical practitioners over the rising professional status of pharmacists, dentists, opticians, and nurses culminated in the Queensland Government introducing The Health Act Amendment Act in 1911. This Act introduced stronger regulation of the nurse workforce and made it unlawful to falsely claim to be a Registered Nurse. Nurses seeking registration were required to have either completed a set period of training in a recognized hospital, or, for nurses lacking formal training, to submit to a prescribed examination. Nurses who could not meet these conditions but were able to demonstrate suitable experience as a nurse could apply for registration through Ministerial discretion. There is no record of Kenny making such a request.

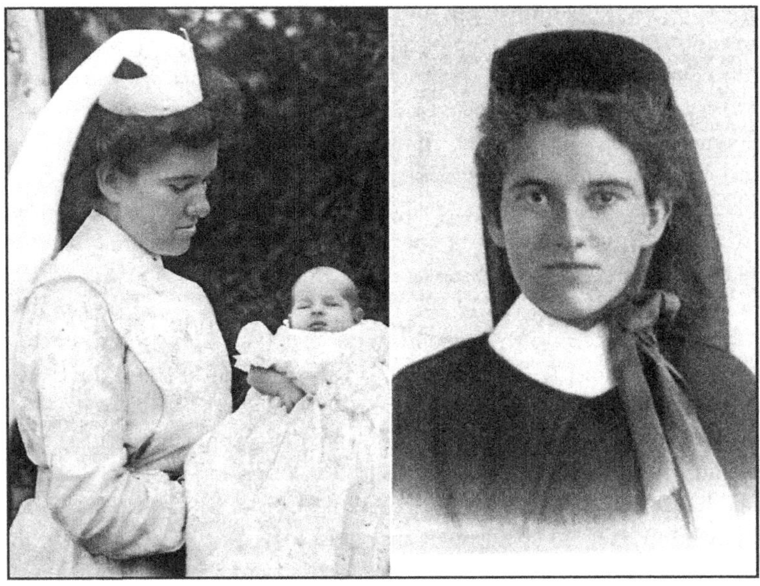

Kenny wearing nurse uniforms c. 1912-1913. Trove NLA.

The Health Act Amendment Act 1911 also set out new arrangements for the registration of private hospitals. Crucially, the Act stipulated '*No person shall be entitled to apply for or hold a certificate of registration of a private hospital unless such person is a medical practitioner or a registered nurse*'.[133] Responsibility for the administration of the registration process was placed with local government authorities. Whilst the impact of this amendment would be slow in taking effect it was a significant milestone on the path which was leading to the institutionalization of nursing practice and the demise of the traditional independent nurse practitioner.

There are many unanswered questions arising from Kenny's decision to present herself as Nurse Kenny to the residents of Nobby rather than returning to the informal home nursing she had left behind three years earlier. Did she seek advice from Aeneas McDonnell, the doctor she later claimed had been an influential mentor in her young adult life? If she had sought his counsel it's likely he would have advised her that she needed to undertake a recognized training course if she wished to pursue a career in nursing. In 1943 she claimed she had consulted him, but the date she provides did not allow enough time for her to heed his advice and complete the three years of training which she claims to have completed.[134] Given most her family lived in a handful of small towns it is inconceivable that they would not know where she, a single woman, was living for the extended period required for her to undertake General Nurse training or Nursery Nurse training. It is also difficult to reconcile the apparent lack of conjecture by her family in Nobby and Guyra on the timing of her nurse training and the reasons for her return to Nobby. These and similar questions can only be answered through the consideration of anecdotal evidence due to the paucity of first-hand accounts of her early life.

As Kenny set out on her journey from Guyra to Nobby in 1910 or 1911 she may have felt confident in her ability to present herself as Nurse Kenny to her anticipated clients in the cloistered community of the Nobby district, but it is impossible to know if she was aware of changes in the wider world which would eventually lead to her subterfuge being discovered. The preceding analysis supports the conclusion that Kenny made a calculated decision to masquerade as a trained nurse in Nobby to escape the ostracism she experienced in Guyra due to her gender non-conformity. Her actions were rational in as much as she possessed basic nursing skills, and she understood the potential for nursing to shield her personal life from external scrutiny and provide her with an independent income and social status. Nonetheless, her actions were also accompanied by risks which she may not have fully assessed.

This chapter is not concerned with judging Kenny's behavior; it is concerned with understanding her behavior by examining the forces which were framing and directing her actions. Elizabeth Kenny's adoption of the Nurse Kenny personae reveals three important personal characteristics. First, it revealed she was willing to claim legitimacy through pretense rather than qualification. Second, it demonstrated her ability to reinvent herself as need and circumstance demanded. Third, it illustrated the extent to which her determination to achieve personal goals was accompanied by a tunnel vision which obscured her recognition of the extent to which her actions could or should be subject to outside scrutiny.

Medical and surgical nurse at your service

The precise date that Kenny first offered her nursing services to the residents of Nobby is not known, but a professional services advertisement in the Clifton Courier, 4 November 1911, declares her availability as a

medical and surgical nurse. Despite her unorthodox preparation for her
new career, Nurse Kenny's arrival in Nobby was a resounding success. In
fact, Kenny's return to Nobby had been so financially successful that within
a year of her return to the district she was able to take control of a small
private hospital in the nearby town of Clifton. The first public record of the
hospital being under Kenny's control is an advertisement in the Clifton
Courier on 13 July 1912.[135] The property, in Norman Street, had previously
been used as a private hospital by Nurse Robson. Kenny called her hospital
St Canice Private Hospital in honor of her father's birthplace in Ireland, but
the choice of name was probably based as much on mercantile
considerations as sentimentality.

Waverton Private Hospital, Clifton, 1915.

There were profound sectarian divisions in Australia society which were
evident in the social structures and provision of services in small towns like
Clifton. Whilst newspaper records for the district do not show direct
evidence of overt social exclusion based on religion, it was commonplace
for private hospitals and nursing homes to be identified by the name of a
Roman Catholic Saint if it welcomed a Roman Catholic clientele, or the
name of an English town or city if it welcomed a Protestant clientele.

Newspaper reports show Nurse Kenny provided medical, surgical, and
midwifery services, and St Canice was equipped with a telephone and
electric room bells.[136] The hospital was located on the south-east corner of
the intersection of Norman and George Streets, Clifton, in a converted

domestic building owned by the Just family.[137] The Queensland Journals of Conveyances and Encumbrances for Clifton for the period 1912 to 1915 contain no record of the building being sold or leased, so it is likely that Kenny rented the property through a private contract with the Just family. There is no extant photograph of St. Canice, but a local historian believes it was probably housed in premises like Waverton Private Hospital, operated by Nurse Pengelly.

The speed of the transition from nursing private patients in their homes to taking control of a small private hospital demonstrates that Nurse Kenny had acquired the confidence of her clients and the support of local medical practitioners. Newspaper reports also confirm she was acquiring the social status which she had been unable to attain as a potato trader in Guyra. An article published in the Brisbane Courier in 1913 reports that Nurse Kenny and other town dignitaries had each donated £1/1s to the local Ambulance fund.[138] This amount is approximately one quarter of the average weekly income for a typical family of four, [139] and represents a sizeable donation for a person who until very recently had no regular income and had been completely dependent on her relatives.

The significance of Kenny's involvement in St Canice is generally unrecognized in past analyses of this period of her life. A thesis written by John Wilson exploring Kenny's views about nursing completely ignores her ownership of St Canice even though it is the only time in her life that she worked in a conventional nursing role. Kenny's biographers are equally neglectful of the importance of St Canice. Despite their knowledge of her lack of formal training, neither Victor Cohn nor Wade Alexander question how she had managed to conduct a hospital without arousing the suspicion of the medical practitioners or qualified nurses who worked in Clifton during the time she ran St Canice. Instead, they focus on rumors of a romance with one of the local medical practitioners. It may be that Cohn and Alexander failed to question the absence of peer review due to a cultural bias which presumed that nurses and medical practitioners who worked in rural Queensland were less educated and qualified than their colleagues in urban areas. In fact, all the doctors who worked with Kenny at St Canice were University trained, and most of the nurses who practiced in Clifton during this period were fully certificated and hospital trained.[140]

For three years Nurse Kenny prospered financially and personally as the proprietor of St Canice Private Hospital, but this episode in her life was about to come to an abrupt end. The long arm of bureaucracy was steadily reaching towards the Darling Downs, and Nurse Kenny was about to find herself being held to ransom by her own subterfuge. Whilst the Health Amendment Act 1911 mandated the registration of all private hospitals, uptake of registration had been slow and there was a lack of clarity in the registration process. Newspaper reports show some hospital administrators believed they had the authority to register hospitals in which they had a financial interest. In December 1914 the Queensland Government acted to enforce the registration process by introducing an amendment to the Act which enabled local authorities to issue certificates of registration to private hospitals. The Clifton Shire Council would now be responsible for the administration of the hospital registration process.

Kenny claimed she closed St Canice because *'the world cataclysm of 1914 closed that chapter of my life'*.[141] It is more likely that her decision was provoked by the impending cataclysm of being exposed as an unqualified nurse by the long arm of health bureaucracy. In 1911 Kenny had been prudent in advertising her services as a *Medical and Surgical Nurse*, but in 1912, when she opened St Canice, she abandoned caution when she claimed to be a *Certificated Medical, Surgical and Midwifery* nurse. Whilst there is no evidence of Kenny directly claiming to be a Registered Nurse, it is very likely that she understood she was unable to apply for registration of the hospital as this would have exposed her absence of qualifications to the Clifton Shire Council.

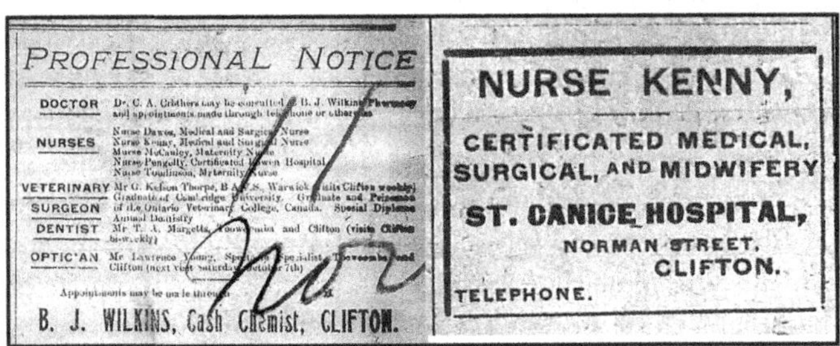

Clifton Courier professional notices November 1911 and July 1912. State Library of Queensland.

Most accounts of this period of her life represent the closure of St Canice as being motivated by her intention to enlist for war service in the footsteps of her brother. This conjoining of motivations for her actions is an anachronistic explanation of her behavior which trivializes the significance of the dilemma which confronted her – should she risk exposure as a fraud for misrepresenting her nursing credentials, or should she abandon the income, status, and respectability she had enjoyed as the proprietor of a successful private hospital? It seems that Kenny found the solution to her dilemma by drawing on lessons from her past.

War nurse

Australia joined the imperial war effort soon after Britain declared was against Germany in August 1914. Kenny's younger brother, William, enlisted on 21st August 1914, and embarked with his regiment, the 2nd Light Horse, for service in Europe on 24th September 1914.[142] The patriotic zeal displayed by William Kenny was not uncommon in Australia at the outbreak of hostilities in Europe, and there are unsubstantiated reports that dozens of Kenny's relatives volunteered to serve during the war. Whilst Australia was mobilizing for war life continued as normal for Nurse Kenny as she managed her private hospital and participated in the activities of the Clifton branch of the Red Cross. Queensland newspaper reports on the military campaign in the Dardanelles praised the gallantry of the Australian and New Zealand expeditionary forces in their *'sanguinary struggle'* against the Turks in the Gallipoli campaign, but there is little evidence of progress despite the mounting numbers of deaths and injuries. Kenny does not offer a precise reason for her decision to join the war effort, but on 29 May 1915 she announced she *'had been accepted for military service'* and would be joining the expeditionary forces to serve King and country.[143]

Kenny continued to treat patients at St Canice until mid-June in 1915.[144] Despite the evident value of a hospital which had provided her with a reliable income for three years Kenny only sold the fittings and fixtures but did not sell the business.[145] Her decision not to sell the business is difficult to reconcile with her demonstrated business acumen, and it is plausible to conclude this may reflect a reluctance to expose her lack of credentials to a prospective purchaser. Whilst the reasons for her hasty departure are not known, her journey to the war front was well publicized. The Clifton Courier reported she received a *'a handsome wristlet watch'* from the Red Cross Society in recognition of her voluntary service in Clifton,[146] while the Brisbane Courier reported she received *'a handsome travelling rug'* on the day of her departure.[147] On 20 June 1915 Kenny bid farewell to friends and family and boarded a train at Clifton bound for Sydney. Six days later she boarded the P&O liner RMS Medina bound for London.[148] The Medina arrived in London on Sunday 8 August after an uneventful journey across the Indian Ocean and through the Suez Canal.

Kenny's memoir states that when she arrived in London she promptly reported to the Australian Imperial Force (AIF) and was instructed to *'proceed to France for a period of special duty'*. In France her *'left knee managed to get in the way of some enemy shrapnel'*, which forced her to return to London to recuperate.[149] After recovering from her injury, she was granted leave to visit her cousins in Ireland. On 8 October 1915 Staff Nurse Kenny embarked on HMAT Suevic bound for Australia on the first of twelve voyages in the service of her country. This is the story which Kenny liked to tell of her war service. It contained seeds of truth.

A more factual account of her journey follows. In May 1915 Kenny abruptly closed her successful business in Clifton and announced she had been accepted for military service. Rather than following in the footsteps of her brother who had enlisted nine months earlier, Kenny was obliged to forge her own path to serve her country – for good reasons. The routine process for a nurse to join the Australian Army Nursing Service (AANS) was to travel to an enlistment office in their nearest regional city or State capital. This routine process was not available to Kenny as she was not eligible to join.[150] Undaunted, and at substantial personal expense, she travelled to Sydney where she purchased a ticket for a sea voyage to London.[151] On the journey Kenny befriended a fellow passenger, Alice Perrott. The two became lifelong friends. Years later Alice recalled in an interview that Kenny travelled in a civilian nurse's uniform and intended to enlist when she arrived in London.[152] Alice also confirmed Kenny had a letter of recommendation from Dr Aeneas McDonnell and was confident this recommendation would enable her to enlist in London. While Kenny may have professed to be confident in her ability to achieve her ambition, it seems quite misguided for a woman equipped only with a nurse's uniform and a letter of recommendation to travel from Sydney to London in the expectation of enlisting with the Australian military.[153] Another, more plausible, explanation is needed if her bravado in setting off to the applause of her family and community is to be interpreted as anything other than a sign of self-delusion.

Kenny's journey from Nobby to London certainly dwarfs her earlier transformational journey from Guyra to Nobby, but she was following a similar script. Experience had probably taught her that appearances could be deceiving, and distance was a formidable ally in concealing her behavior from scrutiny. Most of the eight weeks between Kenny's arrival in London as a civilian and her departure from Liverpool for Sydney on HMAT Suevic is undocumented, but there is reliable evidence she spent some of the time visiting a cousin in Ireland while she was still a civilian.[154] All that is known for certain is that after biding her time in London she obtained an assignment as a nurse aboard HMAT Suevic. In later life she claimed she reported to the Australian Headquarters upon arrival in London and was posted to Ypres, France, where she was wounded. To make this claim plausible she misrepresented her arrival in London as being in the Spring rather than the Autumn. Wade Alexander and Victor Cohn speculated she may have worked with a Red Cross Voluntary Aid Detachment or the Queen Alexandra Imperial Military Nursing Service (QAIMNS), but there is no record of her involvement in the Red Cross or VAD in the Red Cross archives in London. As there was insufficient time for her to travel to France, incur an injury, recuperate in London, and visit her relatives in Ireland in the space of eight weeks it is safe to assume that Kenny invented this story. It is difficult to identify when or why she would invent such a story as there are few surviving accounts of her war service which pre-date the 1940s. If she invented the story while still in London in 1915 she may have intended to use it as an alibi if her much publicized war service did not materialise. If she invented the story in the 1940s she may have believed it would obscure her unconventional transition from civilian life to military service.

All that is known for certain is that after biding her time in London she eventually managed to obtain an assignment as a nurse aboard HMAT Suevic. Her apparent success in enlisting, a term which not applicable to nurses, has been subject to much conjecture as she should have been rejected for failing to hold the required qualifications, and there are inconsistencies in the official record of her war service. Annoying as it may be for historians, it is not uncommon for Army personnel to have incomplete or inconsistent war records. Kenny's war service certificate, which is dated 17 December 1918 in Melbourne, states her date of appointment to the AANS as 30 May 1915. This is clearly incorrect as she was still treating patients at St Canice on this date. The attestation papers held by the Australian War Memorial also record her date of enlistment as 30 May 1915 and her rank as Sister, AANS AIF. These papers were probably created in 1918 as she was not promoted to the rank of Sister until 1917. Other documents in her service records show her date of enlistment as 28 May 1916 and 28 July 1916.

In the mid-1950s Victor Cohn made lengthy enquiries with the AIF to explain her irregular enlistment. Cohn was aware of the requirement for AANS nurses to hold nursing qualifications, but assumed these requirements were waivered because her letter of recommendation from Aeneas McDonnell was a golden ticket. Cohn concluded that in the face of a deteriorating campaign producing boatloads of injured soldiers '*The 1915 Army wouldn't have argued whether she was a bloody trained nurse or not!*'.[155] Whilst there is credence to this explanation, too much of the speculation on her irregular enlistment has focused on her qualifications and too little on the nature of her military posting and the coincidental reorganization of the Australian Army Medical Services (AAMS).

The rapid increase in the number of Australian casualties requiring treatment in England in the summer of 1915 necessitated a review of the standing orders for the treatment and disposal of injured soldiers.[156] In the early stages of the Gallipoli campaign the AIF had implemented a policy of treating Australian casualties in hospitals under its own control, but the logistics of transporting injured troops from the battlefield to hospitals in Egypt and England had been misjudged. At the beginning of the campaign the AIF estimated two hospital ships, or *white* ships, would be adequate for the retrieval of injured troops from the battle front. Hospital ships were known as *white* ships because they were painted white to distinguish them from warships.[157] This level of provision soon proved to be completely inadequate and increasing the number of so-called *white* ships was ruled out due to the cost. The AIF decided to adapt existing transport ships to enable them to be used for the transportation of invalids from England or Egypt to Australia, and the transportation of reinforcements back to England. These transport ships were classified as *dark* ships as they were not protected by the war conventions which defended *white* ships from attack.[158] The AIF believed *dark* ships would be more efficient than *white* ships because they would require fewer medical and nursing personnel to transport '*cases not requiring special treatment on the voyage*'.[159] Typically, a *white* ship would have an establishment of 16-21 nurses, whereas it was estimated that a *dark* ship would only require 6 or 7. Initially, the repatriation of invalid cases to Australia was organized on an *ad hoc* basis, but the surge in casualties returning to England in mid-1915 necessitated a more controlled approach to the clearing of invalid soldiers from the Australian Auxiliary Hospitals. This led to the creation of the Sea Transport Service (STS) in mid-1916.

HMAT Suevic 1919. AWM.

Nurse Kenny had the good fortune to present herself to the AIF in the month that hasty preparations were being made to assemble a medical and nursing crew to accompany 489 invalid cases to Australia on HMAT Suevic. The AIF spent £18,000 converting the troop transport ship into an invalid transport ship in September 1915.[160] The Director General of Medical Services (DGMS), General Fetherston, appears to have been reluctant to assign experienced nurses to the menial duty of chaperoning invalid soldiers on the long sea voyage to Australia as the medical personnel list for the Suevic shows there were only two AANS nurses, Sister Kidd and Staff Nurse Jenkins, accompanied by four nurses with no rank.[161]

The inclusion of nurses of undesignated rank on the Suevic's crew demonstrates the level of improvisation associated with the organization of the voyage. Fetherston had made an earlier attempt to replace orderlies with untrained nurses on the *white* ships but had met with determined opposition from the AANS. Nursing professional bodies in Australia feared the use of large numbers of volunteers and semi-trained staff in Army hospitals would undermine the credibility of their campaign to secure professional recognition and registration for nurses. The AANS prevailed as the AIF were reluctant to engage in a public spat with the AANS which might undermine military recruitment strategies.[162] Invalid transport ships crewed by the STS had '*one medical officer, seven nurses, a dispenser, a masseur, a Staff Sergeant Quartermaster and sixteen other ranks from the Australian Army Medical Corps*'.[163] The Suevic departed Liverpool with two medical officers, a civilian surgeon, six nurses, and twelve orderlies. The fact that some of the nursing personnel were not trained nurses or members of the AANS is enough to demonstrate the expediency which governed the operation of invalid transport at this time.

By means which will probably never be fully understood Nurse E Kenny was on board the Suevic when she departed for Australia. Kenny was accompanied by three other nurses of undesignated rank. After the initial journey Minnie Maxwell served with various organizations in France and Belgium on transport duty and later as a matron in a munitions factory in England. Fannie Jane Moxham served at the Australian Voluntary Hospital in France but returned home after falling ill. Elsie May Smith, recorded as ME Smith, was a member of the AANS but was discharged upon her return to Australia as it was discovered she was not properly qualified.[164]

Kenny is vague in her description of her enlistment status when she made the journey on the Suevic, simply stating she was asked to '*accompany the first Australian wounded on their journey home*'.[165] How and when Nurse Kenny managed to convince the AIF she was suitably qualified to join the AANS remains open to conjecture but taking all the available evidence into account it is likely this decision was taken in Australia in 1916, not in London in 1915 as is widely believed.

Kenny's enlistment with the AANS has been widely misunderstood because many researchers have sought to reconcile the available evidence with Kenny's rendition of the events rather than questioning the veracity or meaning of the story she told. Similarly, the significance of her designation as a nurse on a transport ship has been elevated due to her later appointment as a Staff Nurse and promotion to the rank of Sister, and her efforts in later life to exaggerate the severity of the incapacities of the invalid soldiers. Very few of the invalid cases returning to Australia on the dark ships required complex medical or nursing care for battle related injuries. The major problem facing doctors and nurses on the voyages were epidemics of infectious diseases such as meningitis, typhoid fever, and influenza.

Except for the irregularity of her enlistment Kenny's war service was broadly unexceptional. There is no record of her working in or near a battle zone, and no medical or nursing personnel attached to the STS were killed or wounded through enemy attack. Her promotion in rank from Staff Nurse to Sister appears to have been based on length of service rather than merit as her service records contain no evidence of commendations for exceptional service. At the end of the war she was awarded the standard

Kenny in AANS uniform, 1918. AWM.

trio of British war service medals – 1914/15 Star, British War Medal, and the Victory Medal – issued to all nurses based on their service with the AANS. Neither is there keny evidence she applied for or was recommended for transfer to a hospital ship or one of the Australian Auxiliary Hospitals in England where she could have expanded her nursing skills and knowledge.

Interviews conducted by Victor Cohn in the 1950s reveal her nursing companions considered her to be a competent nurse but were aware of her unconventional techniques and reluctance to talk about her nursing training. Kenny and her colleague Ella Morphett were temporarily attached to the Australian Auxiliary Hospitals at Harefield Park and Southall for short periods while awaiting reassignment to their next voyage. This was the only time Kenny was exposed to the innovative medical and nursing techniques which were developing during the war years. Taking all the extant evidence into account there is little reason to dispute the conclusion that for most of the war she was content to perform routine nursing tasks as a member of a team of trained nurses who possessed a greater range of war time experiences and knowledge of nursing.[166]

The company of women

Kenny's War service bestowed the untrained bush nurse from Nobby with the most important endorsement she received in her life – the title of *Sister*. Although she was never employed as a nurse after her discharge from the AANS she retained the title for the remaining thirty-five years of her civilian life despite the ambiguous meaning of the title outside England and Australia. War service also allowed Kenny to travel far beyond the socially and culturally claustrophobic confines of the Darling Downs and explore the world which she had dreamed of visiting as a young woman. But the War also afforded Kenny with a privilege which has been widely ignored or misunderstood – the opportunity, possibly for the first time in her life, to experience extended periods of personal intimacy with other women.

A troop ship carrying nearly five hundred invalid soldiers may not appear to be the ideal setting for a woman to find intimacy with a handful of other women, but the unique combination of Edwardian social etiquette and WW1 military discipline transformed the inconceivable into reality for Kenny. Joining the crew of the Suevic in October 1915 was a moment of pure serendipity for Kenny as it is probably the factor which facilitated her joining the STS in 1916. The STS also offered her other unexpected benefits. If there were such a thing as *having a good war*, her attachment to the STS came as close as one could get. Life aboard the transport ships was arduous, cramped, and monotonous, but it was relatively agreeable when compared with the conditions nurses experienced in the General and Stationary Hospitals which operated in Egypt and the Dardanelles.

The official history of the AAMS indicates that the small number of deaths on the transport ships was mostly the result of infectious disease, and the main cause of discomfort for the medical and nursing personnel was heat as the ships traversed the equatorial regions. In contrast, nurses posted to the Stationary and General hospitals often worked in appalling conditions, sometimes living and working in tents while experiencing shortages of food and medical supplies. In addition, hospital nurses were subject to the emotional and psychological hazard of dealing daily with horrific battle injuries and high mortality rates due to infectious disease. Until recently the experiences of Australian nurses working in field hospitals on the Eastern Front has been poorly documented, overshadowed by historians' preoccupation with the heroism of soldiers who fought in the Gallipoli campaign. The official Australian war histories produced in the 1930s and 1940s briefly describe the organization of the AANS but pay little attention to the experiences of nurses working in the fields of war.[167]

Kenny aboard HMAT Themistocles, 1916. AWM.

Kenny's memoir, written more than twenty years after the WW1 ended, portrays the selfless dedication of the nurses working on the *dark* ships, and the ever present threat of death and disease, but her recollection of her war service provides little information about the shipboard life which she experienced during the three years she served as a transport nurse.[168] While she exaggerates the risk of death and disease for the nursing personnel, she does acknowledge the camaraderie which existed between the nurses and the invalid soldiers, and there are glimpses of the amusements which could be found on board the ships or on shore leave. As Kirsty Harris observes, remarkably little of the contribution of nurses to the war effort has been documented in official histories of the WW1,[169] but some understanding of shipboard life for nurses in transit between Australia and the War Front is emerging as a result of the publication of nurses' war diaries in academic texts and WW1 memorial websites.[170] The diaries of Annie Bell and Anne Donnell, available from the *Through These Lines* website,[171] depict ship life as orderly, instructive, and comfortable, if not crowded as the transport ships were not designed for carrying equipment and large numbers of military personnel to the war front. The ships were well provisioned and the nurses enjoyed concerts, lectures, and regular shore excursions in exotic locations. In contrast, the return journeys were relatively uncrowded, as the number of invalid soldiers was usually limited to five hundred, but more arduous due to the demands imposed by recurring outbreaks of infectious disease.

Kenny spent two of the three years of her military service working and living in the confined world of a sea transport ship. A photograph taken on the HMAT Themistocles shortly before it landed in London in September 1916 shows Staff Nurse Kenny sitting in the middle of a large group of unidentified officers and soldiers, some displaying evidence of their war injuries. Kenny is the only woman in the scene. She is smiling and appears completely at ease with her life despite her well documented disinterest in the company of men.

It seems quite plausible that the companionship Kenny enjoyed within her small circle of fellow nurses made an important contribution to her contentment during this period. War service records for nurses serving in the No.1 Section STS show that Kenny spent most of the war working alongside and sharing a cabin with three nurses – Irene Kiernan, Ella Morphett, and Edith Trebilcock.[172] These records also show that Kenny and her colleagues were posted to the same Auxiliary Hospitals while awaiting redeployment, and there is some evidence they remained united during their leave from duty.[173] It is impossible to judge the extent to which this sororal assemblage was the product of chance or design, but the war service records of nurses attached to No. 1 Section STS show no evidence of other staff nurses working so closely for such an extended period.

Regrettably, there is no first-hand record of the significance this extended period of intense association with a small group of women held for Kenny, nor is there a body of literature which provides a reference point for understanding the kinds of relationships which nurses formed with each other in the unique conditions created by the operation of the STS during WW1. Lillian Faderman's seminal examination of the changing perception of romantic friendship and homoerotic relationships between women in the late nineteenth and early twentieth century's recognizes the broader social impact of WW1 on women's lives but ignores the unique opportunities for erotic or sexual relations afforded to service women during this period.[174] Recent historical research has explored the role of nurses in the broader reconceptualization of femininity, masculinity and heterosexual eroticism during this period, but does not appraise the potential impact of the war on female homosexual eroticism.[175] Even where research has focused specifically on the social and sexual relations between soldiers and nurses, there is a neglect of the potential for homoerotic or homosexual dimensions within the relationships which nurses formed with each other.

Rebecca Jennings is one of the few historians who directly examines the contemporary portrayal of young women who form relationships with other women during the war years. Jennings observes in *A Lesbian History of Britain* that same sex relationships among nurses has been neglected by nursing historians but acknowledges there is an absence of explicit evidence of how these women viewed themselves. Jennings devotes a substantial portion of a chapter titled *Sapphism and the First World War, 1914-1918* to societal concerns about the impact of the war on female sexuality, concluding *'while some connections were beginning to be made between masculinity, sexual knowledge and lesbianism by some individuals during the First World War, these ideas remained ambivalent and unclear until the 1920s'.*[176]

The invisibility of homoerotic or sexual relationships between nurses in the historical literature may be due to a lack of explicit evidence, but it is still difficult to explain the absence of conjecture in the literature on the possibility of such relationships even existing. American nurse historians Carla Randall and Michele Eliason observe that the nursing professional has been reluctant to acknowledge its lesbian history despite the concurrence of factors which historically predisposed lesbians to join the profession.[177] It may also be the case that little attention has been paid to the potential for homoerotic relationships between nurses during WW1 because they alone did not adopt the practice which has been almost universally interpreted as being the most characteristic outward symbol of sexual transgression among women in the era – the wearing of a military styled uniform. It seems no lesbian history of the twentieth century is complete without a chapter, or two, examining the influence of the military uniform on the sexual emancipation of women during and immediately following the WW1, yet nurses are largely excluded from this literature. It is especially ironic that Laura Doan's comprehensive appraisal of the impact of women adopting male attire in this era does not question why nurses were virtually unique in not adopting a military style uniform, thereby effectively excluding them from her analysis of the development of a modern English lesbian culture.[178]

Whilst little is known of the existence of homosocial or homoerotic relationships between nurses in the war years, glimpses of the social significance of passionate friendships between women may be found in Martha Vicinus' examination of boarding school friendships in England in the early twentieth century.[179] Vicinus prefaces her appraisal of boarding school friendships by claiming lesbian history has been *'overly concerned with external labelling, rather than with the consideration of what homoerotic friendships were like'.*[180] Vicinus claims that in contrast to the preoccupation of male educators on suppressing masturbation and physical expressions of sexuality between young men, passionate friendships between young women were tolerated in single sex educational environments because these relationships promoted societal ideals of women gaining fulfilment through self-denial and devotion. By elevating the spiritual component of relationships over the base pleasure of genital contact Vicinus believes young women were being prepared for the roles women were expected to perform in private and public domains in the late nineteenth and early twentieth centuries. Vicinus completes her analysis of young women's passionate friendships by proposing that the forensic examination of the link between sexual behavior and lesbian identity in the twentieth century has distracted historians from the more important examination of the process by which women's relationships came to be viewed as dangerous in the period leading up to and following WW1.

Elizabeth Kenny would eventually become a prolific narrator of her life story, but she left no personal record of her emotional attachment to the three women with who were her closest companions during most of the war. Further, the stories she later told of her shipboard life disengaged her from the social interactions which surrounded her, giving more prominence to an alleged psychic visitation than the emotional succor she received from her female companions. Nonetheless, the nature of her relationships with her nurse companions is likely to have held more significance for her than she was prepared to acknowledge, as the intimate relationships she would form throughout the remainder of her life would exclusively be with women. The significance of these relationships will be examined in more depth in a later chapter.

Sister Kenny

The Nurse Kenny edifice which Kenny constructed during the 1910s would quickly collapse as she had built her identity on weak foundations. Within one year of being discharged from the AANS the thirty-nine years old retired army nurse would be unemployed, living with her mother, and experiencing bouts of unexplained illness which she claimed were associated with a misdiagnosis of myocarditis. The illnesses were probably psychosomatic in origin as extant medical records suggest she had no underlying cardiac illness.[181] Despite proving her competence as a nurse through her war service the subterfuge which underpinned her identity as Nurse Kenny now prevented Sister Kenny, as she now insisted on being called, from being employed as a nurse or operating a health care facility. Except for supervising a temporary influenza hospital in Clifton in 1919, Kenny would not be employed as a nurse for the remainder of her life. To the outside world Sister Kenny was a retired war nurse who cared for her elderly mother, devoted her spare time to organizing the newly formed Nobby branch of the Country Women's Association (CWA), and did good deeds in the local community. She was adroit at publicizing that she never accepted payment for her occasional home nursing services, but her altruism was in fact based on necessity. As a recipient of a war pension she was permitted to receive payment for living and travel expenses from her private clients, but not allowed to earn an income.

Virginia Hardcastle states *'telling our life stories is a two way street'*,[182] as the more we tell a story the more emotional attachment the story teller will have with the events, whether fictional or not, and the more emotional salience the story will acquire. The corollary of this argument is that stories which are built around emotions which are unpleasant, or undesirable, may be deliberately altered or suppressed to deny the salience of those emotional responses. This proposition partly explains the absence of a narrative which either reflects or constructs Kenny's perception of self in the formative years of her adult life. I believe the subsequent flood of documents recording her personal narrative in later life may have predisposed medical historians and social researchers to anachronistically explain her behavior in the 1910s through the narratives she created in the 1940s.

Elizabeth Kenny's life in the 1910s is far better documented than her narrative of self, but this should not exclude conjecture on the extent to which her self-awareness was shaping her behavior. I agree with Hardcastle's assertion that person and self are not mutually exclusive concepts, rather they are interconnected through an individual's existential journey towards a more unified psychological experience or their search for meaning in life. Despite the appearance of an apparent progression from provincial market trader to bush nurse to hospital matron to war time staff nurse, and contrary to her attempts in later life to present her life story as a journey which started with a chance encounter with a mysterious disease, Kenny's behavior during the period 1907 through to the mid 1920s provides no evidence that she was pursuing a preconceived trajectory for her life. Nor is there evidence of a narrative which weaves her life experiences into a coherent self-identity. Nonetheless, it would be erroneous to conclude she was a hapless victim of circumstance. Her decision to assume the identity of Nurse Kenny by acquiring a costume and performing the role which society attributed to a nurse may be viewed as dishonest, but her actions allowed her to appropriate the authority and independence which society unjustly denied to most women of her age and social class. Similarly, her decision to abandon her secure life in Clifton to pursue a non-existent military commission could either be viewed as delusional or evidence that she felt empowered to pursue goals of her own making. If, as Hardcastle suggests, a sense of self emerges as a person recognizes patterns and repetitions in their own thoughts and deeds, and in turn this recognition leads to a realization of the trajectory of one's life, Kenny's behavior in the years leading to and including the WW1 provides us with evidence that she had found self-awareness and self-confidence in her ability to free herself from the shackles imposed by the societal norms of the era.

Inventor

Victor Cohn observed that by the end of the 1920s Kenny had '*gained some degree of financial security and more experience in living, selling, arguing, and cajoling.*'[183] He omitted to add nursing, and rightly so, because despite assiduously maintaining her wartime title she was as removed from the conventional picture of a nurse as a fifty years old woman could possibly get. Sister Kenny could not be employed as a nurse, but she maintained her nurse identity through her voluntary activity as a first aid attendant with the Clifton Ambulance Brigade and through her membership of the Clifton branch of the Red Cross. In 1922 she found employment as a private nursery nurse for a paralyzed child named Daphne Cregan. Kenny cared for Daphne, partly in her mother's home in Nobby, and partly in Daphne's parents' home in Ben Lomond, NSW. During the time Kenny cared for Daphne she took a keen interest in her medical care and initiated a regime of daily massage and exercises which greatly improved Daphne's ability to walk with the assistance of calipers. The long-term significance of Kenny's treatment of Daphne will be discussed in a later chapter. Despite Kenny's close involvement in Daphne's treatment for several years it is important to note that she did not wear clothing which gave the outward impression that she was a nurse, and there is no evidence that she sought to use her therapeutic skills with any other patients. If Kenny held any interest in extending her involvement in the care of paralyzed children, they quickly evaporated in the aftermath of a freak accident involving a young girl who lived on a farm near Nobby.

On Saturday, 15th May, 1926 Kenny was asked to assist in the transportation of an injured child, Sylvia Kuhn, by ambulance from Nobby to Toowoomba. The accident was reported in the local newspaper the following Tuesday.[184] Sylvia's injuries were sufficiently serious to warrant her transportation from Nobby to a hospital in Toowoomba. Witnesses confirm that Kenny improvised a rigid stretcher from a cupboard door. The improvised device protected the child's injured limbs and improved her comfort,[185] thereby reducing the risk of shock during the journey. The drama did not end with the accident, as the ambulance conveying Kenny and the child was involved in a collision with another vehicle while travelling to Toowoomba. Kenny sustained a shoulder injury, but the child was protected from further injury and eventually recovered from her injuries.

The journey by ambulance to Toowoomba had a profound impact on Kenny's life. Within three months of the accident she had resigned from her role as President of the Nobby branch of the CWA; produced a prototype stretcher with the assistance of a local saddler; instructed a solicitor to file an application to patent the device; agreed a contract with a company to manufacture the stretcher; sought endorsement of the superiority of the stretcher from Dr Rushton Smith, a general practitioner in Clifton; and arranged to exhibit the stretcher at the Brisbane Exhibition Show which opened on 12th August 1926. A more detailed account of these events is presented in a later chapter.

Photograph of Elizabeth Kenny published
in the Australian Women's Weekly, 1927.

Sylvia Kuhn's accident brought Kenny's mundane life in Nobby to an abrupt end. Within weeks of the accident Sister Kenny *retired war nurse* had severed most of her ties with her local community and was presenting herself to a wider world as Sister Kenny *inventor*. The speed of this transition dwarfed her transition from the unqualified proprietor of a private hospital to a staff nurse in the service of the AANS. Kenny's conviction in her new identity was so assured that she arranged to adopt a nine years old child to keep her aged mother company while she travelled Australia promoting her wonderful invention. This arrangement proved to be fortuitous for all involved as Mary McCraken would become Kenny's devoted daughter and acolyte.

Kenny's invention of the Sylvia stretcher is usually framed in the historical literature as a quirky back story which demonstrates her capacity for invention and her flair for entrepreneurialism, but it also provided Kenny with an opportunity to develop her ability to craft a narrative which positioned her in an alternative public identity as an inventor, benefactor, and health care campaigner. Kenny's involvement in the marketing of the Sylvia Stretcher made her a household name in Queensland due to her canny understanding of media management in an era when the concept was not widely recognized. This episode in her life also demonstrated that she could take a cavalier approach to veracity in the narration of her life story. Newspaper articles based on press releases and interviews contain numerous examples of her misrepresentation of her war service, her nursing experience, and her nurse qualifications.

The marketing of the Sylvia Stretcher occupied and financially sustained Kenny for several years, but notably it demonstrated that her attachment to her nurse identity was probably more contingent on the material benefits and social status it bestowed upon her than an altruistic interest in the care of sick or injured children. An episode in 1930 further illustrates the dissonance embedded in Kenny's self-identification as a nurse. Even though she had not worked formally as a nurse for over a decade, in July 1930 she made a submission to the Queensland Government's Royal Commission on Hospitals. In her submission, Kenny describes herself as a member of the Royal British Trained Nurses Association, not, as would be more appropriate, as a member of the CWA.[186] Kenny's submission to the royal commission is notable on several accounts. First; her submission addresses the need for improved ambulance and bush nursing services in the outback without acknowledging her commercial interest in supplying equipment to ambulance services. Second; her submission makes no reference to the care or treatment of children with paralysis despite her later claims that this was her primary occupation during this period of her life. Third; the Royal British Trained Nurses Association did not exist. It is possible that her accreditation as a member of the Royal British Trained Nurses Association may be a misrepresentation of the Royal British Nurses Association or the Australian Trained Nurses Association, but the ATNA and RBNA archives confirm that Elizabeth Kenny was never a member of either organization, and there is no record of Kenny requesting a correction to the erroneous attribution of her nurse credentials in news articles reporting her submission.

Whilst there is some merit in Kenny's claim to have an interest in bush nursing services, the misrepresentation of her nurse credentials to a Royal Commission is breathtaking in its audacity, especially as there was no apparent need for the deception and seemingly nothing to gain from it. Perhaps Kenny's decision to misrepresent her professional status demonstrates the importance of this professional identity to her self-identity, or perhaps years of embellishing and redacting her life story had blurred her perception of the principles which underpinned ethical behavior, leaving her incapable of recognising boundaries in her pursuit of personal ambition.

Conclusion

The person who emerges in this chapter is not the two-dimensional character commonly portrayed in the historical record, or, indeed, fashioned in her own biographical writing. Over a period of twenty years Kenny Elizabeth Kenny forged multiple identities through improvisation, ingenuity, and creativity. Some may consider that her behavior should be described more accurately as dishonest, self-serving, and opportunistic, or that she was Machiavellian in her pursuit of ambitions and interests. Her behavior suggests she was prepared to take substantial risks to achieve personal ambitions and did not hesitate to deceive or dissemble in the pursuit of her goals. I prefer to take a more sympathetic view of a person who achieved material success and social status without the benefit of financial resources or formal education but, nonetheless, demonstrated little of the altruism or nobility which she sought to portray in later life.

In 1930 Elizabeth Kenny was poised, once again, on the threshold of a new decade facing uncertain prospects. Her expectations are undocumented, but her peripatetic life had refined skills and attributes, some enabling and edifying, some not, which would soon be called into action in the most unlikely circumstances. Elizabeth Kenny was unknowingly about to enter the final metamorphosis in her life.

---

[104] Julia Farquarson, interview by Victor Cohn, 19 April 1953, 146.K.8.6F EKP-MHS.

[105] George Knibbs, *Official Yearbook of the Commonwealth of Australia 1901-1907 No. 1 – 1908* (Melbourne: McCarron Bird and Co., 1908).

[106] All Kenny's sisters married local farmers. Minnie Bell and Jack Bell, interview by Victor Cohn, 5 November 1955, 146.K.8.6F EKP-MHS.

[107] Elizabeth Kenny, Unpublished autobiography, manuscript, Reserve 35 EKP-MHS.

[108] Knibbs, *Yearbook*, pp. 439-441.

[109] Palgrave Macmillan (ed.), *International Historical Statistics* (Palgrave Macmillan UK, 2013).

[110] Queensland Office of Economic and Statistical Research, Queensland Past and Present: 100 Years of Statistics,1896–1996, (2009). http://www.oesr.qld.gov.au/products/publications/qld-past-present/index.php

[111] For an appraisal of the employment opportunities for women in the Federation era see the chapter "The Freedom of the Factory" in: Beverley Kingston, *My wife, my daughter and poor Mary Ann: Women and work in Australia*

(West Melbourne: Thomas Nelson, 1975).

[112] See the chapter "She Married Well and Lived Happily Ever After" in Kingston, *Women*.

[113] Cohn, *Sister Kenny*, p. 33.

[114] "The Potato Blight", *Guyra Argus*, 19 August 1909, p. 2.

[115] In her published memoir Kenny described her earnings from the sale of this produce as '*a gift from the men*' rather than as commission or a fee. Elizabeth Kenny and Martha Ostenso, *And They Shall Walk* (New Your, Dodd, Mead and Company, 1943) p. 17.

[116] Kenny devotes two pages of the memoir published in 1943 to describing the event. It is described in more detail in an undated draft manuscript. 146.K.8.6F EKP-MHS..

[117] Minnie Bell also claimed that her husband collaborated with Kenny in her potato selling enterprise. Minnie Bell and James Bell, *interview*.

[118] Kenny Unpublished memoir. Reserve 35 EKP-MHS.

[119] Alicent Woodward, interview by Victor Cohn, 3-4 December 1955, 146.K.8.6F EKP-MHS.

[120] Kenny's preparations to purchase a nurse's uniform are described by Alicent Woodward in an interview by Victor Cohn. Woodward, *interview*.

[121] "Professional Notice", *Clifton Courier*, 4 November 1911, p. 3. State Library of Queensland, Open Access, MFS 0448 (henceforth SLQ MFS 0448).

[122] Kenny and Ostenso, *They Shall Walk*, p. 18.

[123] The cost of the Norland Institute course was £40. Source: "The Home For Babies", *Sydney Morning Herald*, 19 October 1911, page 12, Trove NLA. Catherine Casky, a former patient of Kenny's, told Victor Cohn that Kenny stated her training had cost £45, which was much less than the cost of ordinary nurse training. Cohn, *Sister Kenny*, p. 36.

[124] For an appraisal of the development of nursing in Australia see: Wendy Madsen, *Nursing history: Foundations of a Profession* (Frenchs Forest: Pearson SprintPrint, 2007).

[125] For an appraisal of the social status of nurses in the Australian colonies at the beginning of the twentieth century see Beverly Schultz, *A Tapestry of Service: The evolution of nursing in Australia* (Melbourne: Churchill Livingstone, 1991) and Elizabeth Burchill, *Australian nurses since Nightingale* Richmond: Spectrum Publications, 1992.

[126] For an appraisal of the impact of the Boer War and First World War on the organisation and professionalisation of nursing services in the United Kingdom See Anne Summers, *Angels and Citizens: British women as military nurses 1854–1914* (London: Routledge and Kegan Paul, 1988). For a comprehensive appraisal of the development of nursing education in Australia see Ruth Lynette Russell, *From Nightingale to Now: Nurse Education in Australia* (Sydney: Harcourt Brace Jovanovich, 1990).

[127] Woodward, *interview*, and Minnie Bell and James Bell, *interview*.

[128] Scotia private hospital was under the control of Nurse Sutherland. Kenny's employment as a domestic servant is confirmed in a letter to Wade Alexander by Nurse Sutherland's daughter. Patience C. Moore, to Wade Alexander, letter,

1 February 2001, 143.E.10.9B EKP-MHS.

129 "Women's Work and Bush Nursing", *The Register*, 7 September 1909, p. 9, Trove NLA.

130 "Bush Nursing Scheme", *The Maitland Daily Mercury*, 22 January 1910, p. 4, Trove NLA.

131 The Health Act Amendment Act 1911 mandated that every registered nurse would be issued with a badge which bore the nurse's name and date of registration. Queensland Government, *Health Act Amendment Act 2 Geo. V. No. 26*, (1911), p. 5178.
http://classic.austlii.edu.au/au/legis/qld/hist_act/haaao19112gvn26261/

132 A summary of the history of nurses' badges may be found in: Steven Callander-Grant, "Nurses' badges: archaic symbols or icons of nursing?" *International History of Nursing Journal*, vol. 6, no. 2, (2001), pp. 71-74.

133 Queensland Government, *Health Act Amendment*, p. 5170.

134 Kenny states McDonnell gave her this advice in 1910, but she was running St Canice less than two years later. Kenny and Ostenso, *And They Shall Walk*, p.

135 "Nurse Kenny", *Clifton Courier*, 13 July 1912, p. 3, SLQ MFS 0448.

136 Local newspapers, such as The Clifton Courier and The Warwick Examiner and Times, contain descriptions of St Canice and records of treatment provided to victims of trauma between 1913 and 1915.

137 Shirley Murray, Personal communication to author, 30 July 2015.

138 "Country Telegrams", *Brisbane Courier*, 28 October 1913, p. 8, Trove NLA.

139 George Knibbs, Inquiry into the cost of living in Australia, 1910-1911 (Melbourne, Commonwealth Bureau of Statistics, 1911).

140 The names and qualifications of the doctors and nurses who worked in Clifton between 1910 and 1915 are recorded in the Clifton Courier and annual editions of Pugh's Almanac. Evidence of the standard of medical care in the era can be found in Patrick, *Health & Medicine*.

141 Kenny and Ostenso, *And They Shall Walk*, p. 32.

142 William Kenny's war service is recorded in the Australian War Memorial embarkation and nominal rolls for the First World War.
http://www.awm.gov.au/research/people/

143 "Gossip from Women's Clubland", *Queensland Figaro*, 29 May 1915, p. 14, Trove NLA.

144 A notice in the Clifton Courier on 5 June 1915 reports that Kenny was still treating cases in the hospital in the first week of June. "Personal", *Clifton Courier*, 5 June 1915, p. 3. SLQ MFS 0448.

145 A notice in the Clifton Courier reports the sale of furniture and effects on Wednesday 16 June. "Clearing Sale", *Clifton Courier*, 19 June 1915, p. 3, SLQ MFS 0448. There is no record of sale of the business in the QLD journals of conveyances and encumbrances for Clifton for 1915. A local historian believes the property was vacant for several years, and the buildings relocated to a nearby town after the WW1. Shirley Murray, Personal communication to author, 30 July 2015.

146 "Personal", *Clifton Courier*, 5 June 1915, p. 2, SLQ MFS 0448.

147 "Red Cross Society", Brisbane Courier, 21 June 1915, p. 8, Trove NLA.

[148] Miss E Kenny is listed as a passenger on the R.M.S Medina which departed Sydney on 26 June 1915. "RMS Medina for London", *Sydney Morning Herald*, 26 June 1915, Trove NLA.

[149] Kenny's account of her war service is presented in the chapter "They that go down to the sea" in Kenny and Ostenso, *And They Shall Walk*, pp. 33-51.

[150] The regulations for admission to the AANS include three years training in a recognised civilian hospital and registration with a recognised professional body such as the Australasian Trained Nurses Association. Ruth Rae, Scarlet Poppies: The army experience of Australian nurses during World War One (Burwood: College of Nursing, 2004).

[151] In 1915 a second class rail ticket to Sydney cost £2/2s, and a second class ticket to London on a mail ship cost £25-30. The combined cost of the fares alone was equivalent to approximately two month's income for an average family of four. These costs would have been met by the AIF if Kenny had joined the AANS in Queensland.

[152] Alice Perrott, interview by Victor Cohn, 19 November 1955, 146.K.8.6F EKP-MHS.

[153] Kenny probably understood she had no prospect of enlisting with the AANS, but it is not known whether she was aware of the qualifications required to join the Queen Alexandra Imperial Military Nursing Service (QAIMNS) or serve as a VAD with the Red Cross.

[154] Michael Kenny confirmed that Kenny wore civilian clothes while visiting family in Ireland and was not recuperating from a war injury. Michael Kenny, interview by Victor Cohn, 2 August 1955, 146.K.8.6F EKP-MHS.

[155] Cohn, *Sister Kenny*, p. 54.

[156] In June and July of 1915 around 800 AIF casualties were transported to England from the Gallipoli campaign front. In August the number doubled, and in September the number increased to 4,046. By October 7,764 sick and wounded had been received from the August operations alone. Arthur G. Butler, *Official History of the Australian Army Medical Services, 1914–1918 Volume I*, (1938), p. 500.

[157] For a comprehensive appraisal of the organisation of the Australian Medical Service in the First World War see Chapter XXII in Butler, *Official History*, Vol. I.

[158] For a detailed description of the development of hospital ships in the First World War see: Robert Goodman, *Hospital Ships*, (Brisbane, Boolarong Publications, 1992).

[159] For a full appraisal of the operation of the Seat Transport Service see "Special Problems and Services" in Arthur G. Butler, *Official History of the Australian Army Medical Services, 1914–1918 Volume III*, (1943).

[160] Butler, *Official History Vol. I*, p. 503.

[161] There is no embarkation roll for the Suevic's first journey as a *dark* ship as the journey commenced in England, but Kenny's service records contain a personnel list which records the name and rank of the ship's medical crew. NAA: B2455, Kenny Elizabeth

[162] Christine E Hallett, "Emotional Nursing", in Alison S. Fell and Christine E.

Hallett (ed.), *First World War Nursing: New perspectives* (Abingdon: Routledge, 2013).

[163] Kirsty Harris, "Red reflections on the sea: Australian Army nurses working at sea in World War I", *Journal of Australian Naval History* vol. 6 no. 2, (2009), pp. 51-73.

[164] Kirsty Harris, personal communication, January 2014.

[165] Kenny makes this claim in her memoir published in 1943. Kenny and Ostenso, *And They Shall Walk*, p. 34.

[166] Cohn research notes, 146.K.8.6F EKP-MHS.

[167] See: Ruth Rae, *Veiled lives: Threading Australian nursing history into the fabric of the First World War* (Burwood: College of Nurses, 2009); and Alison S. Fell and Christine E. Hallett (ed.), *First World War Nursing: New perspectives* (Abingdon: Routledge, 2013).

[168] Kenny devotes nearly two full chapters of her memoir to her War experience, but there are few personal anecdotes and she is extremely economical with her description of daily life on the ships. See: "They That Go Down To The Sea" and "Home Is The Sailor!" in Kenny and Ostenso, *And They Shall Walk*.

[169] Harris, *Red reflections*, pp 51.

[170] One such website is *Through These Lines*, published by Cheryl and Bernard Ward. The website contains a bibliography of online and published diaries from the WW1. http://throughtheselines.com.au.

[171] https://throughtheselines.com.au/research.

[172] The war service records for all members of No. 1 STS are held at the National Archives of Australia. NAA Series B2455, First Australian Imperial Force Personnel Dossiers, 1914-1920.

[173] Kenny's nephew claimed she was accompanied by nurses in uniform when she visited him in Ireland on leave during the war. Michael Kenny, interview.

[174] Lillian Faderman, *Surpassing the love of men* (London: The Women's Press, 1981).

[175] Carol Acton, "*Negotiating Injury and Masculinity in First World War Nurses' Writing*", in First World War Nursing: New perspectives, (ed.) Alison S. Fell and Christine E. Hallett, (Abingdon: Routledge, 2013).

[176] Rebecca Jennings, *A Lesbian History of Britain* (Oxford: Greenwood World Publishing, 2007), p. 107.

[177] Randal and Eliason observe that nursing was a professional which almost uniquely offered women who were single and desired to remain unmarried an opportunity for a lifelong career. Carla E. Randall and Michele Eliason, "Out Lesbians in Nursing: What would Florence say?" *Journal of Lesbian Studies* no. 16, (2012), pp. 65-75.

[178] Doan traces the emergence of a modern English lesbian subculture in the early twentieth century, but experiences of nurses are virtually absent in her analysis of the factors shaping the construction of a modern lesbian identity. Laura Doan, *Fashioning Sapphism: The Origins of a Modern English Lesbian Culture* (New York: Columbia University Press, 2000).

[179] Martha Vicinus, "Distance and Desire: English Boarding School Friendships, 1870-1920", in *Hidden From History: Reclaiming the Gay and Lesbian Past,* (ed.) George Duberman, Martha Vicinus and Martin Chauncey, (New York: NAL

Books, 1989), pp. 212-229.

[180] Vicinus, *Hidden from History*, p. 213.

[181] Dr. W. Vinnicombe and Dr. J. Davis to Victor Cohn, personal communication to Victor Cohn, 146.K8.6F EKP-MHS.

[182] Hardcastle discusses the concept of the contribution of personal narrative to the construction of self-identity in Virginia G. Hardcastle, *Constructing the Self* (Philadelphia: John Benjamins Publishing Company, 2008).

[183] Cohn, *Sister Kenny*, p. 75.

[184] "Serious Accident", *Warwick Daily News*, 18 May 1926, p.2, Trove NLA.

[185] Interviews conducted in 1988 by John Pearn with surviving members of the Kuhn family confirm Kenny used a cupboard door to construct the temporary rigid stretcher. Pearn J, "The Sylvia stretcher: a perspective of Sister Elizabeth Kenny's contribution to the first-aid management of injured patients", *The Medical Journal of Australia* no. 149, (1988), pp. 636-638.

[186] "*Hospital Control. Victorian System Explained. Evidence before royal commission*", *Brisbane Courier*, 20 June 1930, p.47, Trove NLA.

3. A DISCREDITED LIFE

'Men! I don't want anything to do with them'
Elizabeth Kenny

Before I start this chapter, I need to talk about labels. Tricky things, labels. Almost certainly they come with a lot of baggage and almost certainly you can never satisfy everyone when you need to use them. So, first up is *gay*, followed closely by *lesbian*. Gay is the label which I find most convenient to describe myself, but by the time you reach my sexagenarian decade it's a label that feels inadequate most of the time. If I was writing a sociology textbook I might grimace and use the *queer* word, but if you know any history at all you'll understand why it's a word I find too hard to use in everyday conversation. Let's move on to lesbian. There's a story that Queen Victoria didn't believe they existed, but that's really a myth. No-one used the 'l' word when the Old Queen was alive, but you know who we're talking about. That's the problem with labels when we apply them to people living in the past, we risk imposing assumptions and meaning which they might not have recognized or understood. So, dear reader, forgive me if you feel offended by my use of labels which you believe to be anachronistic or misguided. My intentions are honorable.

In this chapter I necessarily use terms such as lesbian, heterosexism, and homophobia to help to explain the stigma which shaped the life and work of Elizabeth Kenny. Whilst I will consider Kenny's sexual self-identification in this chapter, I have not set out to prove she was a lesbian because it will almost certainly never be known, and, more importantly, I don't need to know as homophobia is a form of prejudice that operates without a direct knowledge of sexual identity or sexual behavior. Nonetheless, I have set out to offer a new explanation for the intensely personal opposition which she encountered from key members of the medical professional, and to offer a context for significant choices she made in her nursing career.

Hidden lives

Throughout the 1940s Eleanor Roosevelt, wife of President Franklin D. Roosevelt, and Elizabeth Kenny, renowned polio therapist, were voted to be the two most admired women in America in nine consecutive Gallup polls. In 1951 Kenny was voted the most admired woman in America in the national Gallup Poll. The only other non-US citizens to achieve this level of acclaim since 1946 are Mother Teresa, Golda Meir, and Margaret Thatcher. In their lifetimes Roosevelt and Kenny transgressed entrenched societal norms governing the role of women, and they overcame many obstacles to achieve the fame and public adulation they enjoyed as mature women. Prior to the 1980s the investigation of the obstacles faced by Roosevelt was largely restricted to the influence of gender and class, but the discovery in 1978 of an archive of letters between Roosevelt and Lorena Hickock revealed evidence of a hidden lifelong relationship between the two women which was more than a passionate friendship. Roosevelt protected her relationship with Lorena Hickock from public scrutiny during her lifetime through the privilege of her social class and her political power as the First

Eleanor Roosevelt and Elizabeth Kenny, 1944.
Elizabeth Kenny Papers, Minnesota Historical Society.

Lady. Whilst the evidence of Roosevelt's sexual relationship with Hickock is open to interpretation, the posthumous reappraisal and scrutiny of her sexuality has done little to diminish her reputation. In fact, by bringing her life to the attention of a post-feminist generation of women, the debate has probably served her memory well. On the other hand, Kenny's sexual identity continues to be cloaked in a veil of secrecy despite her conspicuous misandry, clumsy attempts to fabricate thwarted relationships in her youth, and evidence of passionate relationships with women during her adult life. I believe the neglect of the relevance of Kenny's ambiguous sexual identity in the analysis of her work may be indicative of a lingering prejudice associated with any challenge to heterosexist assumptions of normality. Countless times I have been asked *'do you have any proof she might have been a lesbian?'*, and equally countless times I have replied *'no more than I have that she may have been straight'*. My point being, that in the twenty first century it is surely presumptuous to assume everyone is heterosexual until proven otherwise.

It is difficult to retrospectively understand the experiences of women who lived in the first half of the twentieth century and might now be thought of as lesbians. Notions of sexual categories and the language we use to discuss sexuality have evolved considerably over the last century, and the way in which sexual identity is constructed differs according to the historical and cultural context. There is, of course, no single lesbian experience. Even so, there is copious evidence to show that women whose primary sexual and emotional attractions are oriented towards other women have for centuries shared the common experience of being forced to lead hidden and isolated lives under the threat of moral, legal, and medical sanctions.

The hidden nature of lesbian lives presents an enormous challenge to historians wishing to understand the relevance and contribution of a subject's sexual identity to their professional life. There are real risks of applying retrospective distortions to the study of private lives from earlier eras, but these risks can be justified to gain a better understanding of the impact of personal and familial factors on scientific, artistic, or political careers, or the development of scientific knowledge. New insights and new question can arise from the retrospective biographical analysis of the impact of homosexuality on an individual's career and achievements even when the person did not publicly embrace a homosexual identity during their lifetime.

Any discussion of Kenny's sexuality must be understood in the context of her public identity during key phases of her life. Unfortunately, our understanding of how she perceived herself is constrained by the near absence of reliable first-hand accounts of her life during her youth and early adulthood. Whilst there is some evidence of Kenny's emerging sense of self as a nurse and inventor in the 1910s and 1920s, this evidence is dwarfed by the wealth of material documenting the decade she lived and worked in the United States. As I have stated before, the disproportionate emphasis on Kenny's public personae in the final decade of her life has skewed the portrayal and consideration of an identity which was more fluid than she portrayed in her autobiographical writing.

Kenny's childhood and early adulthood are the most poorly documented and the least understood periods of her life due to her peripatetic existence moving between New South Wales and Queensland as her father searched for employment as a farm laborer. Family members have done little to assist historians' understanding of her personal life, releasing very little of her copious personal correspondence and none of the diaries she maintained throughout her life. Her memoir published in 1943 allocates one chapter to her youth, and that chapter is redolent with obfuscation and dissembled facts. Kenny portrayed key events which occurred in her late teens as having occurred in her childhood to maintain the deception of understating her age by six years for most of her adult life. She also claimed to have attended schools which did not exist and misrepresented the Darling Downs as a remote region lacking basic medical and health care services. Consequently, all that can be said with certainty about Kenny's formative years is that she had very little formal education, and that she displayed an overt disdain for the conventional fate of marriage and childbearing that awaited most young women of her social class.

The usual explanation for Kenny's outspoken disregard for men and emphatic objection to marriage relies to a great extent on her own carefully manufactured public image as a quasi-religious figure who devoted her life to the care of crippled children. Kenny's lifelong use of the title Sister after only three years of war service reflects her attachment to the public identity the title afforded. In Australia it probably helped to explain her spinsterhood as nursing was still considered a vocation by many people. In the United States it created outright confusion as the title was only used by members of religious orders. Her calling, if there ever was one, apparently came late in life as there is no record of her taking a special interest in pediatric paralysis patients until she was forty-two years old. As there is no evidence that she held any fervent ideological views or political beliefs about the status of women in society, or that she held protofeminist views, or that her parents attempted to dissuade her from marriage, a more plausible explanation is required for the absence of relationships with men in her early adult life.

Notwithstanding the complete absence of evidence of her ever having romantic or sexual relationships with men, there is copious evidence of her preference towards homosocial relationships with women. It is therefore reasonable to extend the speculation in the chapter examining her nurse identity on whether her behavior should be interpreted as signifying that her primary sexual interest lay with women, and whether, she was consequently subjected to homophobic prejudice. Such an exploration offers an opportunity for an alternate interpretation of her life and work, and a basis for examining the extent to which homophobia may have underpinned the overt antagonism demonstrated towards her by members of the medical establishment.

Kenny's sexual identity was as hidden in her lifetime as it is today. There is only a slim biographical record of her private life prior to the 1930s.

Apart from her war service she lived with her mother or close relatives, and she lived with her adopted daughter during the decade she worked in America. Close acquaintances interviewed by Victor Cohn in 1953 recall she was insistent on always being accompanied by a female companion or female member of staff during her constant work-related travelling. To the casual observer these arrangements would not have appeared unusual for a single woman of her age, but it is clear from the personal recollections of her close colleagues that her relationships with her female companions were the primary sources of intimacy in her life.

Changing perspectives of homosexuality

The notion of categorizing identity based on sexual practice did not exist when Kenny was a child; nonetheless it was widely believed that practices such as buggery and masturbation were forms of moral perversion which could result in insanity and the corruption of the flesh. In 1886 Richard von Krafft-Ebing popularized the terms homosexual and heterosexual to differentiate sexual orientation, although the term sexual inversion continued to be used for many decades to describe the perceived reversal of gender roles deemed as normal. The growth in interest among medical practitioners in sexual behavior in the late nineteenth century lead to many sexual practices being classified as diseases, a situation that persisted well into the twentieth century.

In the first half of the twentieth century femininity in men, and masculinity in women, were characteristics almost universally associated with homosexuality. The basis of this perception is vigorously debated in the current era, but during Kenny's youth the received view held by many medical practitioners, researchers, and the general public was that gender role deviation was a cause and a symptom of homosexuality. Those people who held the more tolerant view that homosexuality was not a mental illness or congenital defect, were likely to believe that apparently well-adjusted or productive homosexuals were most likely concealing their inner conflict through bravado or subterfuge.

In 1991 the American historian Lillian Faderman argued that the propensity of American and European sexologists to conflate sex role behavior, gender identity, and sexual object choice profoundly influenced medical practitioners' perception of female sexuality in the early twentieth century. Faderman cited the rapid increase in the number of publications listed in the Index Catalogue of the Library of the Surgeon General's Office 1896-1916 as evidence of the growing medical interest in women's sexual behavior and the sources of beliefs about women's sexual perversion, inversions, and disorders. This growing interest in women's sexual behavior influenced public attitudes towards female sexuality and challenged women to reconsider the social meaning of their homoerotic experiences with other women. Whilst the impact of sexologists' promotion of the objectification of human sexuality is a matter which remains open to debate, they undoubtedly raised awareness that women had sexual lives which could be separated from procreation and conjugal duties. As Faderman eloquently observes; the explanations offered by sexologists *'blew the cover of women whose sexual relationships with other women may have been hidden under the guise of romantic friendship'.*[187]

In 1953 Alfred Kinsey and his colleagues shattered conventional perceptions of the marginality of same sex behavior in women by publishing research which revealed homosexual behavior was far more prevalent among American women than previously recognized. Kinsey was not the first researcher to systematically investigate the sexual behavior of women. In 1929 Katharine Davis, an American sociologist, published the findings of a study of 2200 women, and concluded that a substantial proportion of women had participated in experiences which were sexual in character. Davis' research was groundbreaking, but it did not attract the public attention which Kinsey's research received. Miriam Reumann, an American historian of sexuality and gender, claims that the publications of Kinsey's reports on male and female sexual behavior were events which had an impact on American society comparable to the explosion of the atomic bomb in 1945.

Whilst Kinsey's research has been widely misrepresented and methodologically disputed, it revealed that behavior labelled as deviant, immoral, unnatural, or illegal was in fact common in men and women. Kinsey argued that it was illogical and unjust to criminalize sexual behavior which was common among otherwise law-abiding men and women. The furor surrounding Kinsey's research was fueled in 1956 by the publication of research conducted by Evelyn Hooker which revealed there was no difference in the range of psychological profiles in homosexual and heterosexual men, thereby showing there were no grounds for classifying homosexuality as a mental illness. Her findings were replicated in subsequent studies and eventually led to homosexuality being removed from the American Psychiatric Association's Diagnostic and Statistical Manual of Mental Disorders in 1973. Hooker's research is now viewed as being instrumental in the battle for gay and lesbian human rights during the late twentieth century.

Throughout Kenny's lifetime concepts like lesbian identity or gay rights were an oxymoron. During Kenny's formative years women who were labelled as a sexual invert were at risk of being diagnosed as insane and committed to a lunatic asylum. A small number of artists and philanthropists, such as Romaine Brooks, Hannah Gluck, and Radclyffe Hall, may have publicly eschewed conventional female attire and lived openly with their female sexual partners, but these women had the advantage of being born into families which were immensely wealthy. Women who did not enjoy the protection afforded by wealth or social privilege were, by necessity, careful to project an image of normalcy to avoid public ridicule or being disinherited by their families. Against this backdrop, and bearing in mind the caveats set out earlier, I will use the remainder of this chapter to present an analysis of her life which seeks to unshackle it from heterosexist assumptions of normality.

Sanitised memorials

Kenny's biographers tell her story in good faith, but their accounts sometimes reflect a deference that influences their interpretations of well documented episodes in her life. Indeed, there is evidence which indicates that her nephew, Jack Kenny, who was a journalist in Sydney, may have colluded with Cohn to remove from publication information that could potentially be embarrassing to her memory or challenge her public reputation in America. In 1953 he sent a draft of an article to Cohn with the accompanying request:

> *I should be grateful if you could delete from the article anything which would embarras [sic] the memory of Sister Kenny in Minneapolis or would be inconsistent with what she said or what you have written about her. I know I can trust you to adjust and cut the article as you think fit.* [188]

The article which Jack Kenny subsequently published is structured around conversations with Victor Cohn during Cohn's visit to Australia in 1953. They revisited the theme of Kenny's contemptuousness towards men when Cohn interviewed Jack again in 1955. Jack repeated his assertion that his Aunt had been openly hostile towards men and marriage throughout her life and was unlikely to have ever had a romantic relationship with a man.

The dialogue between Cohn and Jack Kenny encapsulates a theme that is frequently replicated in the notes documenting Cohn's conversations and interviews in the early 1950s with Kenny's friends, family, and associates. These records suggest there was widespread agreement among those close to Kenny that, contrary to her repeated assertion that she was unmarried because she had chosen to devote herself to the cause of fighting polio, she was in fact unmarried because she held no interest in having a romantic or sexual relationship with a man.

Mary McCraken, Kenny's adopted daughter, recalled in an interview with Wade Alexander that '*A lot of reporters couldn't believe how such a voluptuous woman such as she could be so cold where a man was concerned*'.[189] Mary MaCarthy, a screenwriter and close associate of Kenny in the 1940s, told Cohn in 1953 '*I'd bet she (was) never kissed by a man in her life. Sex just didn't mean a goddammed thing to her*'.[190] This rejection of intimacy with men is in stark contrast to the warmth and affection she demonstrated towards her female friends and associates. When interviewed by Victor Cohn, Rosalind Russell, the actress who portrayed Kenny in the film adaptation of her life, recalled with fondness how she and Kenny played in bed together like children when Kenny would visit Russell in Hollywood. [191]

A letter written by Kenny in 1945 provides a rare unguarded glimpse of the depth of the emotional bonds Kenny was able to form with women. Kenny was visiting London when she received news that her secretary, Margaret Odpahl, had resigned to take up a post with the American Red Cross at the close of the Second World War. Kenny immediately wrote to Margaret to express her distress at receiving the news. The letter begins *'Several times I have taken up my pen to write the hardest letter I have ever written in my life That is a letter of farewell to you'*.[192] In the letter Kenny apologizes for her brevity as *'This one has a habit of disappearing in a mist'*. No other surviving record of Kenny's life reveals so candidly the depth of the emotional bond she could form with another person, yet it is equally revealing that, except for her mother and adopted daughter, there is little evidence she experienced this level of intimacy with anyone other than the women with whom she worked.

Valerie Harvey, an Australian nurse who worked as a Kenny Technician in Minneapolis, reflected on the nature of Kenny's emotional relationships with her female employees when she was interviewed by Victor Cohn in 1953. Harvey told Cohn *'I've never known anyone to have a greater fear of being alone as Sister. Secretary or housekeeper had to be with her always'*.[193] Apparently the intensity of Kenny's relationships with her female staff was quite evident to those who met her, as Harvey also claimed that her own mother, who had met Kenny only briefly, warned her not to live with Kenny in America.

A masculine woman in a heterosexist world?

William Hinrichson, a cousin of Kenny, observed to Victor Cohn in 1955: *'She was, what I would say, more of the masculine type in her usual manner, in make up and body build, rather more like a man than a woman.'*[194] Hinrichson's comment is not exceptional. Her close friend, Rosalind Russell, and her staunch antagonist, Dr Alex Duhig, may not have agreed on much, but they did agree she had the manner and appearance of an M4 Sherman tank.[195] Despite the numerous references to Kenny's masculine appearance and manner the significance of this epithet has remained virtually unacknowledged for the past 60 years. Kenny did not transgress the gender norms of her era to the extent of wearing men's clothing, but she presented two faces to the world. Photographic records show that throughout most of her life her attire was reserved and unadorned. Her habit in later life of wearing corsages and flamboyant hats at public occasions became part of her public identity but her personal acquaintances generally viewed this as incongruous with her disdain for fashion and makeup. Kenny's objection to makeup extended to her refusing to allow her adult daughter to wear lipstick when they first lived in Minneapolis. Photographs not intended for public distribution usually portray her with short hair brushed back in an austere style and wearing plain uniform-like clothes. The public flamboyance was in marked contrast to the private disapproval of adornment.

In the Angry Angel series, written by Victor Cohn shortly after her death, the theme of her appearance is always close to the surface.

> *She was, in her prime, strapping, erect, overpowering and positive.*
> *She could be as austere as an iceberg.*
> *'Granite-faced' was a common description.* [196]

On the otherhand, Cohn recognizes her behavior towards patients and close acquaintances could be warm and loving. *'According to those who knew her best, Elizabeth Kenny was a strange and bold woman, with a fierce warmth for people and causes she loved. She could be a saint one minute while treating a child, and two minutes later turn to a doctor and blister him'.*[197] Cohn captures in his characteristic journalist style the contrast between her appearance and behavior in the public and private domains. But it is his observations of her national characteristics which reveal his perception of her true nature. Cohn places great emphasis on her Australian heritage. Australians, we are told:

> *Are no great respecters of pomp or symbols of authority.*
> *They have sharp, witty tongues and will say anything anyplace.*
> *In battle he would fight like a madman.*
> *When an Australian is sour… he is most unpleasantly sour.*[198]

The significance of Cohn's observations is that, without apparent irony, he describes traits which were, and still are, stereotypically associated with Australian men. Perhaps this is not surprising. The dust jacket of the Manning Clark's *A short history of Australia*, published in 1963, states *'This elegantly written and well-illustrated book brings to life the people and events that have shaped Australia's history'*. It should more accurately say the men that have shaped Australia's history. Women are virtually absent in this publication, implying they contributed nothing of value to the shaping of the Australian nation. Beverley Kingston claims that within the Australian zeitgeist prior to the WW2 the only characteristics deemed positive in women were those linked to their capacity for domestic service, home making, and bearing children.

As an American, Cohn might be forgiven for not appreciating the nuances of Australian culture in the 1950s. Nonetheless, Cohn, who knew Kenny well, interpreted her behavior from the perspective of his perceptions of masculinity. Ultimately Cohn is unable to satisfactorily account for Kenny's ambiguous behavior, and enigmatically concludes

'Perhaps there was too much man in her'.[199] The extent to which he understood the irony of this statement is now impossible to know, but it seems unlikely that an educated and urbane journalist would not appreciate the implications of his words.

In 2009 I was fortunate to be able to interview Margaret Ernest (nee Odpahl), who was Kenny's secretary during the early 1940s. As I knew Margaret had been interviewed many times in her life, I decided to start our conversation by declaring I was gay and that I was interested in whether she thought Kenny had shown any indication of being a lesbian or was perceived to be a lesbian. Margaret thought carefully about her response before stating she did not believe Kenny was a lesbian but conceded *'nothing like that ever entered anyone's head in those days'*.[200] Later that year we had lunch together in Minneapolis and the conversation returned to Kenny's sexuality. On this occasion Margaret was very open about describing Kenny's social encounters with gay men and lesbians in Hollywood during the production of the Sister Kenny film. Importantly, she observed that whilst other writers had hinted at their suspicions about Kenny being a lesbian, I was the only person who had directly asked her the question.

A silent foe

The premise that Elizabeth Kenny may have been perceived to be a lesbian does not diminish the validity of previous analyses of her life which have considered gender, class, ethnicity, and professional power. Rather, it provides a new perspective from which to identify and understand the prejudice and opposition she encountered in her life and work, and her evolving life story. Prejudice, by its nature, is often silent or invisible, and almost always based on unexamined beliefs or assumptions of normality. In the first half of the twentieth century the public discourse on homosexuality was so emphatically based on assumptions of heterosexual normality that the language lacked words for the positive portrayal of homosexuality or for the negative portrayal of prejudice towards homosexuals. It is possible that towards the end of her life Kenny may have heard statements imploring tolerance or sympathy for homosexuals, but it is very unlikely that she ever heard any statement that represented an affirmation of any aspect of homosexual practices or the emerging concept of homosexual identity.

As stated earlier, the categorization of a person whose primary sexual and emotional attractions are oriented towards members of the same sex or gender is a relatively recent phenomenon. In the 1960s Erving Goffman, a Canadian born sociologist, used the term stigmatization to describe the attribution of discredited characteristics which differentiated individuals from those possessing a *'normal'* social identity. Goffman argued that stigmatizing individuals leads to the construction of an ideology which explains the inferiority of those individuals and rationalizes animosity and discrimination towards the stigmatized person. In Goffman's world view, homosexuality was very definitely a characteristic which differentiated individuals from '*normals*' in society.

In the present day a much richer language supports a more diverse discourse on the nature of human sexuality. The word most widely used in the present day to represent prejudice and opposition directed towards people perceived to be homosexual is homophobia. The term homophobia was first coined in 1972. Whilst many authors accept the literal interpretation of the term is limiting and misleading, it is now broadly accepted as a catch all term for a wide range of phenomenon and behaviors associated with anti-homosexual prejudice. An Australian researcher succinctly summed up four decades of sociological debate with the simple statement '*It is a new term for an old prejudice*'.[201]

Although it is not surprising that much of the literature addressing the phenomenon of homophobia would focus on its negative impact on the lives of gay men and lesbians, research conducted in Australia in the late 1990s demonstrated that homophobia has far broader societal implications. David Plummer found that homophobia had a profound influence on young men's awareness of socially acceptable male behavior well before they were aware of the concept of sexual identity or how sexual practices differed in homosexuals and heterosexuals. By showing that homophobia is often independent of knowledge of sexual identity or behavior, and not directly related to gender, Plummer provides an explanation for the potential for homophobia to impact on the lives of people like Kenny who do not conform to strict gender norms but do not publicly acknowledge their sexual identity. Plummer's findings have been repeated in research conducted in the United Kingdom by Vicki Stattler for the Lesbian Identity Project.[202] Stattler's interviews with young women who, as adults, self-identified as lesbian, revealed that many recognized the stigma associated with gender non-conformity in women long before they understood the sexual basis of that stigma or the sexual identity of the women in question.

The law reform achieved by the lesbian and gay civil rights movement in the second half of the twentieth century has transformed the lives of lesbians and gay men in many industrialized nations. Nonetheless, most children still grow up in environments in which heterosexism and anti-homosexual prejudice are pervasive, and many experience negative feelings toward themselves when they reach an age where they recognize their own homosexuality. These negative feelings are commonly described as internalized homophobia. Overcoming the cognitive dissonance arising from internalized homophobia is a challenge to psychological wellbeing that is unique to young homosexuals. The struggle many young people have with internalized homophobia is known to lead to depression, feelings of loneliness and isolation, and exaggerated displays of overtly heteronormative behavior, and is believed to be a major contributor to the high rate of suicide among young gay men and lesbians.[203]

If the young Elizabeth Kenny had trouble in reconciling her emerging sexual desires with the values of her family, society, and religion, she would almost certainly have felt a profound sense of alienation and loneliness. Lillian Faderman claimed that in the early twentieth century women who formed passionate relationships with other women usually self-identified in one of four ways:

> *She could refuse to recognise that her own same sex attachments, whether or not they were sexual, had anything to do with sexologists' descriptions of lesbianism.*
> *She could become so fearful of her feelings toward other women that she would deny and repress them.*
> *She could become so fearful of societal reaction to her emotional attachment that she would deny them publicly.*
> *She could accept sexologists' categorisation of love between women and define herself as a lesbian.[204]*

In the near absence of support or sources of affirmation a young woman like Kenny would have few options other than to repress her true needs and desires to avoid ostracism and ridicule. Several incidents in Kenny's later life provide circumstantial evidence that this may have been a choice she confronted.

Passionate friendships

In 1942 Kenny became acquainted with Mary McCarthy, a successful Hollywood screenwriter who was known among her close circle of friends and colleagues to be a lesbian.[205] McCarthy was instrumental in introducing Kenny to Rosalind Russell and conceived the idea of making a feature film of Kenny's life. Kenny became close friends with McCarthy and Elizabeth *'Dickie'* Dickenson who was described by Margaret Ernest as McCarthy's girlfriend. McCarthy and Kenny corresponded regularly with each other during the early development of the film script. The correspondence is written in an affectionate style and shows that Kenny stayed in the home that McCarthy shared with Dickenson in Los Angeles. McCarthy became a close confidante of Kenny's during this period. Margaret Ernest claimed that during the time Kenny worked on the production of the film she attended parties with McCarthy and Dickenson where there were *'gays'* present. Ernest observed that whilst there were plenty of gays and lesbians who worked in the film industry, they needed to be discreet as the studios were wary of attracting the attention of the so-called Hays censors who were responsible for enforcing a set of industry moral guidelines known as the Motion Picture Production Code.

In 1943 McCarthy and Dickenson separated and became embroiled in an acrimonious dispute over the writing credits for the film script. McCarthy's *'non-cardiac heart ailment'*, as she described her woes in a letter to Kenny, exposed her hitherto private life to public scrutiny and undermined her relationship with Kenny and the film's producers. McCarthy's choice of words to describe her separation from Dickenson reveals that even personal correspondence in this era needed to be written in a codified manner. McCarthy wrote a series of letters to Kenny during 1943 and 1944 imploring her to intervene in the dispute with RKO studios, but the

(L-R) Rosalind Russell, Elizabeth Kenny, and Mary McCarthy, 1943.
Elizabeth Kenny Papers, Minnesota Historical Society.

correspondence reveals a noticeable cooling in their friendship. Margaret Ernest claimed the change in Kenny's relationship with McCarthy is likely to have been influenced by Freddie Brisson, Rosalind Russell's husband. Brisson and Russell were also close acquaintances of McCarthy and Dickenson. Ernest claimed that after McCarthy's breakdown Brisson would not allow Russell to travel alone with McCarthy as he feared any association with McCarthy could attract unfavorable publicity for his wife.

In February 1944 McCarthy wrote an affectionate and reassuring letter to Kenny, explaining that many of her financial and personal troubles were now behind her, but her efforts to enlist Kenny as an ally were in vain. In August 1944 Kenny severed her ties with McCarthy in a stinging letter which contained the advice:

> *You have many splendid qualities and good brains which I admire and respect along with your great kindness of heart. You have other characteristics which I detest, and cause me deep grief and sorrow. Turn over a new leaf. Go back to your God and your religion, and your brain shall carry you through forever.*[206]

I believe the '*characteristics*' which Kenny claims to detest is almost certainly a reference to McCarthy's homosexuality. Kenny had shown no public objection to McCarthy's lesbian relationship during their extended period of close collaboration, so the ferocity of this outburst may be an indication that Kenny's feeling of internal dissonance was pushed to its limit by McCarthy's homosexuality becoming publicly evident during her separation from Dickenson. I believe Kenny's veiled advice to McCarthy to renounce her homosexuality and find solace through her religious faith may very well have been born of personal experience.

The historical portrayal of Kenny's relationship with McCarthy carries as much significance as the relationship itself. Documents held in the Elizabeth Kenny Papers in Minneapolis provide clear evidence of Kenny's relationship with McCarthy and Dickenson but nothing published about this episode in Kenny's life contains conjecture on the significance of McCarthy's sexuality in her relationship with Kenny. The notes of Cohn's interview with McCarthy in 1953 indicates they engaged in a lengthy discussion about Kenny's lack of interest in having a physical relationship with a man, but he leaves no record of them discussing the possibility of Kenny having romantic involvements with women. When Cohn asked McCarthy why Kenny describes in her memoir having relationships with men McCarthy replied '*Because she's no different from any other human being. They like their fictional life better than real one, and start to embellish it.*' Cohn's interview notes provide no evidence of an off the record conversation with McCarthy. Perhaps, to paraphrase Margaret Ernest's words, nothing like that entered Victor Cohn's head in those days. It seems improbable. Cohn's daughter thought it unlikely that her father would have felt prejudice towards lesbians or have been oblivious to their presence as he was university educated, worldly, and tolerant of different lifestyles.[207]

The most visible evidence of Kenny's self-awareness of her gender role nonconformity can be found in her attempts in later life to portray romances with men in her youth. Kenny's marital status was, arguably, her Achilles' heel. It, rather than her lack of nursing qualifications, proved to be the aspect of her life that she found most difficult to protect from examination in the final decade of her life. During the 1940s Kenny made repeated attempts to convey the impression that she had forsaken personal happiness in marriage to pursue her calling to battle the scourge of infantile paralysis. Her nephew, Jack Kenny, recalled that when he was young she would tell stories about being courted by eligible bachelors, but would say '*Men! I don't want anything to do with them*' when asked why she had not married any of them. During the time she lived in America Kenny's personal life came under increasing scrutiny, and the inconsistencies in her comments about her youthful romance appears to have fueled journalists' curiosity.

The 1943 memoir, co-written with Martha Ostenso, alludes to a romance with a man named Dan. This story appears to be the one she stuck with for the remainder of her life. Ostenso confirmed to Victor Cohn in 1955 that the romance depicted in the memoir was fictitious and was included to make the book more interesting. Kenny's ongoing attempts to portray her alleged romance became increasingly convoluted, and eventually descended into farce. On separate occasions she confided to Rosalind Russell, Valeria Harvey, Mary McCarthy, and her adopted daughter Mary McCracken, that she had experienced an illfated relationship with a man named Dan, but she failed to give any of these close confidantes an unambiguous description of his identity, or when and where the alleged romance had occurred. Not a difficult task if it is to be believed that this was the one genuine relationship she experienced in her youth.

Valerie Harvey recalled in an interview after Kenny's death that in late 1945 Kenny came to her room in a state of distress clutching a piece of paper which Harvey thought to be a telegram. Harvey recalled Kenny '*crying, really crying*' and saying '*No-one would even believe I was interested, and now he is dead.*' Shortly afterwards a copy of a telegram reporting the death of Daniel Montgomery was published in the Minneapolis Tribune. The cable stated that on his deathbed the deceased had requested a message be sent to Kenny; '*Here in the silent hills you loved so well I wait for thee.*' A copy of the telegram survives in the Elizabeth Kenny papers at the Minnesota History Center.

Victor Cohn investigated the source of this telegram after Kenny's death and was unable to find any record in Australia of the firm of solicitors who allegedly sent the telegram, the person named as the deceased, or the place of death. Cohn concluded that the telegram was probably a publicity stunt organized by RKO Studio ahead of the release of the Sister Kenny movie. As Kenny did not object to the publication of the fake telegram, and had a copy in her possession, I believe it is reasonable to conclude she was complicit in a deceit which raises serious doubts about her ethical standards. Nonetheless, the loyalty of her family protected her from being confronted as a counterfeiter and dissembler. Kenny's adopted daughter believed the story for the rest of her life, but thought the alleged suitor was a man who had lived and died in South Africa.[208] Victor Cohn appears to have conceded to accept McCracken's belief as he cites a memoriam to the deceased in the Courier-Mail in Brisbane on 16 April 1946 as evidence of the death occurring in South Africa. I remain unconvinced as my examination of the digital archives of every newspaper published in Queensland between 1945 and 1947 failed to locate a memoriam or death notice for anyone who died in South Africa during that period.

The testimony of the women with whom Kenny formed close relationships demonstrates she could not simply be dismissed as emotionally dysfunctional or incapable of forming loving relationships. Victor Cohn observed that '*Something, or many things, turned her constantly inward*'[209] but he shied away from speculating on the source of her detachment other than to say he believed '*she never quite trusted the great outside world*'.[210] These words were written at the end of her life, and were informed by Cohn's personal observation of a woman who he believed emitted bitterness like a beacon. Cohn, and many other historians, pursued a fruitless search for evidence that Kenny experienced a thwarted heterosexual relationship in her youth, but ignored or trivialized the significance of the deep and lasting relationships she formed with women. Perhaps this is because those relationships were few in number. I believe it is because they were always with women.

Taking all the available evidence into consideration, I believe it is plausible to conclude that Kenny's primary emotional attachments were oriented towards women even though there is no evidence of her having a sexual relationship with anyone in her life. The uncertainty surrounding Kenny's sexuality is not surprising as coming out was not a lifestyle option for most of women of Kenny's class and means at the beginning of the twentieth century. Such a public declaration would certainly have resulted in her being ostracized by her family and could easily have resulted in her being diagnosed as insane and committed to a lunatic asylum.

A battle on two fronts

Elizabeth Kenny lived in an era where an accusation of sexual impropriety could not be made unless it could be supported by credible proof; to do otherwise would lead to charges of libel or slander. Nonetheless, the invisible forces of innuendo and prejudice could have an equally, if not more, devastating impact on a person's reputation. There is no extant record of overt speculation on the nature of Elizabeth Kenny's sexual orientation, but there is evidence that speculation on the reasons for her not marrying continued well into her old age, and there is evidence she was considered and described as masculine in an era where the meaning of this epithet was unambiguous.

The conventional account for the intensity of the opposition displayed towards Kenny by the medical profession is based on her gender, professional status as a nurse, and absence of formal education. Whilst there is compelling evidence that she experienced rejection because of all these factors, she was not alone in her struggle. Kenny's gender was undoubtedly a source of disadvantage at a societal level, but the acclaim afforded to Isabel Morgan, Dorothy Horstmann, and Dame Jean Macnamara demonstrates that gender was not an insurmountable obstacle in the field of polio research. Isabel Merrick Morgan (1911-1996) proved that killed polio virus protected monkeys against polio. Morgan's contribution to polio research is commemorated in Polio Hall of Fame at Warm Springs, Georgia. Dorothy Horstmann (1911-2001) demonstrated that the poliovirus was transmitted through oral intake and contributed to the development of the Sabin oral vaccine. Horstmann was the first woman to be appointed as a Professor at Yale University. Jean Macnamara (1899-1968) was an Australian pediatrician and scientist who was awarded a DBE for her work with Frank Macfarlane Burnet in identifying there were three strains of polio virus.

Many authors have argued that medical practitioners, especially those in Australia, rejected Kenny's concepts due to their prejudicial view that it was inconceivable that a Nurse could be capable of independently developing a therapy which was superior to conventional medical care. This argument is usually accompanied by the qualification that those who were prepared to overlook their medical snobbery simply couldn't understand her uneducated attempts to explain her techniques in medically acceptable language. The historical literature does show that opposition to Kenny's concepts may be partially explained by these factors, but prejudice and snobbery are not unassailable, and do not fully account for the personal nature of the criticism she faced. Using the uptake of Kenny's methods in Australia and New Zealand as examples, Kerry Highley observes that Kenny's concepts were more positively received when she had less direct contact with members of local medical unions and professional associations, which implies that disapproval of her as a person was a factor which may have contributed to opposition to her methods.

An Australian doctor who helped to publicize her work in the early 1930s described her as *vain, secretive, and jealous*,[211] while a senior member of a government committee examining her work in the 1930s described her as a person *with a curious and occasional criminal obsession about her ability to cure poliomyelitis in all stages*.[212] Even her alleged mentor, Aeneas McDonnell, was not alone in describing her as *That bitch Kenny* in his private communication with colleagues.[213]

Key figures associated with the medical establishment in America spoke of her derisively and behaved with a level of rudeness that cannot simply be attributed to discrimination on the grounds of gender or professional status. Soon after her arrival in America Kenny met Basil O'Connor, President of the National Foundation for Infantile Paralysis (NFIP). O'Connor appears to have taken an instant dislike to Kenny, a dislike which intensified the longer he knew her even though the NFIP provided substantial financial support for Kenny's work in America. O'Connor openly admitted to Victor Cohn that he found her a detestable person.[214] When O'Connor learned that Kenny had been granted a private audience with President Roosevelt in 1943, he frantically attempted to persuade Major General Edwin Watson, the President's Appointment Secretary, to cancel the meeting. Confidential communication between O'Connor and Watson reveals O'Connor requested, and was granted, a private meeting with Roosevelt ahead of the audience to inform him of *things about Sister Kenny that I should tell him*.[215] No record of the private meeting is extant, but it is difficult to imagine which aspects of the life of 63 year old polio therapist could be so sensitive that they could only be communicated to the President in private. O'Connor's dislike of Kenny was so intense that shortly before her death he refused to shake her hand when they met at an official reception. He later claimed to be proud of this ignominious act.[216]

Margaret Ernest recalled that at a meeting she and Kenny attended with Morris Fishbein, editor of the highly influential Journal of the American Medical Association (JAMA), Fishbein sat with his feet on the desk, smoking a cigar throughout the meeting. After a short discussion he told them to leave his office and shut the door on the way out.[217] Displaying such rudeness to a woman during a business meeting was unconscionable in the 1940s. I believe Fishbein's behavior was more than rude, it was symbolic of his opinion of Kenny; if you present yourself as a man, I will show my disrespect as I would to a man.

Passing

As Kerry Highley observed, Kenny concealed many aspects of her past during her lifetime. This chapter shows that some were concealed on her behalf, some will remain forever concealed, and some reveal themselves in the stories she told of her life. When considered in isolation, the characteristics and behaviors appraised in this chapter could be, and have been, interpreted as the unrelated quirks and foibles of a complex person who attracted unreasonable criticism or pedantic analysis for daring to challenge the medical status quo. Alternatively, these disparate traits and behaviors could be interpreted as being evidence of a lifelong quest by a stigmatized individual to project a personal identity which was socially acceptable.

Stigma is easily trivialized by people whose lives conform to social norms, but the victim of stigmatization is often painfully aware of its ability to undermine their identity, self-reliance, and social relationships. Erving Goffman's seminal essay on stigma, published in 1963, provides a useful guide for understanding the stigmatization of an individual based on their discredited personal attributes.[218] Goffman argued that an individual will manage their communication of information about a personal attribute which they believe is deemed to be socially unacceptable. This process of managing a social identity is known as passing. The attribute could be hidden, such as mental illness or religious beliefs, or it could be visible, such as physical disability or racial characteristics. For a person whose primary sexual interests are in members of the same sex, an individual may attempt to minimize the impact of the discrimination by attempting to pass as heterosexual in social interactions. Goffman argued that stigmatized homosexuals used strategies such as concealing overt displays of flamboyant or feminine affectations, correcting their abnormality through psychotherapy, or defy normal social conventions and obstinately proclaim the legitimacy of their social identity. Whilst Goffman's characterization of homosexual behavior and identity appears naïve by modern standards, it should be remembered he was writing before homosexuality was declassified as a mental illness, and decades before it was decriminalized in most English-speaking countries.

There are a range of characteristics associated with Kenny's public identity which may have been recognized by her peers and professional colleagues as discreditable personal attributes. These included: her masculine demeanor; daring, by her own admission, to do work usually restricted to men; choosing to be unmarried; her preference for same sex intimacy; her outspoken misandry; and her assertions that medical men were unwilling to be directed by a woman. Kenny also possessed characteristics associated with ethical and moral integrity which may have been recognized as discredited personal attributes. These included: claiming to hold qualifications which she did not possess; misrepresenting the ideas of others as her own; making false claims about the efficacy of her treatment; and a propensity to dissemble and dissimulate the portrayal of key life events.

Whilst there is circumstantial evidence which supports the hypothesis that Kenny's primary emotional attachments were formed with women, there is no direct evidence that she understood or sought to inhabit an idealized lesbian identity. Nonetheless, her behavior, previously dismissed as idiosyncratic or defensive, suggests she was self-aware of the incongruence between prevailing social norms and her preference for same sex intimacy. I believe this gives credibility to the conclusion that Kenny's behavior should be understood as performances which represented her attempts to project her alignment with the values and norms of the society which she inhabited.

Sanctuary in the clinic

I believe that Kenny's response to the stigma she encountered in her

adult life may usefully be explained by considering the idea of heterotopia –
a concept described by the French philosopher Michele Foucault in a
lecture given to architecture students in 1967. The word heterotopia is an
English approximation of the French term *espace autres* (literally; other
spaces) that Foucault used in the lecture. The lecture was not available in
the public domain until an English translation was published in 1984.
Foucault argued that heterotopias are real spaces which invert the prevailing
order within society. In other words, they are real spaces where idealized or
unconventional behavior or customs are permitted. Heterotopias may be
thought of as the opposite of utopias, which are idealized spaces that do
not exist. The rules which govern normal social interaction within the social
world are set aside within heterotopic spaces but are nonetheless easily
understood by participants and observers. Hence, behavior which is
deemed as socially unacceptable in the normal context is permitted and
common place in a heterotopia.

Foucault uses the example of prisons to illustrate how heterotopias
function. A prison isn't a building with locked doors and barred windows; it
is a space where rituals of punishment are performed, and the inhabitants
are obliged to relinquish conventional social roles. All the participants in the
prison understand, albeit unwillingly, their roles in the heterotopic space. A
hospital is another example of a heterotopia as it is a space where rituals of
healing and death are enacted, and lives are transformed. I believe a hospital
is the most easily understood example of a heterotopia – which probably
explains the universal appeal of situation comedies and drama set in
hospitals. The English concept of hospital derives from the German for
klinik, itself from the French for *clinique*, via the notion of bedside medical
education. The modern sense of a clinic as a physical space is thus a reversal
of the classical sense when a clinic was a service which came to the patient.
I will use the generic term clinic to describe the range of spaces recognized
as health care facilities where rituals and performances transform the lives
of individuals.

Elizabeth Kenny inhabited several heterotopias in her life but the
principal and most enduring of these was the clinic. The clinic is defined by
the social relationships and rituals which are performed by the participants,
rather than physical characteristics of a building. The clinic is the type of
heterotopia which Foucault defined as heterotopias of deviance.
Heterotopias of deviance are institutions where the inhabitants deviate from
normality (for example; due to illness or criminality) and need to be spatially
isolated. The clinic fulfils several important characteristics which Foucault
ascribed to heterotopias: the ritualisation of entry requirements; the ability
to recreate a microcosm which reflects the wider world; and the ability to be
refashioned over time whilst maintaining their overarching purpose.

The heterotopia of the clinic is a consistent thread in Kenny's life story.

In characteristic fashion, Kenny did not submit to the formal rites of entry to the nursing profession, or seek the required permissions, but she enacted the rituals of entry by adopting the uniform and learning the language of the profession to the extent that her masquerade was never unmasked in her lifetime. In her foray as the proprietor of St Canice Private Hospital, Kenny gave a physical form to the heterotopia of the clinic, wherein she interacted with her community through the institutionalized rituals of birth, illness, and death. Through her adoption of the personae of a nurse, Kenny could perform a social role within the heterotopia of the clinic which was congruent with her decision to remain unmarried and her rejection of the conventional roles of wife or mother.

The heterotopia of the clinic also enabled Kenny to prolong her identity as a nurse long after her brief experience of nursing in traditional institutional settings came to an end. After returning from war service Kenny inhabited a virtual heterotopia for almost a decade through her peripatetic employment as a children's nurse, and her adoption of the role of health advocate whilst marketing the Sylvia first aid stretcher. In this period of her life she adopted the classical role of a clinician taking her services to the patient in a manner which explained her social identity. The turning point in her career as a polio therapist occurred when Kenny created her clinic in Townsville in 1934. The Townsville clinic may have been a makeshift affair housed in the veranda of a hotel, but as a heterotopic site it allowed her to confirm her identity as a health care professional and legitimize her therapeutic regime. By offering her services through the recognizable structure and organization of a clinic, Kenny demonstrated to the world that she was neither a faith healer nor a quack.

The Sister Kenny Clinics which were subsequently established in Australia and America during the 1930s and 1940s were examples of the ability of heterotopias to allow unorthodox practices to be employed within a setting which in most respects mimicked conventional health care facilities. In fact, Kenny placed a great deal of emphasis on her claims that her techniques were radically different from conventional or orthodox therapy, whilst carefully maintaining recognizable roles of therapists and nurses, and mimicking the appearance of a conventional health care facility.

The clinics which Kenny created throughout her adult life were spaces which permitted potentially discreditable attributes, such as her marital status and her nonconformist approaches to therapy, to be normalised. These clinics also provided a space which enabled her to acquire social recognition; as a healer of stricken children, a campaigner for social reform of care services, and as a person who possessed knowledge which transcended medical orthodoxy.

Kenny's life was also significantly shaped by the heterotopia of the ship. Foucault claimed the ship is the 'heterotopia par excellence' as ships are organized according to their own self-serving rules but have a unique ability to connect with real spaces which permit the inhabitants to experience multiple alternative cultures and assume multiple identities. There are many aspects of Kenny's life during the years of her war service which embody the habitation of the heterotopia of the ship. As argued in the chapter which examines the development of Kenny's nurse identity there is evidence that Kenny experienced personal liberation and fulfilment during her war service due to the serendipitous combination of circumstances which permitted women to participate in hitherto prohibited activities and roles. Even though the effect of the suspension of conventional social norms during the WW1 is examined in an enormous body of literature, the emotional liberation Kenny experienced during the three years she served as a transport nurse has received inadequate recognition. Troop transport ships provided a unique opportunity for a small number of women to inhabit a space that had previously been the exclusive domain of men. The expectation that the female nurses would not form personal relationships with their fellow officers, crew, and patients, protected their homosocial relationships from scrutiny.

For a brief period, the ship was the site of an idealized life for Kenny; she had income, a protected homosocial environment, status, and autonomy. The ship also served as a space which exposed Kenny to other spaces which were beyond her reach in conventional life. It is this capacity of a ship to be a space which enables wider experiences which places the ship at the heart of Foucault's notion of heterotopia. When her war service came to an end Kenny returned to the socially restricted life she had experienced during her young adult life. The episodes of psychosomatic illness which she experienced on her return to civilian life suggests that it was an existence which brought her little joy.

The final heterotopia associated with Kenny's life, whilst not a place or site in the conventional sense, is the virtual realm of the news media; the cyberspace of the mid-twentieth century. Foucault does not address the concept of cyberspace or virtual reality directly in his lecture on heterotopia, but he uses the analogy of a mirror to explain how a heterotopia can function as '*a sort of counteraction on the position that I occupy*'. The news print media of the mid-twentieth century fulfilled the function of a mirror to the real world, as it directs the individual's gaze towards the virtual space portrayed on the page, which in turn directs attention back to reconstituted selves with a refashioned understanding of the world. The newsprint media is not a place in the conventional sense, but it should be recognized as a space which connected geographical, sectarian, occupational, and political communities of interest just as the internet does in the current era.

The analysis of Kenny's interaction with the newsprint media throughout the 1920s, 1930s, and 1940s, usually portrays her as the subject of a fierce debate, but this is a gross misrepresentation of her relationship with the news media. In reality, she was actively constructing her public identity through her astute and masterful use of press statements, interviews, and letters to editors. Crucially, the newsprint media gave Kenny the ability to engage with a global community of interest – the parents of children who were stricken with polio – which no longer recognized the sovereignty of the medical profession as possessing the knowledge or skills to defeat polio. For a brief time, Kenny could challenge the ability of the medical profession to enforce sanctions on her behavior by reframing the public discourse on the treatment of polio.

The virtual heterotopia which Kenny embraced through her media activities allowed her to connect, albeit through a non-digital platform, with a global network of spaces and communities. The heterotopic space which Kenny inhabited could be considered as a socially produced *espace autres* that had no conventional physical borders or socially recognizable attributes, but nonetheless existed in real time and space. Memoirs produced by polios provide evidence that Kenny's authorship of her personal narrative and her conception of polio therapy created an alternate paradigm for experiencing polio. Kenny, and her collaborators, created an alternative discourse to the conventional medical discourse; a discourse which framed her as healer whose knowledge was sourced from experiential knowledge and evidenced by the experience of her patients. The demise of this heterotopia was a product of the gradual loss of her ability to communicate with her global virtual community, and the eradication of the disease through mass immunization. From 1945 there are clues to the growing impact of her undiagnosed Parkinson's disease on her ability to manage her media profile. Her thought processes were becoming less responsive and more dogmatic, and she was becoming less animated in her personal interaction. Victor Cohn notes that she was defensive and repetitive in her press communication, and increasingly isolated from the journalists who she depended upon as a conduit to the news media. By the early 1950s the medical profession in America was growing confident that an effective vaccine was within the grasp of medical scientists and became more adept at shifting the public discourse away from treatment towards the more optimistic objective of eradication.

Conclusion

In this chapter I have argued that in an era where attitudes towards homosexuality differed from those held today, Kenny's gender nonconformity and open contempt for men could have been interpreted as a sign of her homosexuality and provided a focus for covert homophobic prejudice. Whilst there is no direct evidence that she understood or sought to inhabit an idealized lesbian identity, her behavior, previously dismissed as idiosyncratic or defensive, suggests she was aware of an incongruence between her preference for same sex intimacies and the prevailing social norms. I believe Kenny's behavior should be better understood as the performances of a stigmatized individual seeking to project a personal identity that was socially acceptable.

I have also drawn attention to the strategies which Kenny used with varying credibility and success to project an impression of adherence to social norms and to avoid being labelled as a discredited individual. The most important of these strategies was her decision to adopt the personae of a nurse and seek refuge in the heterotopia of the clinic. The clinic provided Kenny with a sanctuary in which her otherwise discredited attributes were normalised, and her quest for social acceptance was enabled.

---

[187] Lillian Faderman, *Surpassing the love of men* (London: The Women's Press, 1981).

[188] Jack Kenny, to Victor Cohn, letter, 11 June 1953, 146.K8.6F EKP-MHS.

[189] Mary McCracken and Stewart McCracken, interview by Wade Alexander, 30 July 2000, 143.E.10.9B EKP-MHS.

[190] Mary McCarthy, interview by Victor Cohn, 4 April 1953, 146.K.8.6F EKP-MHS.

[191] Cohn, *Sister Kenny*, p. 204. Also, Rosalind Russell, interview by Victor Cohn, 18 August 1953, 146.K.8.6F EKP-MHS.

[192] Elizabeth Kenny to Margaret Ernest, letter, 10th August 1945, 143.E.10.3B EKP-MHS.

[193] Harvey to Cohn, 27 August 1953.

[194] William Hinrichson, interview by Victor Cohn, 3 December 1955, 146.K.8.6F EKP-MHS.

[195] Victor Cohn research notes, 146.K.8.6F EKP-MHS.

[196] Victor Cohn, "Angry Angel: The real story of Sister Kenny, Series 3.", 143.E.10.9B EKP-MHS.

[197] Victor Cohn, "Angry Angel: The real story of Sister Kenny, Series 2." 143.E.10.9B EKP-MHS.

[198] Victor Cohn, "Angry Angel: The real story of Sister Kenny, Series 3.", 143.E.10.9B EKP-MHS.

[199] Victor Cohn, "Angry Angel: The real story of Sister Kenny, Series 8.", 143.E.10.9B EKP-MHS.

[200] Margaret Ernest, interview by author, 17 May 2009.

[201] David Plummer, One of the boys: masculinity, homophobia and modern manhood (Binghamton: Harrington Park Press, 1999), p. 6.

[202] Vicky Statler, Lesbians on… Choosing our icons (LIP publishing, 2010).

[203] APA Task Force on Appropriate Therapeutic Responses to Sexual Orientation, *Report of the Task Force on Appropriate Therapeutic Responses to Sexual Orientation* (Washington DC: American Psychological Association, 2009), p. 6.

[204] Faderman, *Odd Girls*, p. 3

[205] Ernest to author, 4 September 2009.

[206] Elizabeth Kenny to Mary McCarthy, letter, 12 August 1944, 143.E.10.6F EKP-

MHS.
[207] Phyllis Beetsch (née Cohn) to author, personal communication, 2 September 2009.
[208] Mary McCracken, interview by Victor Cohn, 15 April 1955, 143.E.10.6F EKP-MHS.
[209] Cohn, Angry Angel: Series 2.
[210] Cohn, Angry Angel: Series 3.
[211] Dr Philip L K Addison, interview by Victor Cohn, 21 October 1955, 146.K.8.6F EKP-MHS.
[212] Duhig to Cohn, 16 Nov 1955.
[213] Cohn claims McDonnell's hostility towards Kenny was *'generally* confirmed' by McDonnell's son John but qualifies the claim by describing Dr McDonnell as *'beginning to ail, and his mind was slowing'*. Cohn, *Sister Kenny*, p. 99 and p. 278.
[214] Basil O'Conner interview by Victor Cohn, 20 June 1955, 146.K.8.6F EKP-MHS.
[215] Basil O'Connor to Major General Edwin Watson, *correspondence*, 143.E.10.9B EKP-MHS.
[216] Basil O'Connor, *interview*, 20 June 1955.
[217] Ernest to author, 4 September 2009.
[218] Erving Goffman, *Stigma: notes on the management of spoiled identity* (London: Penguin Books, 1963).

4. CREATING THE LEGEND

'I want them rags that wells my legs.'
Elizabeth Kenny

All stories have a life of their own. Many have multiple authors. Most reveal little of their provenance. Most lives are represented by multiple stories which may or may not form a coherent narrative. Some lives, especially those which attain fame or notoriety, may be overwhelmingly represented by a single story. The simplicity of many enduring stories often belies the complexity of their meaning and the purpose for which they were crafted. In this respect, the story of Elizabeth Kenny's first encounter with infantile paralysis is no exception. Elizabeth Kenny's entry in the Australian Dictionary of Biography contains a synopsis of the story which defines her life.

> *In 1911 she used hot cloth fomentations on the advice of Aeneas McDonnell, a Toowoomba surgeon, to treat symptomatically new cases, diagnosed by him telegraphically as infantile paralysis (poliomyelitis). The patients recovered.*[219]

The longevity of this unassuming story is partly the product of good authorship and partly the result of a decade of refinement by Kenny throughout the 1940s. Despite there being no record of the story before 1940, and no witnesses to the event which is portrayed, the story is widely regarded as an autobiographical record of an historical event. Stories do not break out *'like a dose of measles or chickenpox'*,[220] they incubate from personal experiences and are communicated through the language which defines our perception of existence. Even stories which are imagined are based in reality.

In this chapter I will examine two separate and apparently unrelated stories which Kenny narrated more than 15 years apart and to entirely different audiences. The analysis of the historical evidence will reveal that treatment discovery story which Kenny narrated in the 1940s is the product of an invention story which she used to market an ambulance stretcher in the 1920s. This chapter sets out the foundation for my claim that the treatment discovery story should be understood as a personal identity narrative rather than a personal account of an individual's recollection of a chance encounter in the Australian bush.

A story is born

When Elizabeth Kenny arrived in America in April 1940, she brought with her an effective but poorly explained therapy for treating the effects of polio. She also brought a wealth of experience in managing the presentation of her life story in Australian newspapers. Kenny developed her skills in the 1920s through writing press statements and managing media events during her involvement in the Queensland Branch of the Country Women's Association and later through her marketing of the Sylvia Stretcher. In the 1930s she was prolific in producing press releases which endorsed the superiority of her therapeutic techniques or refuted any criticism of her work. Between 1934 and 1939 she was cited, or her activities were reported, in a quarter of the 14,000 news articles on the topic of infantile paralysis in the three main States of Australia. [221] Elizabeth Kenny could easily have given the Kardashian family lessons in self-promotion.

After an initially cautious reception her methods were soon endorsed by prominent doctors in Minneapolis, and favorably reported in the prestigious Journal of the American Medical Association. News of her work in Minneapolis exposed her to an unprecedented level of public interest. The American public were eager to learn about the Australian nurse who claimed to be offering a new treatment for a disease which was greatly feared. Sensing the presence of a good story, American newspaper reporters were keen to interview Kenny as she appeared to be something of a conundrum – she called herself Sister Kenny, but did not appear to be a member of a religious order; and, although she claimed to be a nurse, she did not dress or behave in a manner which corresponded to the conventional public image of a nurse.[222] American journalists found Kenny to be an eager and prolific source of *copy*, but they quickly discovered she was not an easy assignment and had no tolerance of inaccuracy in the reporting of her work. She preferred press conferences to individual interviews as she considered them to be more efficient, and she had a disconcerting habit of asking journalists to read out their notes so she could check they had not made errors or omissions.[223]

The earliest record of the discovery story appears to be an article published in the August 17, 1941 edition of The American Weekly.[224] The article was written by the Science Editor, Robert Potter. The American Weekly was a weekly supplement which was distributed nationally in newspapers published by Randolph Hearst. In the Potter version, which is set in the Australian bush, a frantic woman knocks on the door of the home of the district nurse known as Sister Kenny. A paraphrased summary of the article follows.

A mother visits Kenny's private hospital. *'I've come to find a doctor. My little boy is ill. Is there a doctor here?'* Kenny replies *'I'm sorry but the nearest doctor is 100 miles away. I'm the nurse here and I have to act as doctor, dentist, midwife and nurse.*

What seems to be the matter with the lad?' The desperate mother answers *'I don't know. I'm worried. He had a bit of a fever, a pain in his back, and now his legs hurt.'* Kenny answers *'I'm afraid there is no doctor here, but if you wish I'll come and look at the boy.'* Kenny accompanies the worried mother to the farm south of the town, where she examines the stricken child. After completing her examination Kenny explains to the mother that the symptoms seem to be those of infantile paralysis, but she will send a telegram to the doctors 100 miles away to see what they think. Hours pass until finally the telegraphic response is received. Tearing it open they read *'Case appears to be infantile paralysis. No known cure. Carry on as you are.'* The frantic mother pleads with Kenny to do something. Kenny replies *'I haven't any splints, braces or other things, but I think I can offer help.'* But Kenny cautions her *'I must warn you that this is my own method.'* *'The usual thing is to consider the muscles as dead and so doctors bind the afflicted parts in rigid splints and braces and try to prevent muscle injury which would lead to deformities.'* *'I try to use hot, moist packs to relieve the pain and I try to start the training of the muscles to do their job again. I try to get the patient to relearn to control his muscles.'* Although she has doubts, the desperate mother replies *'Do what you can. I'll believe in you. Tom will too. We'll pray and hope and work with you.'* The article ends with Kenny describing how she helps the young boy to recover and regain control of his stricken legs. Fortunately, we are told, the boy's father was a friend of the Premier of the State, and through his interest Kenny was sent hundreds of patients, half of whom were restored to a normal life.

This early version of the story contains interwoven themes which are biographical – Kenny's status as a district nurse, and her possession of her own fully formed treatment regime; contextual – the location of the patient in a remote rural home, and the absence of local medical practitioners; and performative – the verification of the diagnosis by telegram, and the recognition of her success by a senior politician.[225]

Five months later Robert Yoder reported a different version of the story in an article written for the January 17, 1942 edition of the Saturday Evening Post.[226] Yoder's version is set in the region of South East Queensland known as the Darling Downs. The following paragraphs summarize Yoder's article.

In 1913, in the sparsely settled Australian outback, real doctors were few and far between, and a good deal of emergency surgery was likely to be performed by *'jack-knife wielding amateurs'*. A medical consultation in these remote areas was often only available via a telegram, and most care was delivered by hard working, *'two fisted women'* known as bush nurses. Here, in the settlement of Pilton Hills, a young bush nurse is called to the assistance of a child *'desperately ill with a brand-new malady – new, that is, to the nurse who had to treat it.'* Unable to diagnose the cause of the child's illness, Kenny sends a telegram to the nearest physician, Aeneas McDonnell, 40 miles away in

Toowoomba. His reply: *'Symptoms you describe clearly indicate infantile paralysis. Use your best observation and judgement.'* Within days the young bush nurse has three more cases to deal with. Not knowing the conventional treatment for the disease her common sense tells her to treat the pain, which she does by using hot packs made from strips of torn blankets. When the pain subsides *'she does whatever she can to get the children to move their rebellious arms and legs again'*. Later, when her patients have recovered, the young bush nurse demonstrates her impromptu treatment to Dr McDonnell. He expresses surprise as *'It was thoroughly unconventional, and was based on a completely different conception of what happened to the muscles in the early treatment of the disease.'* Still, it seemed to work, and despite the improbability of a young bush nurse scooping the entire medical profession in discovering a treatment for infantile paralysis, he encourages her to *'Keep it up'*.[227]

The story as told to Yoder retains key performative themes – the medical verification of the diagnosis by telegram, and the recognition of the originality and success of her treatment by a person of authority; and introduces a new performative theme – her discovery of a remedy through experimentation, and a new biographical theme – her ignorance of conventional therapy. Kenny emphasized her prior lack of knowledge of conventional treatment by stating that if she had known about the standard treatment *'I would have been out tearing bark off the trees to make splints'*.[228] This comment may have been deliberately provocative or it may be an indication of how much she believed her revisionist memory of her past as she had used splints constructed from bark to treat a paralysis patient in the early 1920s.[229] This statement is a rare example of Kenny straying off-script in her telling of the story.

Eighteen months later a similar version of the story appears in an article written by Stewart Robinson for the July 30, 1943 edition of *The Family Circle*.[230] Robinson prepared for the interview by sending Kenny a letter with a list of questions, one of which asked for clarification of the date of her first polio case as he had noticed a discrepancy in the dates previously reported in news articles.[231] Robinson's article includes a rendition of the story which closely matches Yoder's version except that this version specifies the event took place in 1910. There is no extant record of Robinson's meeting with Kenny, so the reason for the change of date of the event is unknown.

It is probably no accident that Robinson's rendition of the story was the most succinct account thus far circulated, as it coincided with the publication of Kenny's memoir, *And They Shall Walk,* written with the assistance of Martha Ostenso.[232] Most of the memoir was written in 1942 while Kenny was working in Minneapolis. Whilst the versions produced by Robinson and Kenny retain the core description of her encounter, they place a different emphasis on the response of Aeneas McDonnell to the recovery of her patients.

Robinson writes:

(McDonnell) was frankly amazed when he was told they were as good as new. Sister Kenny's description of her treatment so impressed him that he immediately turned over one of his own patients to her while the hospital staff of doctors and nurses rallied round to watch. Off came the restraining splints; on went the hot foments; deftly to work went Sister Kenny's hands. And in a few weeks the child had recovered. From that day until his death many years later, Dr. McDonnell, a man above jealousy and one who could see beyond the dogmatic theory of the day, was one of Sister Kenny's most loyal advocates.[233]

Whereas Kenny writes:

Elizabeth, you have treated those youngsters for symptoms exactly the opposite of the symptoms recognized by the orthodox medical men of today.
Then he fetched from his library some impressive-looking tomes that dealt with this baffling disease. What I discovered in their pages left me speechless with astonishment. It simply could not be that I, in contraposition to wise authorities, had blundered upon a treatment that had met with success![234]

Although the version presented in Kenny's memoir is the most widely cited version it was subject to revision while Kenny and Ostenso were preparing the manuscript for publication. Victor Cohn, Kenny's biographer, owned holograph copies of sections of a handwritten draft of the memoir. Only two pages of this version are extant. [235] The handwritten description is consistent with the version which eventually reached print, but with the noteworthy exception that in the original draft the patient is a young boy.

In 1944 Kenny further refined the story in a series of articles she wrote for the American Weekly titled *God Is My Doctor*.[236] The American Weekly paid Kenny $2,500 (equivalent to $36,000 in 2018) to provide factual material concerning her observations.[237] Kenny changed *observations* to *discoveries* in the contract which was signed on 31 December 1943. The description of the incident in *God Is My Doctor* is generally consistent with the 1943 version except the patient is named Amy McNeil and the date of the incident is now June 12, 1910. Placing the encounter in a winter month in Australia is noteworthy as polio infections usually peak in the summer months, hence the disease being known colloquially as summer plague. Most Americans would not have questioned this date as it coincided with their own experience of the disease occurring in summer.

Press releases prepared by Kenny in 1950 for distribution to American newspapers provide evidence that the form of the story reached stasis near the end of her life.[238] The prose is more flowery and self-congratulatory, but the key themes and gender of the patient remain consistent. The noticeable enhancements to these final renditions of the story are the greater emphasis placed on a divine inspiration guiding her response to the child's suffering, and greater detail in her description of her therapeutic actions. The following extract picks up the story at a recognizable point.

> *The message read: 'Infantile paralysis. No known treatment. Do the best you can with the symptoms you see.' What was I to do, alone in the Bush of Australia, away from all medical assistance? I must think, and, looking towards the East where dawn was breaking into day, the still small voice of my Mother came to me, as it were, over the air when as a child I was given a task I thought was beyond my strength, she would place her hand upon my head and looking into my face, repeat one of her favorite passages, which has stayed with me and supported me through many an hour of trial and weakness, the words of that grand old English bard:*
>
> > *'He who of the greatest work is finisher*
> > *Oft does it by His weakest minister.'*
>
> *With an unvoiced prayer to the Great Physician, I returned to the bedroom in that humble cottage in the backwoods of Australia, to lay the foundation stone of a work that one day was to receive recognition in the great halls of learning throughout the medical world.*
>
> *What took place during those hours and days of suspense and fight with this little girl and five of the twenty children who comprised the neighborhood could not be written. How the soft, moist heat applied soothed pain and made the part that was invaded by the virus of this dread disease receptive to the treatment which had to be evolved; how my knowledge of surface anatomy came to my assistance and helped me to restore again the mental pathway to those once tortured areas; how I had to evolve a means of restoring again the true mechanical action of the parts that had been so disturbed and beaten down by the invasion of this enemy; how my knowledge of the architecture of the human frame, learnt in a peculiar way from childhood, came to my aid, it seemed to me that some mysterious Higher Power had shaped my destiny even from childhood in order that I may be of help to the helpless.[239]*

Unravelling fact from fiction

For more than sixty years researchers, historians, journalists and chroniclers of polio in the twentieth century have based much of their analysis of the life and work of Elizabeth Kenny on the assumption that a story which she crafted during the final decade of her life is a reliable account of her first encounter with infantile paralysis. Kerry Highley is the only researcher to have questioned the authenticity of the discovery story. The story has a naïve charm, and is rich in drama and pathos, but it lacks internal consistency, and has never been reliably corroborated. A century has passed since the events described in the story are alleged to have occurred, but enough evidence survives to allow a balanced examination of the five key themes embedded in the story's multiple iterative forms: the time and place of the encounter; the diagnosis of infantile paralysis; the originality of the method of treatment; the involvement of Aeneas McDonnell; and the recovery of her patients. The analysis of the factual claims which are embedded in the treatment discovery story is a necessary starting point to understanding the historical context of the narrative and the life of the narrator.

Time and place of the encounter

The date of Kenny's first encounter with a case of infantile paralysis is impossible to state precisely as there are no records of the event other than Kenny's personal testimony. Between 1941 and 1952 Kenny claimed the encounter occurred in 1909, 1910, 1912, and 1913. Victor Cohn initially suggested the first encounter took place in '*1911 or so*',[240] but later broadened this to '*somewhere between 1910 and 1913*'.[241] Kenny's residence in the Clifton district can only be confirmed from 1911 onwards. A local medical practitioner suggested that she may have treated children with infantile paralysis while she was the proprietor of St Canice from 1912 to 1915, but his recollection was vague.[242]

If the story is to be believed it is remarkable that there is no record of an outbreak of the size described by Kenny. When Victor Cohn interviewed Kenny's acquaintances, family members, and professional colleagues shortly after her death in 1952 he was unable to determine a reliable date for the alleged event or obtain the names of any of the alleged patients. As Kenny was a local hero, and one of the most famous Australians of the twentieth century, it is very difficult to understand why no-one has ever claimed the honor of being one of her first patients.

Infantile paralysis was uncommon at the time but was sufficiently well known to attract the attention of the local print media of the era. The main newspaper in the district, the Warwick Examiner and Times, regularly reported births, deaths, and the treatment of burns and trauma at Nurse Kenny's private hospital in Clifton, but only one case of infantile paralysis was reported by the Sanitary Inspector between 1905 and 1915, and this was in Warwick in 1914.[243] The Clifton Courier also contains reports of deaths and births in Clifton in the period 1909 to 1915, but there are no reports of cases of infantile paralysis.

The lack of records of Kenny's initial encounter with poliomyelitis is not, as she frequently claimed, associated with the remoteness of the rural location in which the events are set, or the lack of medical interest in the disease. Kenny may have lived in a small village, but the rural arcadia she describes in her memoir was not especially isolated or unsophisticated by Australian standards. During the Federation period the Darling Downs was a prosperous region with a thriving rural economy. In 1912 the Darling Downs produced around 95% of all the cheese and wheat for the State of Queensland.[244] The region had an extensive telephone and telegraphic network, and the towns of Nobby and Clifton were linked to the nearby city of Toowoomba by a rail line. Clifton is 38 miles from Toowoomba, not 100 miles as she claimed. The town had resident pharmacists, dentists, medical practitioners, and two private hospitals during the period she owned St Canice. One of the first changes Kenny implemented when she took control of her private hospital in 1912 was to have the telephone connected.[245]

The story Kenny told her American audience portrayed Australia as an unsophisticated society which lacked modern transport, communication, and health care infrastructure. The cultural framing which Kenny employed in the telling of the discovery story assisted her American audience to conceptualize the challenge she faced as a lone nurse working in a hostile environment, and to believe, or at least not question, her claims that she faced a hitherto unknown foe.

Diagnosis of infantile paralysis

In the period leading up to the WW1 health care services were highly regulated in Queensland, and a comprehensive disease surveillance system had been operating since 1900. The science of medicine in pre-WW1 rural Queensland may have been rudimentary by today's standards, but the administrative systems supporting the provision of health care were in many respects comparable to those which exist in the current era. Infantile paralysis was made a notifiable disease in Queensland in 1909,[246] thereby making it compulsory for medical practitioners to notify central health authorities and local government authorities of their diagnosis of every case involving the disease. Prior to 1909 cases were monitored by the Commissioner of Public Health. The first recorded epidemic of infantile paralysis in Queensland occurred during the summer months of 1904-1905, with 108 cases reported in the Annual Report of the Commissioner of Public Health.[247] The next significant epidemic involving 332 cases did not occur until the summer of 1915,[248] by which time Kenny had closed St Canice and set sail for England. Consequently, it is difficult to believe Kenny's claim she treated six infantile paralysis cases in one small geographical area when only five cases were notified for the whole of Queensland in 1912.[249]

One version of the discovery story describes Kenny treating a child with infantile paralysis in St Canice Private Hospital. In common with the more familiar version of the story the case is diagnosed by a local medical practitioner, and Kenny improvises her treatment. If this had occurred the medical practitioner should have notified the case to the local health authorities. No notification exists. Kenny states in her memoir that there are no records of the disease because at the time it '*had not won any special attention from the medical men*'. [250] Publishing such an explicit deceit was foolhardy as the deception could have been exposed through a relatively simple enquiry. As it turns out the gamble paid off as her assertion escaped cross examination by her contemporaries and many subsequent chroniclers of her life and work.

A complication in understanding the true prevalence of polio in this era stems from the similarity of the symptoms of the disease to those present in other viral diseases. The flaccid paralysis that is so characteristic of the acute stage of poliomyelitis is also characteristic of diseases such as Guillan-Barre syndrome, transverse myelitis, or encephalomyelitis.[251] Indeed, it has recently been argued that Theodore Roosevelt's paralysis, diagnosed in 1921 by the eminent physicians George Draper and Robert Lovett, was more likely to have been caused by Guillain-Barre syndrome than polio.[252] Even if Kenny's claims to have treated paralysis while working in Clifton are factual, these cases were not necessarily cases of paralytic poliomyelitis.

Recovery of the patients

Kenny's claim that all her early infantile paralysis patients recovered from their illness is the most consistent theme in the discovery story, and it is easily the most contentious claim within the narrative. To understand the significance of this claim, it is important to consider it was made at a time when the superior efficacy of her treatment regime was receiving wider acceptance. Nonetheless, many medical practitioners remained sceptical due to Kenny's propensity to exaggerate claims about the success of her method and the absence of clinical trial data. By claiming her method had produced a full recovery in all her early cases, and then endorsing this claim through the alleged admiration of a respected medical practitioner, Kenny was demonstrating behavior which was characteristic of a dissembler.

In 1943 it was common knowledge that some patients with the acute paralytic form of polio were left with no residual disability after their illness had subsided. Kenny was aware of the unpredictable outcomes of the disease, so by claiming her patients had recovered she was not, as she was quick to point out, making a claim to be able to cure the disease. Kenny tells the reader all her patients recovered but does not explain the extent of the recovery. By avoiding any explicit description of the residual physical function of her patients Kenny allows the reader to draw their own conclusions about the outcome of the story. The lay person might interpret recovery as meaning a complete absence of residual disability, whereas a nurse might interpret recovery as including a range of residual disabilities which allowed close to normal function for the patient. The careful phrasing and choice of words in the story allows Kenny to artfully imply her approach could produce results which were beyond the effects of chance, whilst minimizing the potential for the claim to be objectively scrutinized.

The debate over the increased efficacy of the Kenny method continues to this day. During her lifetime there were limited opportunities to conduct clinical trials as it was difficult to predict the occurrence or size of outbreaks, and clinical trial methods were primitive by modern standards. By the time clinical trial protocols were sufficiently refined to provide a valid evaluation of polio treatment the number of cases had fallen to low levels. Then, as now, the debate centers on the uncertain level of residual dysfunction once the patient has passed the acute paralytic phase of the illness. Kenny's description of the cases she allegedly treated circumvents this aspect of the disease.

Involvement of Aeneas McDonnell

The depiction of Aeneas McDonnell's role in the discovery legend is significant for several reasons. Whilst his involvement is universally accepted, I believe it is probably a fabrication. At the time of the alleged incidents Kenny had known McDonnell for more than a decade. They had met when McDonnell treated Kenny for a broken wrist when she fell from a horse. The precise date of the accident is not known but family members claimed it occurred sometime during 1897 or 1898 when her family were living at Headington Hill, a property near Clifton. After treating the broken wrist McDonnell apparently invited Kenny to recuperate at his home in Toowoomba. Kenny portrays these events in her memoir as occurring when she was a child rather than as a young woman.

Kenny placed great importance on her relationship with McDonnell. She claims he provided her with access to an extensive medical library which she used to develop her knowledge of anatomy and physiology.[253] Later he provided her with valuable mentorship and referrals to her private hospital,[254] and in 1915 he furnished her with a reference which has often been attributed as having facilitated her recruitment to the AANS. Despite his modest professional background as a rural General Practitioner, McDonnell eventually became a highly respected and influential member of the Queensland medical establishment. Kenny's decision, after early prevarication, to cast McDonnell as a central figure in the discovery story is most likely a ruse designed to enhance the perception that something significant had been discovered during the encounter.

McDonnell performs three important roles in the discovery narrative – he confirms the diagnosis of infantile paralysis, he authorizes Kenny to improvise her own treatment, and he validates the success of her approach. As an actor in the story he is cast as the learned and unbiased authoritarian figure whose initial incredulity is replaced by belief in her ability. In short, he is Kenny's first convert. In the real world, it seems McDonnell's alleged incredulity lasted longer than the story suggests. He left no record of the encounter, never adopted her techniques in the treatment of his own patients, and never publicly expressed or published any formal support for Kenny's methods throughout a long and distinguished career. Indeed, McDonnell's son claimed that while his father admired Kenny's determination to improve the after care of polio patients, he was keen to disassociate himself from Kenny in later life due to her propensity to exaggerate the effectiveness of her treatment. [255]

McDonnell's inclusion in the story is indispensable to Kenny's claim to the originality of her conceptualization of the disease and its treatment. McDonnell's alleged declaration of powerlessness in the face of the disease serves to exalt Kenny's intuitive responsiveness, whilst admonishing medical practitioners for their lack of humility in the face of truth. McDonnell's views on how he is portrayed in the story will never be known as he died four years before its first publication.

Originality of the treatment

Putting aside the questions of when and what Kenny was treating, and whether or not a doctor was involved in the diagnosis, the theme which is most consistent throughout all iterations of the story is the claim her discovery of a new treatment is based on her resourcefulness and intuitive response to her patient's pain and physical deformity. Early versions of the story make explicit reference to the use of hot stupes to ease pain, and the early introduction of muscle training to enable the muscles to remember their function. Neither of these practices were especially contentious. A stupe, or foment, is a hot moist cloth or sponge, sometimes medicated, which is applied to the skin to ease pain or relax muscles and joints. The term hot pack is used in the United States. The third and most controversial aspect of her method, the avoidance of immobilisation, is included less consistently. The reasons for Kenny's prevarication in declaring the full extent of her discovery is unclear, but it is possible she was testing the response of the American public to her claims.

Rigid immobilisation of limbs for extended periods was standard practice in the treatment of many forms of paralysis. For reasons which are not known Kenny abandoned the use of rigid splints around the time she set up her first makeshift clinic in Townsville in 1933. It may have been a response to a change in her conceptualization of the pathology of paralysis, or it may have been a deliberate attempt to strengthen her public identity by dispensing with a practice which was synonymous with conventional methods of treatment. Both arguments are plausible, but neither are supported by a credible evidence base. The simplest explanation, and one which has been completely overlooked in the literature, is that she didn't use splints because she didn't have any to use. The clinic which she established in Townsville started its life under a veranda at the rear of a hotel. Kenny states that her equipment consisted of a few beds and tables, a tin bath, and a kerosene fueled water heater.[256] Whilst some of her early patients were admitted to the clinic with their own rigid splints,[257] Kenny had no money to purchase additional medical equipment, and there are no records of splints being purchased when the clinic later received funding from the Queensland State Government. Kenny's radical change in the treatment of polio may have simply been an improvisation based on necessity.

Reports produced by medical observers in 1934 and 1935 provide conclusive evidence that Kenny did not have a consolidated system for treating polio when she commenced treating patients in the improvised Townsville clinic in mid-1933. Kenny is known to have used an *under water method of treatment*, or hydrotherapy as it is now known, to treat Maude Rollinson for three months in 1931.[258] Whilst she used warm water baths when the Townsville Clinic was established,[259] this type of therapy had been abandoned by 1935, and replaced by the routine use of hot packs.[260] Independent reports by Dr Rae Dungan and Sir Raphael Cilento confirm she promoted the early introduction of passive exercise and avoided, but not completely abandoned, the use of rigid splints at the Townsville Clinic.

The cautious endorsement which Kenny received from Raphael Cilento in 1933 turned into vociferous public spat in 1934. Cilento accused Kenny of copying her ideas from Wilhelmine Wright, a therapist who had published an influential paper in 1912 on muscle training in the treatment of infantile paralysis.[261] This paper was reprinted several times through the 1920s, and probably explains Cilento's suspicion that Kenny had plagiarized Wright's ideas. The accusation exacerbated a fractious relationship, and, with the benefit of hindsight, Kenny's indignation was justified – her ideas had little in common with those held by Wright. On the other hand, Kenny's ideas had a lot in common with those published by Charles MacKay in the British Medical Journal in 1920.[262] MacKay was Officer-In-Charge, Muscle Re-education Department, Alder Hey Special Military Surgical Hospital, where he studied the work of Sir Colin Mackenzie.[263] By necessity, rehabilitation techniques progressed rapidly during the First World War in response to the large number of amputations following battle injuries. Mackenzie's techniques were adopted at the Australian Auxiliary Hospitals in England which were under the control of the Australian Army Medical Corps. Kenny worked on a temporary basis at the two Auxiliary Hospitals during 1916 and 1917,[264] and it is likely she observed the massage and muscle re-education therapies which were used to treat injured soldiers at these hospitals. The paper MacKay published in the BMJ presents ideas which are similar to those presented by Kenny a decade later, especially those related to the concepts of alienation and incoordination of muscles affected by polio. MacKay argued that *'Muscle must now be restored to its rightful and prominent place in the treatment of disorders of the neuromuscular system'*. Whilst there is no evidence that Kenny had read MacKay's paper, she repeatedly claimed throughout the 1930s that she had developed her techniques while nursing invalid soldiers during the WW1.[265]

Silent witnesses

Victor Cohn's research notes show that the identification of witnesses to her early work was an important objective in his biographical project. To date, no investigator has identified a patient who was treated for an acute case of polio by Kenny prior to 1934. The absence of witnesses to this key event in Kenny's life is a challenge to scholars attempting to understand the origin of her method, but an even more significant obstacle is presented by scholars who suppress the testimony of witnesses which is inconsistent with pre-existing views.

In 1955 Victor Cohn interviewed Dr Alex Horn, a general practitioner who worked in Toowoomba from 1908 until his retirement. Horn claimed Kenny had sought his advice on treating paralysis when she owned her private hospital, asserting Aeneas McDonnell had told her *'I don't know a damned thing about this'*. Horn claimed he advised Kenny to use stupes and early mobilization to treat her patients as this was the approach he had been taught during his medical training in Scotland. Horn also claimed Kenny had deliberately omitted references to his assistance from her memoir because at the time he was working as a lodge doctor. The term lodge doctor is derived from the colloquial name for benevolent societies and fraternal societies which employed doctors to provide medical services for their members. Private medical practitioners were critical of lodge doctors because they reduced demand for their fee-based services. Medical unions in Australia and America waged a fierce publicity campaign during the 1920s to discredit the quality of health care provided by lodge doctors.

According to Horn, Kenny gave prominence to McDonnell in the story because *'She wasn't going to attach the name of any but a man like McDonnell who had a private practice. She chose that arrangement for a story; it fitted in and looked better'*.[266] Cohn dismissed Horn's claim that he had assisted Kenny on the basis that Horn was unable to provide a precise date for offering the advice and remained silent about Horn's conjecture on his low status. Horn's claims are acknowledged by Wade Alexander, but he does not question the reasons for the inconsistencies between Horn's claims and Kenny's reporting of the events. In the summary of his discussion of Kenny's early treatment of polio Alexander concludes *'In all the versions of this story, Nurse Kenny observed her patients, listened to them, gently placed her hands on them to enhance her perceptions and then found a way to help those children in a new and creative manner.*[267] Alexander deftly precedes his conclusion with the observation *'it is impossible to confirm that they actually had polio'.*

Cohn and Alexander either disregard or marginalize Horn's claims because they do not conform to Kenny's telling of the story, rather than questioning the story because it did not conform to available facts. Cohn dismissed Horn's testimony because it suggested Kenny was seeking advice about the treatment of paralysis in the 1920s, not in the 1910s as Kenny had claimed, even though Cohn knew Kenny had treated Daphne Cregan's paralysis during the early 1920s. Horn's absence in the story might also be attributed to the fact that, unlike McDonnell, he was still alive when it was published, and was, therefore, in a position to challenge the facts as they were portrayed.

Taking all the available evidence into consideration I believe it is highly unlikely that Elizabeth Kenny treated children with acute polio, or discovered a method of treating acute polio, whilst working as an independent nurse practitioner in the Clifton district prior to WW1. This conclusion led me inevitably to questioning why Kenny created the discovery story in 1940, and what inspired her to construct the story in the form which it takes. As noted earlier, stories don't break out like a dose of measles or chicken pox, they are actively crafted from personal experiences and familiar narratives. The source of the inspiration for the treatment discovery story therefore lies in understanding the story as more than a personal account of an individual's recollection of a chance encounter in the Australian bush.

The Sylvia stretcher invention story

If the polio treatment discovery story is not a personal account of an historical event, why did Kenny create it and what was its purpose? This conundrum preoccupied my thinking for many years. I knew she had claimed to her Australian audience in 1935 and 1937 that she developed her therapeutic techniques while nursing injured soldiers during the WW1, and I knew she had repeated these claims to her American audience in the early 1940s. Therein lies the rub. How could both explanations be presented to an American audience, but only one to an Australian? I was mindful that my interpretation of the evidence could be skewed by the imbalance in the availability of historical records in America and Australia, but I felt certain that an explanation could be found. The solution to the problem came after reflecting on the tutelage I received from Professor Simon Chapman when I was studying public health at the University of Sydney. Where would Simon look for evidence of Kenny's discovery in the public discourse on infantile paralysis? The news media, of course!

Feeling inspired I decided to undertake a content analysis of newspaper reporting of polio and Sister Kenny in Australia prior to her journey to America in 1940. Such an undertaking would once have been logistically impossible, but the development of the Trove web portal now allows full text-based searches of digitised copies of hundreds of Australian newspapers published in the first half of the twentieth century. I initially focused on news reports featuring a discussion of Kenny and polio which were published between 1934 and 1939 in the three States with the highest prevalence of polio; New South Wales, Victoria, and Queensland. This search revealed no evidence of Kenny making any reference to treating the acute symptoms of polio prior to her war service. I then extended the search period to cover the period 1919 to 1932 to identify the existence of contemporary records of her treating paralysis cases. This content analysis also revealed no evidence of Kenny treating paralysis patients throughout the specified period, but it did reveal a spike in news reports which focused on her involvement in the invention of an ambulance stretcher known as the Sylvia Stretcher. I was already aware of her involvement in the invention and marketing of the ambulance stretcher, but the scale of reporting surprised me and suggested that the episode may have held more significance than I previously recognized. The remainder of this chapter examines Kenny's involvement in the invention of the Sylvia Stretcher and the contribution of the venture to her evolving personal story.

A little girl's accident

On Saturday 15th May 1926 Kenny was asked to assist in the first aid treatment of Sylvia Kuhn, a child who had been injured in an agricultural accident on a farm near Nobby. The incident was reported in a local newspaper the following Tuesday.[268] The child's injuries were sufficiently serious to warrant her transportation to a hospital in Toowoomba. Witnesses confirm that Kenny improvised a rigid stretcher from a cupboard door. The improvised device protected the child's injured limbs and improved her comfort, thereby reducing the risk of shock during the journey.[269] The drama did not end with the accident, as the ambulance conveying Kenny and the child was involved in a collision with another vehicle while travelling to Toowoomba. Kenny sustained a shoulder injury, but the child was protected from further injury and eventually recovered from her injuries.

Sylvia Kuhn's accident had a profound impact on Kenny's life. Within three months of the incident she had resigned from her role as President of the Nobby branch of the CWA,[270] produced a prototype stretcher with the assistance of a local saddler,[271] instructed a solicitor to file an application to patent the device,[272] agreed a contract with a company to manufacture the stretcher,[273] sought endorsement of the superiority of the stretcher from Dr Rushton Smith, a general practitioner in Clifton, [274] and arranged to exhibit the stretcher at the Brisbane Exhibition Show which opened on 12th August 1926.[275] Marketing the Sylvia stretcher would be an all-consuming preoccupation for Kenny for the next five years.

The Sylvia stretcher proved to be a successful business venture due to Kenny's ingenuity in utilising the network of CWA branches to promote sales of the stretcher to local ambulance brigades. Its success also owes much to her creativity in keeping the story alive in the news media over an extended period despite there being little new content in her press releases and interviews as sales began to decline. Kenny set herself apart from her contemporaries by demonstrating an exceptional talent for linking the Sylvia stretcher story with her own life story.

Devices as varied as the cardiac pacemaker, surf ski, notepad, armored tank, and rotary hoe were invented by Australians between 1900 and 1930, yet none of the inventors are household names, and none earned significant royalties from their inventions While fellow Australian inventors remained content with refining the technical features of their inventions and shunned their commercial exploitation, Kenny nurtured a public image with the zeal of a politician engaged in an election campaign.

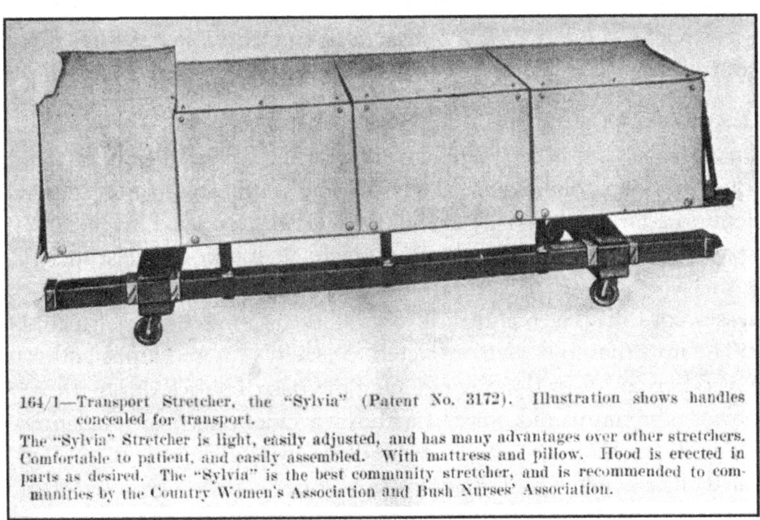

Catalogue listing for the Sylvia Ambulance Stretcher.

The experience of Eady Hart provides a sobering insight into the approach to self-promotion typically taken by female Australian inventors in the 1920s. Working alone in her home kitchen, Hart developed a process for manufacturing organic dyes from indigenous plants. She patented the process in 1921. Despite the commercial viability of her production methods, and the technical and aesthetic superiority of her dyes,[276] the company failed. Hart died a pauper in 1931.[277] Whilst Hart is one of only three women categorized as inventors in the 12,000 entries in the Australian Dictionary of Biography, her invention was barely visible in the news media during her lifetime.[278] Unlike Kenny, Hart showed little understanding of the importance of identifying her invention with her personal story despite possessing a life story which combined hardship, tenacity, creativity, and entrepreneurial determination.

An evolving story

The story of Kenny's invention of the Sylvia stretcher is narrated almost entirely through newspaper articles written by journalists using notes of interviews with Kenny or press releases written by Kenny and distributed through telegraphic *wire* services. The only known version written entirely in the first person is included in her memoir published in 1943. The story, as reported in the Queensland newspapers, evolves throughout the five-year period Kenny actively engaged in marketing the stretcher. A news report published in August 1926 is typical of the early form of the story.

Boon To Sufferers. New Ambulance Stretcher. Lady Inventor Demonstrates.

Some time ago a little child fell, breaking both legs, and two of its toes were actually severed. An improvised litter was arranged by Sister E. Kenny, of Warwick, upon which the child was carried from Nobby to Toowoomba. With such comparative comfort was the child moved that it actually fell asleep, and its rapid recovery after only nine weeks in hospital was ascribed to the singularly comfortable character of the litter. So much praise was bestowed upon the stretcher that Sister Kenny was induced to perfect it, and under her supervision was evolved the Sylvia stretcher, named after the little Nobby patient.[279]

Over time the story was embellished, but a version published in 1928 is consistent with the version Kenny included in her memoir published in 1943.

Romance of C.W.A. President's Invention

In her work among people in her country district Sister Kenny found the regulation ambulance stretcher not as efficient as could be wished and she experimented with doors and mattresses until she found a stretcher that counteracted the effects of shock — the most dangerous attribute of all accidents. This she patented and called it after a little girl whose was the first the stretcher was instrumental in saving.

This child was riding on a plow driven by her brother when she fell and was terribly mangled. The brother rode 30 miles on his motor cycle for Sister Kenny, whom he took out behind him, and the little sufferer was conveyed to the hospital on an improvised Sylvia stretcher placed on a motor lorry. Nearing the town a touring car knocked into the lorry,

> *slightly injuring Sister Kenny and the young man, and knocking the stretcher off on to the road. When they lifted the cover of the stretcher, fearing the worst, Sylvia was asleep! Sister Kenny, like so many more members of the C.W.A., had done the work that lay nearest her and she had made a discovery of incalculable value to mankind.*[280]

There are four key themes embedded in this invention story. These are: Kenny's response to a child in crisis; her intellectual ownership of the invention; the expert verification of the superiority of the invention, and her altruism in marketing the stretcher.

A child in crisis

'*Little Girl's Ordeal*' the headline proclaims; a child is seriously injured on a farm near Nobby, and Sister Kenny, local ambulance attendant, is called to tender first aid.[281] Early reports place emphasis on the ability of Kenny's improvisation to provide comfort for the child and protect her from further injury.[282] Kenny reinforced the connection between the stretcher and a child's suffering by naming the stretcher after the first patient it conveyed. Then as now, the suffering of a child commanded special media attention; especially in Queensland where the idealization of Australia as '*young, white, happy and wholesome, and in constant need of protection*'[283] was resonant with the demographic profile of the population. Between 1901 and 1921, 60-65% of the Queensland population were aged under 25, but the birthrate was declining and population growth was frequently reliant on overseas and interstate migration.[284]

The power of the presence of an injured child in the invention story appears to have distracted newspaper journalists from questioning her claim that the improvised stretcher had contributed to the child's rapid recovery. Kenny's claim may have been made in good faith, but this *ex post facto* judgement ignores the potential for an equally valid critical evaluation of the stretcher if the child had died from shock, hemorrhage, or sepsis. The probability of Sylvia's recovery was not high. [285] John Pearn drew the safe conclusion that the child made an uneventful recovery due to '*the resilience of youth and to fracture immobilization*'.[286] Whatever informed her claims, a year later Kenny stepped up the rhetoric by claiming the stretcher had saved the child's life.[287]

In 1927 the child, Kenny, and the stretcher form a triad in the consolidated invention story:

> *A year ago, Sister E. Kenny, of Nobby, on the Darling Downs, patented her idea of a comfortable stretcher for ambulance transport work, and called her invention the "Sylvia" stretcher, in remembrance of a little patient, whose life was saved by the use of the stretcher.*[288]

By 1930, Kenny takes the central role in the story, and the stretcher is relegated to the function of qualifying her credentials as a globally recognized advocate for improving health care for people living in rural Queensland:

> *According to letters received from England, Sister Elizabeth Kenny had just returned from a visit to the continent, where, in Paris, it was arranged that she should meet M. Clousot, the Chief of the Secretariat of the International Red Cross Committee, in connection with Sister Kenny's "Sylvia" stretcher.*[289]

Intellectual ownership of the stretcher

Elements of the invention story suggest that Kenny felt compelled to demonstrate her intellectual ownership of her stretcher and validate her identity as an inventor. Eye witness accounts suggest that the improvisation of the rigid stretcher was a collaborative exercise, and Kenny required the assistance of the child's father and a local saddler to produce a prototype.[290] There is additional evidence that Kenny was assisted by an engineer who had gained public attention for inventing an ambulance stretcher used in WW1.[291] Nonetheless, within weeks of the accident she was asserting her identity as the inventor of the stretcher by publicly declaring she was taking out a comprehensive patent on the design.[292] A patent application for an '*improved transport stretcher*' was submitted in 1926 and accepted on 15th March 1927,[293] and an associated patent for a '*surgical appliance for supporting the injured members of patients' bodies during their transport*' was accepted on 4th June 1929.[294]

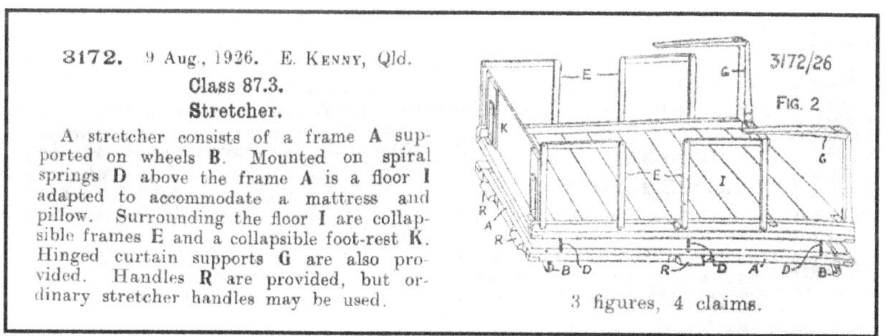

Intellectual Patent for the Sylvia Stretcher.

Whilst Kenny was not obliged to take out a patent or lodge a trademark to manufacture and sell the stretcher, lodging an application publicly demonstrated that her invention met the criteria for obtaining a patent; the invention had to be novel, useful, and involve an inventive step. In addition to protecting her rights to manufacture the device, the patent also verified her intellectual ownership of the invention and provides evidence of her understanding of the narratives which shaped the public understanding of the concepts of invention and discovery during the 1920s.

The differentiation between invention and discovery was a topic of public interest in the 1920s. David Miller argues that an artificial differentiation between discovery – the revealing of the natural states of the world, and invention – the creative product of man, lay at the core of a fractious debate about the recognition of the concept of *scientific property* in the 1920s.[295] Proponents of scientific property argued that discovery was a creative process manifested through the production of an artefact or idea. Opponents to scientific property argued that invention and discovery were binary opposites. This differentiation between invention and discovery remains unresolved to the present day.

Australian newspapers regularly published reports of the discussion of intellectual property rights throughout the 1920s. The inequality in the rights of artists and inventors is a recurring theme in the news media.

> *Authors, musicians, or inventors, can obtain financial compensation for their work, but to the scientist who discovers some truth from which humanity will derive great lasting advantages the present laws grant nothing.*[296]

Whilst there is no direct evidence of Kenny's awareness of this debate, the rhetoric of recognition and reward for a gift to humanity is strong within the life story she presented.

Kenny's use of the intellectual property laws to confirm her claim to be the inventor of the Sylvia Stretcher demonstrates her understanding of the conceptual framing of invention. This raises questions about the absence of clarity in her framing of her first encounter with polio. In the 1940s Kenny states she evolves, experiments, develops, and employs her knowledge of symptomatic treatment, but she never uses the terms invent or discover to describe the process which leads to the production of her method. Her use of terminology should not be interpreted as a semantic accident; Kenny possessed knowledge of the intellectual patent system and the benefits it endowed on acknowledged inventors. By abstaining from using the term *invent* in her treatment discovery story Kenny minimizes the potential challenge to the originality of the techniques she employed in her treatment of polio. By avoiding the term *discover* in her treatment discovery story she avoids the pitfall of her ideas being classified as knowledge which rightfully belonged to a scientific community. Rhetorically, Kenny treads a middle path. Nonetheless, stylistically, she frames her first encounter with polio as a scientific discovery.

A superior contrivance

Patenting the stretcher demonstrated her invention was useful, novel, and inventive, but it did not demonstrate it was superior to other ambulance stretchers. The invention story shows that Kenny was not content to represent the Sylvia stretcher as different from existing devices; she wanted to show it was better. Early versions of the story imply the stretcher contributed to the rapid recovery of the patient and prevented shock from the stress of transportation. Both claims relied on the fortuitous recovery of the patient. Unfettered by current day concepts of product testing or quality standards, Kenny presented a prototype of her allegedly superior device at the 1926 Brisbane Exhibition Show and convinced a Brisbane firm to commence the manufacture of the patented design.

Kenny's claims of the superiority of her stretcher were primarily supported by expert verification, although her choice of experts was sometimes questionable,[297] and their observations were entirely restricted to assumptions based on the features which the design incorporated. Later news reports cite the endorsement of medical practitioners and nurses who confirm the stretcher *'is as different from and superior to the ordinary medical stretcher as can be imagined'*,[298] but do not interrogate the evidence which forms the basis of these claims. Putting aside the qualifications of the expert witnesses who endorsed the superiority of the stretcher, it is important to recognize that the standard of evidence which informed these opinions was not uncommon by contemporary standards. In the 1920s medical devices were routinely tested through heuristic evaluation rather than clinical trial.

Kenny promoted the stretcher in Australia for two years before embarking in 1929 on an ambitious marketing exercise in the United Kingdom and the United States. By the time she arrived back in Australia in 1930 sales had declined due to the improved standard of ambulance vehicles, changes in first aid practices, and inherent design limitations of the stretcher.[299] Pearn estimated that less than 200 stretchers were sold over the five year production run; indicating that the invention was evidently not the solution to *'the last great problem of the transport of invalids'*.[300]

A gift to mankind

While the stretcher ultimately only saw modest service within Australia it served Kenny's interests remarkably well. At a time when a senior qualified nurse was paid between £100 and £150 per year for working 44 to 48 hours a week,[301] Kenny received a guaranteed dividend of £150 per year from the manufacturer whilst still receiving her war pension. *'One woman's gift to suffering mankind'*[302] was, to use the parlance of her era, a nice little earner for a woman who consistently claimed she only patented the device *'to prevent anybody from using it as a means of making excessive profits'*.[303] There are no extant records which show whether the sale of the device generated any profits for the manufacturer, but Kenny claimed *'half the money will go to the treatment of crippled kiddies'*.[304] Considering Kenny's proficiency in using press releases to publicize the stretcher, the absence of news articles reporting the distribution of profits is compelling evidence that none were distributed.

Kenny's positioning of herself as a public benefactor in the invention story is a peculiar inversion of the concept of *noblesse oblige*. Her behavior during the four years she spent promoting the stretcher bears little resemblance with philanthropy and is more revealing of a propensity for self-promotion than altruism. Arguably, Kenny's gift to mankind, and the proper purpose of the story, is the revelation of her noble self, not the reporting of the circumstances of her discovery. The focus of the story is Kenny, not the child or the stretcher, as she is the component of the story which endures.

Kenny's invention of the Sylvia stretcher is usually framed as a quirky back story which demonstrates her capacity for invention and her flair for entrepreneurialism but is unrelated to the development of her therapeutic regime or her campaign to reform the rehabilitation of paralysis patients. This content analysis of press reports shows that the invention story provided Kenny with an opportunity to develop her ability to craft a narrative which created an alternative public identity as an inventor, benefactor, and health care campaigner. This analysis also demonstrates her awareness of the nuances in the ownership of intellectual property rights and explains the source of her perception of the heuristic testing being equivalent to clinical evaluation. All these factors were evident in the approach she took to negotiating with health officials, medical practitioners, and the news media in her subsequent career as a polio therapist. Finally, this content analysis reveals similarities in the structure, content, and plot of the invention story and the discovery story which will be examined in the following chapter.

Conclusion

My analysis of news reports from the 1920s shows that Kenny's invention of the Sylvia stretcher is more than a quirky back story that is unrelated to her campaign to reform the rehabilitation of paralysis patients, or the development of her treatment of paralysis. The story which Kenny crafted around her marketing of the Sylvia stretcher demonstrated her ability to construct a narrative which created a public identity as an inventor. Further, I believe the available evidence leaves little room for doubt in concluding that it is highly unlikely Elizabeth Kenny treated children with acute polio, or discovered a method of treating acute polio, whilst working as an independent nurse practitioner in the Clifton district prior to WW1. I have no doubt that Kenny created the discovery story soon after arriving in America in 1940.

I believe that attributing the discovery story as having originated in the 1910s has distracted attention from the contribution of important life events to the development of her therapeutic regime and her personal identity. The analysis in this chapter demonstrates that the stretcher invention story and the treatment discovery story are equally important in establishing the narration of Kenny's life story and her identity as an inventor and scientist.

[219] Ross Patrick, "Kenny, Elizabeth (1880-1952)", Australian Dictionary of Biography vol 9 (1983).

[220] Holstein, James A., and Jaber F. Gubrium. "Narrating the Self". In *The Self We Live By: Narrative Identity in a Postmodern World*, pp. 103-123, Oxford: Oxford University Press, 2000

[221] Allan Hildon, "War of Words", paper presented at 14th Biennial Conference of the Australian and New Zealand Society of the History of Medicine, Sydney, 30 June 2015.

[222] There is no photographic record of Kenny wearing a nurse's uniform after she was discharged from the AANS in 1919.

[223] Source: Victor Cohn's research notes. 146.K.8.6F EKP-MHS.

[224] Robert D. Potter, "Sister Kenny's Treatment for Infantile Paralysis", The American Weekly, 17 August 1941, pp. 4, 5, 13. 143.K.8.5B EKP-MHS.

[225] The term performative refers to the extent to which the reader perceives the story to be a performance or an enactment of real events.

[226] Robert M. Yoder, "Healer From The Outback", *Saturday Evening Post*, 17 January 1942, pp. 18-19, 68-70. 143.F.2.5B. EKP-MHS

[227] Yoder, *Healer*, p. 19.

[228] Yoder, *Healer*, p. 68.

[229] Kenny's use of bark splints is confirmed in a letter written by Daphne Cregan to Victor Cohn in 1956, EKP-MHS. The bark of iron-bark eucalypt trees, so named due to its strength and rigidity, is still recommended for first-aid splinting of injured limbs where medical devices are not available.

[230] Stewart Robinson, "Sister Kenny", *The Family Circle*, 30 July 1943, pp. 4-6, 18-19. 143.F.2.5B. EKP-MHS

[231] Stewart Robinson, to Elizabeth Kenny, letter, 19 February 1943, 143.E.10.6F EKP-MHS.

[232] Martha Ostenso was hired by Kenny to edit the first draft of the memoir.

[233] Robinson, *Sister Kenny*, p.5-6.

[234] Kenny and Ostenso, *And They Shall Walk*, p. 29-30.

[235] A holograph is an early form of photocopy. Cohn donated his holographs to the Smithsonian Institution in Washington. Correspondence between Cohn and the Smithsonian reveal that the Smithsonian lost all but two of the donated images. Elizabeth Kenny, Holograph copies of draft memoir, Reserve 35 EKP-MHS.

[236] Elizabeth Kenny, "God Is My Doctor", *The American Weekly*, 26 March 1944, pp. 18-19. 143.K.8.5B EKP-MHS.

[237] Contract between The American Weekly and Elizabeth Kenny, 146.K.8.5B EKP-MHS.

[238] Typed manuscript inscribed 3-8-50, and typed manuscript inscribed 3-28-50, 146.K.8.5B EKP-MHS.

[239] Typed manuscript inscribed 3-8-50, 146.K.8.5B EKP-MHS.

[240] Victor Cohn, "Angry Angel, Series 9", p.2. 143.E.10.9B EKP-MHS.

[241] Cohn, *Sister Kenny*, p. 274.

[242] Dr. Alex Horn, interview by Victor Cohn, 29 November 1955. 146.K.8.6F EKP-MHS.

[243] "Town Council, Thursday General Meeting, Sanitary Inspector's Report", *Warwick Examiner and Times,* 12 December 1914, p. 6. Trove NLA.

[244] Source: Centre for the Government of Queensland, University of Queensland.

[245] "Nurse Kenny", *Clifton Courier,* 13 July 1912. p. 2. Trove NLA.

[246] Cumpston, *Health and Disease*, p. 398.

[247] Patrick, *Health and Medicine*, p. 238.

[248] Cumpston, *Health and Disease*, p. 326.

[249] Cumpston, *Health and Disease*, p. 326.

[250] Kenny and Ostenso, *And They Shall Walk*, p. 30.

[251] Margery Kennett, Vicki Stambos, Ann Turnbull, Aishah Ibrahim, Heath Kelly. "Report of the Australian National Polio Reference Laboratory, 1 July to 31 December 1999", *Communicable Diseases Intelligence* vol.24, no. 5, May 2000, pp. 118-121.

[252] Goldman, *Franklin Delano Roosevelt*, p. 240.

[253] Kenny and Ostenso, *And They Shall Walk*, p. 12.

[254] Alexander, *Sister Kenny*, p. 27, citing interview by Victor Cohn with Thomas Thompson, 1956.

[255] John McDonnell, interview by Victor Cohn, August 1955. 146.K.8.6F EKP-MHS.

[256] Kenny's description of the clinic is corroborated by the description given by Doris Rollinson and Lydia Rollinson-Cully in an interview by Victor Cohn, 9 Dec. 1955. 146.K.8.6F EKP-MHS.

[257] Harold Kenny, Elizabeth Kenny's nephew, told Wade Alexander he had seen a room full of discarded splints in the Townsville Clinic. Kenny stated his Aunt boasted that the owners of the splints had been admitted '*stiff legged, held straight, irons on*' and walked out of the clinic with no further need of their splints. Harold Kenny, interview by Wade Alexander, 30 July 200, Wade Kenny Archive, Sister Kenny House, Nobby, Queensland.

[258] Her use of '*under water*' therapy is reported in "A daughter of Alfred Deakin", *Evening News*, 23 September 1931, p.12.

[259] Rae W. Dungan, *Report on work done by Sister Kenny at the muscle re-education clinic, Townsville,* (1934). Dungan RW Box, 1 Folder 9, UQFL354.

[260] Rae W Dungan, *Report on Elizabeth Kenny Clinic at George St. Brisbane and Kenny wards general hospital Brisbane.* Dungan RW Box 1 Folder 10 UQFL354.

[261] Wilhelmine G. Wright, "Muscle Training in the Treatment of Infantile Paralysis", *Boston Medical and Surgical Journal* vol. 167, (1912), pp. 567-574.

[262] Charles MacKay, "The place of muscle re-education in the treatment of anterior poliomyelitis (Infantile Paralysis)", *British Medical Journal* vol. 2, (1920), pp. 513-515.

[263] Mackenzie published The Treatment of Infantile Paralysis: A Study on Muscular Action and Muscle Regeneration in 1910, and The Action of Muscles: Including Muscle Rest and Muscle Re-Education in 1918.

[264] Kenny's statement of service issued by the Australian Imperial Force Base

Records Office in 1953 shows she was temporarily assigned to the hospitals at Southall and Harefield Park several times during 1917 and 1918. NAA: B2455 Kenny, Elizabeth.

[265] In 1935 Kenny claimed her method was a *'treatment for all kinds of paralysis'* which she had discovered when nursing soldiers during the war. "Generous Action of Queensland Nurse", *Australian Women's Weekly*, 23 February 1935, p. 4. In 1937 she elaborated on this theme by claiming she had developed her ideas on a troopship while nursing meningitis patients. "Sister Kenny's Treatment for Infantile Paralysis" *Australian Women's Weekly*, 27 November 1937, p. 3. Trove NLA.

[266] Dr. Alex Horn, *interview*.

[267] Alexander, *Sister Kenny*, p. 27.

[268] "Serious Accident", *Warwick Daily News*, 18 May 1926, p.2, Trove NLA.

[269] John Pearn, "The Sylvia stretcher: a perspective of Sister Elizabeth Kenny's contribution to the first-aid management of injured patients", *Medical Journal of Australia* vol. 149, (1988), pp. 636-638.

[270] "Nobby's Loss Sister Kenny Farewelled", *Daily Mail*, 20 August 1926, p.12, Trove NLA.

[271] Pearn, *Sylvia stretcher*, p. 636.

[272] Victor Cohn and John Pearn separately confirm that Kenny instructed E.G. Abell to assist with the patent application.

[273] Victor Cohn states she initially agreed a contract with Laycock, Littledike, & Co., bedding manufacturers in Brisbane, but later agreed a contract with Elliott Bros. Ltd. in Sydney. Cohn claims Elliott Bros. agreed to pay Kenny a dividend of £150-£200 per annum for the rights to sell the stretcher. Cohn, *Sister Kenny*, p.72

[274] "To Aid the Sick", *Warwick Daily News*, 9 August 1926, p.4, Trove NLA.

[275] "Ambulance Display", *The Telegraph*, 11 August 1926, p12, Trove NLA.

[276] Hart's display at the British Empire Exhibition in London in 1924 was awarded a gold medal. "Olla Podrida", *Muswellbrook Chronicle*, 18 December 1925, p. 6, Trove NLA.

[277] Weston Bate, "Hart, Eady (1848–1931)", *Australian Dictionary of Biography*, (National Centre of Biography, Australian National University, 2005). http://adb.anu.edu.au/biography/hart-eady-12965/text23197.

[278] Between 1920 and her death in 1931, Hart's invention is reported in 16 newspaper articles in 890 Australian newspaper titles indexed in the Trove database. Half of these articles appear to be based on a single press release which was syndicated in late 1925.

[279] "Boon to Sufferers", *Daily Standard*, 11 August 1926, p.8. Trove NLA.

[280] "Romance of C.W. A. President's Invention", *Tweed Daily*, 8 September 1928, p.6. Trove NLA.

[281] "Little Girl's Ordeal", *Western Star & Roma Advertiser*, 26 May 1926, p.4. Trove NLA.

[282] "New Ambulance Stretcher", *Daily Standard*, 11 August 1926, p.8. Trove NLA.

[283] For an appraisal of the cultural tropes associated with Australian identity in the early twentieth century see "Growing Up" in Richard White, *Inventing Australia*

(Sydney: Allen & Unwin, 1980), pp. 140-156.

284   Australian Bureau of Statistics, *Australian Historical Population Statistics*, cat. no. 3105.0.65.001, 2014. http://www.abs.gov.au/ausstats/abs@.nsf/mf/3105.0.65.001.

285   In 1925 accidents were the most common cause of death in children aged 5-15 years in Australia, accounting for 25% of all deaths. Cumpston, *Health and disease*. p. 111.

286   Pearn, *Sylvia stretcher*, p. 637.

287   "Sylvia Stretcher Sister Kenny's Invention Appreciated", *Daily Standard*, 25 February 1927, p.2, Trove NLA.

288   "The 'Sylvia' Stretcher", *Townsville Daily Bulletin*, 23 August 1927, p.6, Trove NLA.

289   The letter was probably written by Kenny as it characteristically uses commas in the name of the stretcher. "Improved Stretcher Sister Kenny's Invention", *The Brisbane Courier*, 10 January 1930, p.3, Trove NLA.

290   Pearn, *Sylvia stretcher*, p. 636.

291   Alexander Worsfold was an engineer who designed and patented the Transporter stretcher which was used by the A.I.F. during the WW1. The timing of Worsfold's involvement is not known as Kenny did not publicly acknowledge Worsfold's assistance until three months after she lodged her second patent application in January 1929. "Sylvia Stretcher Inventor Going Abroad", *Queensland Times*, 15 January 1929, p.4, Trove NLA.

292   "To Aid the Sick, *Warwick Daily News*, 9 August 1926, p.4; "Ambulance Display", *The Telegraph*, 11 August 1926, p12, Trove NLA.

293   IP Australia, Patent no. 3172/26. *Australian Official Journal of Patents*, 5 March 1927.

294   IP Australia, Patent No. 1928 016293. https://www.ipaustralia.gov.au/

295   David P. Miller, "Intellectual property and narratives of discovery/invention: The League of Nations' draft convention on 'scientific property' and its fate", *History of Science* vol. 46, (2008), pp. 299-342.

296   "Scientific Works", *Queensland Times*, 23 August 1923, p. 5, Trove NLA.

297   Early endorsement mostly came from public dignitaries, such as the Governor General and his wife, or senior members of organizations, such as hospital boards and ambulance organizations, who were potential customers.

298   "'Sylvia' Stretcher Sister Kenny's Invention Appreciated", p.2

299   Pearn states the stretcher was heavy and difficult to clean when contaminated with body fluids such as blood and vomitus. Pearn, *Sylvia stretcher*, p. 638.

300   "*Sylvia Stretcher Inventor Going Abroad*", p.4

301   "Nurses Award", *The Queenslander*, 13 November 1930, p.20, Trove NLA.

302   "*Sister Kenny's Invention Appreciated*", p.2

303   Kenny and Ostenso, *And They Shall Walk*, p. 77

304   "*Sister Kenny's Invention Appreciated*", p.2

5. MYTH, METHOD, METAPHOR

In the preceding chapter I examined the veracity of the factual claims which are stated or implied in the discovery story and concluded that it should not be read as a first-hand account of a historical event. Whilst I am confident in my appraisal of the historical basis to the story it would be remiss of me to simply debunk the myth without offering my assessment of its meaning and purpose. To ensure this assessment is not viewed simply as a personal opinion, even if subjectivity is inescapable, I will set out an edited description of the analytical process which will inform my assessment of the meaning and purpose of the story. In addition to examining the internal organization of these stories, I intend to step outside the structure of the narrative to consider who produced the stories, where they were produced and reproduced, what were their purpose, who were their audiences, and how they became narratives with a life of their own.

The analysis set out in this chapter shows that the treatment discovery story is far more than a personal account of a life changing event. It should be understood as the culmination of Kenny's personal myth at the end of her life, a myth which defines her identity, illuminates her values, and embodies her quest for personal truth – a truth which is an amalgamation of myth, method, and metaphor.

It's all about the plot

A life story evolves throughout a person's life span as they collect experiences, language, and imagery from their cultural environment. Dan McAdams uses the analogy of the rings of a tree to illustrate how we may read the chronology of the events and imagery embedded in a personal myth to understand the relationships between those ordered events.[305] The ordering of a sequence of events within a story is generally known as emplotment, but the term plot is so ubiquitous in everyday language that story and plot are often used interchangeably. I like to define plot as the ordering or arrangement of events and actions within a story to explain motivations and predict the consequences of those actions. In this context, plot guides the reader's expectations or understanding of the narrative by signposting the extent to which the story conforms to a known genre. Plot, therefore, is the mechanism which translates the events of a story into a narrative which has social meaning.

The analysis presented in chapter five may be used to signpost the key elements within the stretcher invention story and the treatment discovery story. These elements are presented in table 1. The table shows there is a striking congruence in content of the stories and the ordering of the events. The similarity in the content of the stories is, by itself, not the feature which give the stories a shared narrative purpose. It is the ordering of the elements, or shared plot, that leads the reader to a conclusion which, in this

Table 1. Plot structure of actions and events

Stretcher invention story	Treatment discovery story
Remote rural setting	Remote rural setting
Kenny receives call for help	Kenny receives call for help
Patient is a child	Patient is a child
Kenny appraises the condition of the child	Kenny appraises the condition of the child
Kenny decides orthodox transportation would be inadequate	Doctor authorises Kenny to use her judgement to treat the child
Kenny improvises the care of the child	Kenny improvises the care of the child
The child's discomfort is reduced	The child's discomfort is reduced
The child recovers	The child recovers
A medical practitioner endorses the superiority of Kenny's improvisation	A medical practitioner endorses the superiority of Kenny's improvisation
Originality of the improvisation is endorsed by a recognised authority (patent office)	Originality of the improvisation is endorsed by a recognised authority (medical practitioner)
Kenny makes a commitment to share her invention for the betterment of mankind	Kenny makes a commitment to share her discovery for the betterment of mankind

case, is not immediately obvious. One of the key binding characteristics of these stories is their capacity to lead the reader into a probable future – Kenny's commitment to share her invention or discovery with the world – beyond the immediate outcome of the events – the recovery of the child. In both stories a causal relationship is established between Kenny's improvisation and the recovery of the child, but the purpose of both stories is to extend this causal relationship to Kenny's humanitarian future. As this *future* is the present for the discovery story, the reader is assured that the protagonist's situation was engineered through her own actions. The analysis in chapter five shows how Kenny manipulated the plot in the invention story over several years to alter it from a report of events to a story which may be understood as a *'probability design'* which has the ability to change *'what readers accept as likely outcomes between the beginning and the end of a narrative'*.[306] Whether or not her decision was taken consciously, it is not surprising that fifteen years later Kenny employed the same plot structure to craft a story which would be pivotal in defining her identity as the bearer of a gift to the American people.

From story to narrative

The terms discourse, narrative, and story are widely used and often interchanged in everyday communication. This is no less the case in many academic publications. I like to think of stories, which can be conveyed orally, or through performance, writing or visual expression, as being a vehicle for conveying a message. I find it helpful to understand narrative in terms of its linguistic origins *narrare* to tell, and *gnarus* to know. Hence, story is telling, whereas narrative is knowing and telling. The consensus presented in the academic literature is that narrative and story are inextricably linked as instruments which allow individuals to create meaning and purpose in their lives, construct personal identities, and reimagine the past. The ability of stories to recreate and the past is essential to the human experience of time as history is a reinterpretation of the absent world. History is a reorganization of events, actions and stories into an intelligible plot. Ergo: history is narrated

Choosing an appropriate form of narrative analysis can be daunting as there has been a proliferation of techniques in recent decades. As I am interested in stories which already exist, I will focus on the internal organization of those stories. The systematic deconstruction of stories for elucidating the narrative themes is a practical, albeit subjective, method for understanding the purpose of stories. The techniques I have used follow the approaches described nearly fifty years apart by William Labov and Shaul Shenhav. Labov's approach to narrative analysis was originally developed with Joshua Waletzky in 1967.[307] Labov and Waletzky proposed that a fully developed personal experience narrative contained five key elements, or clauses, which could be identified by asking simple questions: what is the story about, what unusual action occurred, what is the point of the story, what happened as a result of the action, and how is the story connected to the present time? These elements are then coded as: orientation (O), complication (CA), evaluation (E), resolution (R), and coda (C). There are variations in the questions which may be used to codify the actions, but all link to the same five linguistic features. The purpose of the narrative is revealed by examining the positioning of the clauses within the narrative structure

Shaul Shenhav takes a less formulaic but equally structured approach to

Table 2. Narrative clauses in the invention story

Code	1926 version	1943 version
A	Some time ago a little child fell, breaking both legs, and two of its toes were actually severed.	On a beautiful morning in 1926… a young share farmer… demanded that I should hurry to his father's house, where his little sister had "broken both legs and torn off two toes".
O	An improvised litter was arranged by Sister E. Kenny, of Warwick,	Since the stretcher that had been brought along was of the standard type, I asked if I might be permitted to substitute transport equipment of my own devising.
O	upon which the child was carried from Nobby to Toowoomba.	My request was granted
CA	With such comparative comfort was the child moved	and I was gratified, after a few miles of our journey,
E	that it actually fell asleep,	to see the little girl's body relax and her eyes close in sleep.
E	and its rapid recovery after only nine weeks in hospital was ascribed to the singularly comfortable character of the litter.	Six weeks later the little girl's father brought her to see me on his way home from the hospital. No visible sign of her misfortune remained other than the missing toes.
R	So much praise was bestowed upon the stretcher that Sister Kenny was induced to perfect it,	…the kindly hearted surgeon suggest that I seek a patent for my stretcher and make it available for ambulance services in centers remote from city hospitals.
C	and under her supervision was evolved the Sylvia stretcher, named after the little Nobby patient.	Thus the Sylvia Stretcher came into being.

the analysis of narratives.[308] Shenhav believes narrative meaning may be revealed by examining the key features of a social narrative; text, story, and narration. Text is the mode in which the story is conveyed – written, spoken, or visual; story is the chronological sequence of events constructed from text; and narration is the process of communicating the story. To this conventional typology Shenhav adds the concept of multiplicity; *'the process of repetition and variation through which narratives are reproduced at the societal sphere in order to become social and influential'.*[309]

Multiplicity is the feature of stories which allows them to be reproduced or adapted over time. A narrative's adaptability through multiplicity helps to explain how stories achieve a life which can extend beyond the original author because of its incorporation by new social groups over extended periods of time. This feature is especially relevant to the study of the polio discovery story.

An analysis of the clauses in the stretcher invention story is set out in table 2. The analysis uses versions of the story published in 1926,[310] and 1943.[311] It is now impossible to confirm the authorship of the 1926 version, but its prosaic style distinguishes it from the original press reports written closer to the event. The two versions adhere to near identical structures, but it is not known if this is because Kenny contributed to the authorship of the early news report or if she appropriated and incorporated the story into her own identity narrative.

The analysis shows that the linear sequence within the invention story is characteristic of the normal form of a personal experience narrative. The events within the narrative adheres to a temporal sequence which leads the audience from the abstract, through the orientation, to the complicating action. The evaluation establishes the real importance of the narrative. The story ends with the narrator stating the resolution to the dilemma which the complicating action created, and a coda which brings the audience back to the present time. The placement of the complicating action in the sequence is essential to the evaluation of the key messages within the narrative.

The analysis of the invention narrative suggests that it serves two crucial functions: it confirms that Kenny's improvisation made a material difference to the welfare of the child *'With such comparative comfort was the child moved'*; and it places responsibility on Kenny to share her invention to prevent further unnecessary suffering *'So much praise was bestowed upon the stretcher that Sister Kenny was induced to perfect it'*. The significance of Kenny's improvisation is established by the evaluative statements *'it actually fell asleep'* and *'its rapid recovery after only nine weeks in hospital was ascribed to the singularly comfortable character of the litter.'*

An analysis of the clauses in the treatment discovery story is set out in table 3. The analysis uses two versions of the discovery story, a press release

Table 3. Narrative clauses within the discovery story

Code	1950 version	2009 version
A	I had received an urgent call to hurry to the spot where six months before I had ushered into the world Australia's best immigrant native born a little son.	In 1909, a young Darling Downs lass called Elizabeth Kenny, aged just 23, made what appeared to be a remarkable breakthrough.
O	I thought the call was in connection with some teething problem or some minor ailment… (The child) was stricken with one of the most feared of all diseases to the hearts of Motherhood – the disease infantile paralysis, and I, at the age of 22	The unqualified bush nurse, the daughter of an Irish vet who migrated to NSW,
CA	was confronted with the problem of battling this enemy of childhood	was handed an infant girl in agony from twisted limbs.
O	The only physician available was one hundred miles away and very busy… The only communication was by telegraph.	She was at a loss about the mysterious ailment the girl's father called cow disease.
CA	Ruth's condition was carefully recorded and sent away to my guide, philosopher and friend, the late Dr. Aeneas John McDonnell,	Kenny saddled up and rode to the nearest telegraph station where she cabled a doctor friend,
CA	the telegram read: 'Infantile Paralysis. No known treatment. Do the best you can with the symptoms you see.'	who diagnosed infantile paralysis
E	The thought came to me: 'How could I, humble nurse in the backwoods of Australia, do anything when the medical world had decided there was no known treatment?'	and informed her nothing could be done.

Table 3 cont. Narrative clauses within the discovery story

Code	1950 version	2009 version
CA	… my first endeavour was to relieve this shortening and bring back again the life giving oxygen by restoring the circulation so much needed. After many trials and much error, of applying heat, I at last found the soothing influence of the moist heat, applied per medium of the warmth of a part of a woollen blanket wrung tightly out of boiling water.	Undeterred, she applied warm, moist strips of cloth.
R	Gradually the shortened area began to relax, the lifeblood started flowing more freely, bringing a soothing influence to the areas that had been starved for the lack of oxygen. The agonizing look of fear gave place to one of confidence, the moans of pain gradually ceased, and the lids closed on the blue eyes of Ruth; and sleep, gentle sleep, nature's soft nurse, had come to my assistance.	The next morning the girl's limbs were better.
E	The foundation of a great discovery had taken place – not in the Halls of Science, but in the remote bush land of Australia.	Authorities tried to debunk the method, but after it was endorsed by US experts,
C	As I sat by the bedside of this little girl in the lonely watches of the night I was grateful for a kindly Providence who had prepared me in a most unusual way for the rugged path that lay before me in the years ahead.	her fame took off.

written by Kenny in 1950,[312] and an article published in the Courier Mail newspaper in Brisbane in 2009.[313] The Courier Mail version is reproduced exactly as published. The version written by Kenny is an extract of the original press release. The original press release is burdened with extraneous detail, which is characteristic of Kenny's affected writing style, but in a redacted form it remains useful for analysis because it is written in the first person and adheres to the structure which Kenny used in the memoir published in 1943.

The analysis of the discovery story shows that the linear sequence within the story is characteristic of the normal form of a personal experience narrative. The structure of the discovery narrative shows that it serves two crucial functions: it confirms the helplessness of the medical profession and inadequacies of medical knowledge *'the telegram read: Infantile Paralysis. No known treatment. Do the best you can with the symptoms you see.'*, and it places responsibility on Kenny to use her nursing knowledge to resolve the problem *'Undeterred, she applied warm, moist strips of cloth'*. The significance of these elements of the story is established by the evaluative statements *'and informed her nothing could be done'* and *'How could I, humble nurse in the backwoods of Australia, do anything when the medical world had decided there was no known treatment?'*.

As stated previously, the purpose of a personal experience narrative is to assert that the events in the narrative took place in the order described by the narrator. The authenticity of the account is underpinned by its reportability, credibility, and causativeness. The most reportable event is the event which has the greatest impact on the needs and desires of the participants. In the invention story the requirement for Kenny to perfect her invention is the resolution of the narrative, but the most reportable event is Kenny's initiative in making the improvisations which improve the comfort and safety of the child. In the discovery story the recovery of the patient is the resolution of the narrative, but the most reportable event is the necessity for Kenny to assume responsibility for finding the means to relieve the suffering of the child.

The concept of reportability has a direct impact on the credibility of the narrative. Credibility is the extent to which the audience believes the events occurred as described. In the invention story the causality is established by linking the orientation clause *'a little child fell, breaking both legs, and two of its toes were actually severed'* and the resolution clause *'so much praise was bestowed upon the stretcher that Sister Kenny was induced to perfect it'* with the action taken *'an improvised litter was arranged by Sister E. Kenny'*. Whilst the reason for the recovery of the child is attributed to the *'comfortable character of the litter'* this statement is unnecessary as reporting the recovery of the child is not the main purpose of the story. The recovery of the child simply adds credibility to the resolution that Kenny had a duty to share her wisdom with the world. In the discovery story the causativeness, or causality, is established by linking the orientation clause '*She was at a loss about the mysterious ailment the girl's father called cow disease*' and the resolution clause '*The next morning the girl's limbs were better*' with the action taken by the narrator '*Undeterred, she applied warm, moist strips of cloth*'. Bearing in mind that the audience knows that the use of hot packs was a characteristic component of Kenny's method, the inclusion of the reference to '*warm, moist strips of cloth*' is enough to confirm causality in the narrative. This in turn reinforces to the audience that the events did occur. Both iterations of the discovery story end with a coda which reminds the audience of the purpose of the story. In the later iteration Kenny reminds the reader that the origin of the method lay '*not in the Halls of Science, but in the remote bush land of Australia*'. She also invites the audience to empathize with her subjective position within the narrative by reflecting on her emotional response to being chosen by providence to tread '*the rugged path that lay before me in the years ahead*'.

The narrative analysis of these stories serves to illustrate Shaul Shenhav's proposition that some narratives may possess a multiplicity which enables them to define reality for a given population, and to integrate speakers, texts, and audiences across space and time.[314] The quality of multiplicity is derived from the reproduction and dissemination of core elements which are constant across the subsequent iterations of a narrative. The preceding analysis shows there are core narrative elements within the invention and discovery stories which remained constant over many decades, and in varying social contexts, signifying that these core elements have enduring social meaning for the narrators and the audience, and define the perception of the reality of the events which are the focus of these narratives.

The longevity of the discovery story is testament to its instrumentality in cementing Kenny's identity within the public consciousness and demonstrates the ability of a good story to resist critical analysis due to its capacity to appear to tell the *truth*. The truth, or authenticity in the discovery story, is established by Kenny presenting herself as the sole witness to events which the audience can understand. Truth, of course, is a highly subjective concept. I believe the analysis of the structure and content of the discovery story tells us that the truth of the story lies in the prophecy it offers in 1910 being fulfilled in 1940. This suggests to me that the discovery story should properly be considered as a parable which is constructed from metaphors sourced from Kenny's life rather the report of an historical event.

Meaning from metaphor

The difficulty Kenny experienced in communicating her ideas to qualified health professionals is usually attributed to her lack of formal qualifications and ignorance of medical terminology. While this explanation may be partly true, it assumes her ideas could be communicated in the technical language of her era, and it assumes there is only one heuristic framework for knowledge production. In the 1930s and 1940s the business of science was the verification of a priori reasoning and rendering observable the hidden facts of reality. The idea that metaphor could be constitutive of theory or knowledge creation, rather than merely explanatory, was not a credible proposition in this era. I believe that in the absence of a meaningful technical language, expressing her ideas through metaphorical language was Kenny's only option.

Narration facilitates sensemaking, but the sense or purpose of the discovery story cannot be imputed from the structure alone, for this we need to explore the role of metaphor in conveying the conceptual meaning of the language or imagery from which the story is constructed. As explained in the introduction chapter, metaphor is not simply a linguistic device which embellished everyday communication; metaphor is fundamental to how humans perceive and interpret their existence. Metaphors build links between concepts which are familiar with ideas which are new, complex, or contested. Metaphors, which are most often words, can therefore influence decisions and actions by shaping beliefs about their consequences within the real world.

Whilst the explanatory function of metaphor is now widely accepted, the process of metaphor production remains open to conjecture. The French philosopher, Paul Ricoeur, suggests that metaphor arises from a *'paradox of fiction'* whereby an alternative reality is created through the productive use of imagination which endows verbal icons with augmented meaning. The use of verbal icons in stories, fiction, and the portrayal of utopias, augments our understanding of reality and expands our perception of the world.[315] Alternatively, the Lithuanian philosopher, Saulius Geniusas, presents an Aristotelian argument that the concept of metaphor implies an intuitive perception of the similarity in dissimilarity, and without this intuitive perception there would be no metaphors.[316] The Italian philosopher, Gemma Fiumara, conceives of metaphoricity as a fundamental feature of human life, whereby metaphorical projections connect biological life to dialogic existence.[317] Crucially, Fiumara's anthropomorphic concept of metaphoricity offers a means to explain the process which connected Kenny's life experiences to her conceptualization of a disease and its treatment.

In order to identify the presence of metaphors within the treatment discovery narrative I turned to the metaphor identification process developed by a group of scholars with the improbable title *The Pragglejaz Group.* This group suggested that a metaphor could be identified within

Table 4. Metaphorised icons within the discovery story

Icon	Generalised metaphors	Entailments
Illness	Illness is a being. Disease is an enemy. Psychological forces are physical forces	Polio is an external threat which invades or overwhelms the individual. Metaphysical threats mimic the action of human beings. Experience of prejudice or social alienation is similar to the experience of illness.
Child	Life is suffering. Believers are infected. Society is a body. The body is a battleground. The self is fragile.	Kenny's intervention is a counterfoil to the absurdity of polio. The intervention restores order where disorder has reigned. Belief will ease physical and psychological suffering.
Doctor	Ignorance is bliss. The past is a captor. Compliance is adherence.	Conventional wisdom is powerless in the face of a new malady. Conformity is valued more than originality.
Parents	Life is struggle. Hope is light. The unknown is a wilderness.	Polio threatens the homeostasis which parenting seeks to achieve. The crisis can only be overcome through belief.
Nurse	Knowing is seeing. Choosing is being. Knowledge is power. Knowledge is liberation.	Authenticity is choosing to act as one believes is correct. Choice brings consequences. Choosing sets one apart from society.

a discourse if it satisfies the following conditions: the word or phrase can be understood beyond the literal meaning in context of what is being said; the literal meaning stems from an area of physical or cultural experience – the source area; which in this context is transferred to a target area. The meaning of the metaphorised word or phrase is assessed in the context of its use in the wider narrative on the subject.

Applying this process to the reading of the discovery story reveals the presence of several metaphorised words which transform the meaning of the narrative. These metaphorised words and their entailments are set out in table 4. The entailment of a metaphor is the logical consequence or implication arising from the use of the metaphor. The analysis reveals the story contains words which represent iconic characters which have been metaphorised: the disease is symbolic of the silent prejudice and social alienation Kenny encountered as a young woman; the child personifies the absurdity of the random of human suffering; the parents are symbolic of the powerlessness of individuals faced with an existential threat; the doctor represents society's disregard for nonconformity; and the young nurse represents Kenny's realization that she was alone in choosing how to act authentically. This analysis of the discovery story demonstrates the ability of metaphorical icons to represent reality beyond the literal representation in the narrative. In this sense, the discovery story may be understood as being metaphorical because the vicissitudes of Kenny's lived experience are symbolically condensed to create a novel perspective on reality which the audience can appreciate.

Method as metaphor

Kenny produced the discovery story in the final decade of her life, during a period of reflection on her life achievements,[318] but there are recurring themes in her extant autobiographical writing which indicate the centrality of metaphor in her evolving conceptualization of her method of treating polio patients. My exhaustive but nonetheless selective reading of the corpus which Kenny produced between 1934 and her death in 1952 suggests there are systematic metaphors which shaped Kenny's practice and her conceptualization of polio.

The term systematic metaphor is used in the generic sense to describe a group of metaphors which can be recognized as sharing a collective meaning or forming a recognizable pattern.[319] Identifying systematic metaphors in a discourse on a topic provides an insight into the way a speaker or writer conceptualizes the world, and allows us to *'draw inferences about their thoughts and feelings, their conceptualizations and communicative intentions, from the language they used'*.[320] The systematic metaphors which I conclude are associated with the Kenny method are: method as revelation, method as liberation, and method as transformation. The entailments of these metaphors are set out in table 5.

The method as revelation metaphor is simultaneously the most ubiquitous and the most complex of the method metaphors. Examples of this metaphor emerge in the earliest commentary on her clinic in Townsville in 1934 and remains prominent throughout the 1940s in her press statements, autobiographical, and technical publications. The revelatory nature of the method is communicated through the act of revealing her unique and original knowledge of the disease to unsuspecting health officials and incredulous medical practitioners, and her confidence that the superior efficacy of her techniques would be self-evident through the act of observing her therapy being administered. As she frequently stated – *'Believe what you see with your own eyes'*.[321]

Kenny appears so convinced of the entailment between seeing and knowing that a chapter in her memoir, in which she castigates the medical profession for refusing to accept the visible improvement in her patients' condition, is given the title *Eyes have they but they see not*. In her posthumously published second memoir she uses familiar words:

> *The conditions present in the tissues were not those which were recognized throughout the medical world*
> *Where medicine saw strong normal muscles pulling against weak affected ones, I saw tightened, shortened structures pulling against weak affected ones.*
> *Where medicine saw a loose, flaccid paralyzed muscle, I saw one whose activity was, in some way, cast aside...*[322]

To enhance the credibility of her claims that the method was superior, Kenny agreed to medical practitioners observing the operation of the Townsville and Brisbane clinics. Her press statements indicate she was confident the visible improvements in her patients' physical function would be acknowledged by these observers. At the same time, she produced several films which she used to demonstrate her techniques to medical practitioners in Australia. To her dismay and irritation, medical practitioners dismissed her films as propaganda, and claimed they saw no evidence of the superiority of her patients' recovery.

The method as revelation metaphor is reflected in Kenny's insistence that her patients believed in the restoration of control of their limbs through an act of faith shared with the therapist. This duality in the belief in recovery by the patient and the therapist placed Kenny in opposition to the assumed passivity of the patient in the traditional nurse/patient and doctor/patient roles. The Kenny method required the patient and the therapist to believe in recovery in a manner which is reminiscent of a shared religious experience. Whilst the repetitive application of hot packs is the signature characteristic of Kenny's method, the symbolism of this ritualized behavior has not previously been recognized. Viewing the process as a performative metaphor enables the method to be understood in the context of a wider metaphor of healing through faith.

Table 5. Systematic metaphors of Kenny's therapy

Metaphor	Entailments and implications
Method as revelation	<ul><li>Seeing is knowing.</li><li>Truth is revealed.</li><li>Knowledge requires faith.</li></ul>
Method as liberation	<ul><li>The method frees the body from the physical constraints of orthodox practice.</li><li>The method frees the practitioner from the constraints of orthodox thinking.</li><li>The method frees the body from the constraints of the illness.</li></ul>
Method as transformation	<ul><li>The patient is transformed from a state of imperfection to a state of perfection.</li><li>The method gives purpose to the practitioner.</li></ul>

The method as revelation metaphor is strengthened during the 1940s by Kenny capitalizing on the misconception in the United States that she was a member of a religious order. In magazine articles which she authored or exerted editorial control she is referred to as the *'healer from the outback'* and reported as having *'God as her doctor'*. The message to the American audience was that her knowledge of polio and her mission to reveal the superiority of her method was guided by an authority higher than science. The framing of Kenny's story within a divinity narrative has received little attention in the literature, but it did not go altogether unnoticed. The American sociologist JE Hulett observed in 1945 that the widespread acceptance of Kenny's claims of the superiority of her techniques was based on her ability to use language which framed her concept of polio as a divine revelation,[323] but the significance of Hulett's observation remained virtually unrecognized in the polio corpus.

At an elementary level, the narration of Kenny's method aligns with the widely recognized entailments of the medicine is war metaphor: illness attacks the body; doctors use technology to fight disease; the war with disease inevitably involves sacrifice and privation. The medicine is war metaphor also implies that there are multiple potential outcomes of warfare: defeat, truce, or liberation. Of these outcomes the method as liberation metaphor has an importance resonance with the Kenny method. Crucially, the method as liberation metaphor provides an explanation for the most enigmatic and fiercely contested feature of the Kenny method – her abandonment of prolonged immobilisation of paralyzed limbs. The use of immobilisation to correct deformity and promote healing was hegemonic in the treatment all forms of paralysis in the early twentieth century, yet Kenny abandoned conventional immobilisation for no apparent reason.[324] Kenny's insistence that recovery was aided by removing splints and casts attracted entrenched opposition from medical practitioners in Australia, America, and the United Kingdom, but may have underpinned support from patients and their families for her techniques. The Australian nurse, Edith Hall, speaks passionately about loneliness and isolation imposed on children by the constraints of conventional care,[325] and the memoirs of polio survivors are redolent with descriptions of the psychological and physical liberation of being treated with Kenny's method. Hall argues that Kenny's approach was liberating because it literally freed the patient's body from the imprisonment of orthodox therapy.

The families of polio patients also found liberation in Kenny's conceptualization of polio and its treatment. Kenny's approach to therapy gave families a sense of hope and a sense of control, as the Kenny method involved visible and repetitive actions which would lead to recovery, rather than the imposed passivity of conventional treatment. Kenny shifted the focus away from the medical fascination with the action of the virus, to a new focus on rehabilitation and the patient's ownership of healing through cooperation and belief in recovery.

The method as liberation metaphor is also recognizable in narratives which portray the liberation of the practitioner from the constraints of orthodox thinking. Kenny believed her method could only be understood if medical practitioners and nurses abandoned preconceptions of the disease which had been imposed by their formal training. Kenny's insistence that medical practitioners must purge themselves of ingrained prejudice to allow her truth to be revealed is viewed by Hulett as further evidence of her role as a charismatic cult leader. Hulett's interpretation of Kenny's behavior is insightful as she made no apology for insisting that her trainee technicians were undergoing a process of indoctrination and initiation.[326] To her own detriment she failed to recognize that many potential trainees were not persuaded to become one of her novitiates.[327]

The concept that the patient is transformed from a state of disorder to a state of order through the therapeutic process is prominent in all of Kenny's treatment and discovery narratives. This metaphor of method as transformation is strongly aligned with the entailments associated with wider metaphors of illness and disease: polio produces mayhem within the body; recovery requires the restoration of order and control; recovery is achieved through self-discipline; recovery requires re-education of alienated muscles. Kenny's avoidance of the word *cure* to describe a patient's recovery from polio has been interpreted as semantic pedantry, but neither cure nor recovery is consistent with the concept of the method as transformation. The entailment of the method as transformation metaphor is that a person stricken with polio has their homeostasis disrupted. Kenny's treatment transforms the person into a new state of homeostasis which enables them to live an approximation of a normal life, thus making the concept of recovery redundant.

The method as transformation metaphor also incorporates the recurrent narrative that the method bestows a purpose on the practitioner. Rather than sitting passively in witness to the misery of children, practitioners of Kenny's method are given a gift which will enable them to '*dedicate the labor of their hands and the devotion of their hearts to the end that healing may be brought to the suffering children of every land, of every creed, and of every race*'.[328] Kenny's words suggest she believed that the life of the practitioner of her method would be transformed as hers had once been:

> '*As dawn broke on that far-off day and the rays of the rising sun shone upon the mountain tops, I received a message which altered the whole course of my existence and set my feet upon the thorny path which I have trod for forty years.*'[329]

Kenny's long journey was, of course, metaphorical as her polio career was less than twenty years in duration. Nonetheless, debunking the literal accuracy of her words is not the primary point of this analysis. As Fiumara observes, '*the boundary between the poetic use and the heuristic use (of metaphor) must ultimately remain vague*'.[330] My appraisal of Kenny's use of metaphorical language, and the representation of systematic metaphors within the conceptualization of her method, is intended to elicit an understanding of the way Kenny conceptualized her method and conceptualized her world. The extent to which Kenny possessed an insight into her metaphorical portrayal of her method, and her metaphorical portrayal of her discovery of her method, is impossible to know. Kenny frequently griped about the curiosity displayed towards her personal life, claiming '*the work*' was all that mattered,[331] but others observed that her method was confined to her personal relationship with each of her patients – in other words, *she* was the work. Most importantly, the exploration of the role of metaphor in Kenny's conceptualization of polio and her work offers an insight into the inseparability of scientific enquiry and the lived experience of the individual person.

Conclusion

This chapter presents the findings of an analysis of two stories which

Kenny narrated during her lifetime. The analysis shows the invention story and the discovery story are problem-resolution personal experience narratives with shared plot structures and narrative functions. Both stories predict the author's destiny following life changing events, and both stories use the medium of newspaper reports as their primary mode of dissemination. Both stories are performative in that they enact the truth which they claim to represent. The treatment discovery story, which has universally been considered as a record of an historical event, should properly be interpreted as a narrative which embodies the conceptual and systematic metaphors that communicate Kenny's understanding of the disease and her therapeutic system.

---

[305] See chapter four "Becoming the Mythmaker" in: Dan P. McAdams, *The stories we live by: Personal myths and the making of the self* (New York: Willian Morrow, 1993), pp. 91-115.

[306] Karin Kukkonen, "Plot". In *The living handbook of narratology*, (ed.) Peter Hühn (Hamburg: Hamburg University Press, 2014).

[307] William Labov and Joshua Waletzky, "Narrative Analysis: oral versions of personal experience", in *Essays on the verbal and visual arts: proceedings of the 1966 annual spring meeting of the American Ethnological Society*, (ed.) June Helm (University of Washington Press, 1967), pp. 12-44.

[308] Shaul Shenhav, *Analyzing Social Narratives* (New York: Routledge, 2015).

[309] Shaul Shenhav, "Reply" in Ronald R. Krebs, Michael D. Jones, Myron J. Aronoff and Shaul Shenhav SR, "Review Symposium: Analysing Social Narratives", *European Political Science* vol. 16, no. 4, (2017), pp. 577–589.

[310] "Boon to Sufferers", *Daily Standard*, p.8

[311] Kenny and Ostenson, *And They Shall Walk*, pp. 74-75.

[312] Typed manuscript inscribed 3-8-50, 143.E.10.3B EKP-MHS.

[313] O'Malley, "*Bush nurse*".

[314] Myron J. Aronoff, "Narratives and multiplicity" in Ronald R. Krebs, Michael D. Jones, Myron J. Aronoff and Shaul Shenhav SR, "Review Symposium: Analysing Social Narratives", *European Political Science* vol. 16, no. 4, (2017), pp. 577–589.

[315] For an appraisal of iconic metaphor see: George H. Taylor, "The Phenomenological Contributions of Ricoeur's Philosophy of Imagination", in *Social Imaginaries vol. 1, Issue 2*, (ed.) Jeremy Smith and Suzi Adams, (Bucharest: Zeta Books, 2015), pp. 13-31.

[316] Saulius Geniusas, "Between Phenomenology and Hermeneutics: Paul Ricoeur's Philosophy of Imagination", *Human Studies* vol. 38, no. 2, (2014), pp. 223-241.

[317] See "Connections between language and life" in Gemma C. Fiumara, *The metaphoric process: Connections between language and life* (London: Routledge, 1995), pp. 1-12.

[318] Extant handwritten drafts of the memoir show that she began writing about her early adult experiences soon after arriving in the United States in 1940.

[319] This definition of systematic metaphor is proposed in Robert Maslen, "Finding

systematic metaphors" in *The Routledge Handbook of Metaphor and Language*, Elena Semino and Zsófia Demjén (ed.) (Abingdon: Routledge, 2017). The term systematic metaphor is also used to describe the process of systematic metaphor analysis – a schema for analysing metaphors within discourse analysis.

[320] Maslen, *Systematic metaphor*, p. 89.

[321] "Kenny Institute Beacon of Hope to Polio Victims), *Washington Times-Herald*, September 3, 1944.

[322] Kenny, *My Battle and Victory*, pp. 18-19.

[323] Hulett, *Kenny Healing Cult*, p. 366.

[324] Her abandonment of conventional immobilisation is discussed in chapter three.

[325] Hall, *In the ward*.

[326] Kenny first reported her dissatisfaction with nurses who refused to relinquish their orthodox views when she was defending her inability to train technicians in Townsville in 1934. She used the terms indoctrination and initiation to describe her training in autobiographical publications throughout the 1940s.

[327] Kenny only managed to train twelve technicians in the first seven years she worked in Minneapolis despite the investment of hundreds of thousands of dollars by the NFIP and Kenny's own fundraising for the Elizabeth Kenny Institute. Levine, *I knew Sister Kenny*, p. 65.

[328] Kenny and Ostenso, *And They Shall Walk*, p. 281. Kenny repeatedly used the term gift to describe her method and her invention of the Sylvia Stretcher.

[329] Kenny, *My Battle*, p. 15.

[330] Fiumara, *Metaphoric process*, p. 12.

[331] Kenny used the term *the work* as a catch all phrase to describe her campaign to disseminate the use of her therapy.

6. REWRITING THE LEGEND

In this final chapter I will show that Kenny's discovery story works as a narrative glue which binds together the disconnected phases of Kenny's life and her episodic habitation of the heterotopia of the clinic to provide an illusion of continuity to her disconnected life. I will also show how the credibility of the story is bolstered by its conformity with persuasive and compelling cultural tropes which appealed to its American audience, and the portrayal of idealized characters who were universally recognized as metaphorical icons. Finally, I will show how the widespread acceptance of the story as a factual representation of her discovery may have inadvertently undermined the scientific credibility of the method, thereby easing the incorporation of her techniques into conventional medical care.

A narrated life

The analysis presented in the previous chapter shows the invention story and the discovery story are problem-resolution personal experience narratives which share a common plot structure and narrative function. Both stories predict the author's destiny following life changing events, and both stories use the medium of newspaper reports as their primary mode of dissemination. Crucially, both stories are performative in that they enact the truth which they claim to represent, even if the veracity of the event are open to dispute. Nonetheless, as William Labov wisely observes; *'tall tales, myths and outright lies'* never stood in the way of a good story.[332]

These stories are also linked by their contribution to the personal myth which Kenny was authoring. Dan McAdams, who had no apparent knowledge of Kenny, could be writing the dust cover of her life story when he describes the plot of a romantic myth.

> *We embark on a long and difficult journey in life in which circumstances constantly change and new challenges continually arise. We must keep changing and moving if we are to win in the end. But we are confident that we will win'*[333]

The discovery story embodies the culmination of Kenny's personal myth; a myth which defines her identity, illuminates her values, and embodies her personal truth. The idea of creating a personal myth should not be interpreted as an exercise in narcissism, rather it should be understood as a commonplace product of an individual's quest for the meaning of their existence. In this context Dan McAdams argues that a personal myth may be endowed with noble and enabling qualities. Crucially, McAdam's concept of the purpose of stories in building a personal myth over a lifespan, and the process by which they are embedded in our lives, provides a mechanism for explaining the reciprocity between the individual and the society in which they live. Further, the mythic tone of the stories which we hear throughout childhood and in our youth, creates a predisposing framework for understanding the events which shape our lives, and provides a template for telling the stories which communicate our existential search for meaning. Whether or not Kenny consciously chose a mythic form for the discovery story is a matter of conjecture; but I believe there can be little doubt that her audience understood its underlying truth – something great and noble occurred in a remote farmhouse in rural Australia.

No life is narrated through a single mythical form. Whilst the romantic tone is dominant in Kenny's telling of her life story, the narrative also presents her as a tragic heroine whose quest is thwarted by the indifference and the vanity of her antagonists. Early iterations of the discovery story emphasize the romance of the Australian bush, and the plucky inventiveness of the young nurse bringing hope to a sick child. Later iterations, typified in the film *Sister Kenny*, accentuate the personal cost of her battle with medical orthodoxy. The final iteration, published posthumously in 1955, was written while she was experiencing the depressive symptoms of advanced Parkinson's Disease. The tone of her final attempt to present her life story is melancholic and tinged with bitterness that her gift to mankind had not been universally applauded.

> *The sun is low on the horizon and I am also nearing life's sunset.*
> *Looking back on the stormy years that have passed, I am ever grateful*
> *that a kindly Providence endowed me with a tenacity of purpose that led*
> *me to hold on to my beliefs until they had been placed in the hands of*
> *those members of the medical profession with the mind and heart of the*
> *true physician, who will use this knowledge for the benefit of humanity.*[334]

The stories which Kenny told of her invention and discovery integrate her knowledge of rehabilitation, incrementally accumulated over a period of decades, with her emerging self-conception of her identity as a nurse, within the context of the personal myth which gave her life purpose and meaning. Conventional analysis of the Kenny treatment controversy has relied on the assumption of narrative objectivity in the discovery story to guide the interpretation and analysis of Kenny's approach to the treatment of poliomyelitis, as if her stories were akin to a photographic record of the events. The detailed analyses of the invention story and discovery story presented in chapter five is not designed to simply denounce their factitiousness, rather, it liberates them from the constraints of the tradition of empiricism as the highest source of knowledge. The power of the stories which Kenny authored lies not in the objective facts or events they purport to depict; it stems from our interpretation and understanding of the meaning of the stories.

The stories which Elizabeth Kenny told about her life are part of her life. As George Rosenwald and Richard Ochberg succinctly conclude '*what is told and what is lived promote each other*'.[335] This beguilingly simple statement represents a complex proposition which has great resonance for the role of the discovery story in Kenny's life. Rosenwald claims that the life stories which people tell are only comprehensible when those stories have a meaning, or '*intelligibility*' which is understood within their culture.[336] Therefore, stories which conform to prevailing cultural norms are recognized as being sensible, and those which do not are either disregarded or rejected as being implausible. Kenny's formulation of her discovery story incorporated fragments of personal experience organized by a narrative of discovery which reflected a known social role and resonated with the persona which Kenny presented to her American audience. The refinement of the recorded narrative which is evident in the newspaper articles is a product of the acceptance and reinforcement of the credibility of the story by the positive response of the American audience.

The credibility of the discovery story also derives from its quality as an idealized representation of characters, rituals, and relationships within a heterotopic setting. In the story, idealized characters – Kenny, the child, the doctor, and the parents – inhabit a real, but heterotopic, construction of a past which is both alien and familiar to the audience. The arcane rural landscape, whilst not an obvious place of deviance, is the location of a disruptive revelation which will change the natural order outside the heterotopic setting. The discovery story aligns with Foucault's categorization of a heterotopia of crisis – a place where individuals are brought together by an imposed crisis rather than a shared characteristic or interest. The heterotopia portrayed in the story is stripped of artifice and technology, making it timeless and recognizable at the same time. The audience, once drawn into the idealized space, can imagine themselves joining in the rituals and sharing in the experiences of the inhabitants, and imagine the possibility of recovery in the real world.

The longevity of the Kenny discovery story suggests that it embodies a narrative which had the capacity to resonate far beyond the needs and interests of a polio weary American public. The discovery story has in fact outlived the memory of the storyteller and the disease which inhabits the core of the story. In essence, the discovery story has achieved a life of its own and is an example of the capacity a story to possess its own agency, or, in the words of Arthur Frank, to become an *actor* possessing its own capacities and capable of working with humans to enable social relations.[337]

The extent to which the discovery story has overshadowed the contribution Kenny made to the development of rehabilitation therapy can be demonstrated through the following personal anecdote. In 2014 I was contacted by Susan Latta, a writer based in Minneapolis, who was seeking advice on obtaining historical records which would assist her to write a biography of Sister Kenny for an intended audience of young people. Susan explained she was concerned that the current generation of young people were unaware of the work of '*a great lady*'.[338] I provided Susan with some bibliographic recommendations and a copy of a conference paper I had written for a history of medicine conference. The paper included a discussion of the absence of evidence to corroborate the alleged discovery in 1911. Two weeks later Susan contacted me again to express her dismay at learning that the story of the discovery was a '*falsehood*', and stating she was struggling to imagine how she could convey this to children. Susan rightly observed that it would be difficult to discuss the significance of Kenny's work without reference to the story as it made such a good '*jumping off point*'. I replied with an assurance that my analysis of the available evidence was open to challenge by other researchers and should not be interpreted as an incontrovertible truth. Whilst my assurances were given in the spirit of academic collaboration, the episode was a stark reminder to me of the consequences of questioning the plausibility of a noble reputation.

Arthur Frank argues that a primary capacity of a story is its ability to enact the truth by showing that something new, original, or important has happened with the full significance that the story bestows on it.[339] I believe this is true for Kenny's discovery story, but there is the added dilemma which arises from her need to reveal a truth which, in Frank's words, would '*ring true*', with her need to authenticate her ownership of her therapeutic techniques. In doing so the story has achieved a symbolic meaning which has overshadowed the proper memorialization of its author. The anecdote presented above suggests that the significance of Kenny's contribution to polio rehabilitation continues to be dependent on, or possibly secondary to, the story of its discovery.

Hell is full of good intentions

The meaning of the oft misquoted and misunderstood aphorism *l'enfer est plein de bonnes volontés ou désirs*, or *hell is full of good intentions or desires*, could not be better demonstrated than in the creation of the Kenny discovery myth. The aphorism was originally interpreted as meaning there is no value in good intentions unless they are acted upon, but in the current era it is interpreted as meaning action that is based on illconceived good intentions can lead to perverse or unexpected results. Within months of arriving in

America, Kenny's methods were being adopted by influential medical practitioners in Minneapolis and receiving a cautious endorsement by the NFIP. Nonetheless, many moderate practitioners remained sceptical or unconvinced. With the assistance of her benefactors in Minneapolis, she set to work on the production of her second attempt to explain the principles and methods of her therapeutic system, [340] whilst simultaneously embarking on a public relations campaign to promote her discovery story through the American news media. This two-pronged approach to asserting her credibility, and the credibility of her techniques, seems counterintuitive as there were risks in claiming that the fortuitous application of an arcane home remedy was the foundation of a therapy for a viral illness which had confounded medical science for decades. Would sceptical medical practitioners believe, in the absence of a scientific explanation, that hot rags could promote recovery from infantile paralysis?

There are several factors which may have contributed to Kenny giving prominence in America to her discovery narrative to support her claim to have discovered a new and more effective treatment for polio. Despite her attempt to produce a coherent appraisal of the clinical foundations of her therapeutic techniques in Australia,[341] she had failed to convince a sceptical Australian medical profession through an intellectual argument that her techniques were new or original. Kenny had built her personal credibility as a nurse with knowledge of rehabilitation techniques on her war time nursing experience. Despite her public profile in the Australian news media throughout the 1930s, and the political support for the network of state sponsored clinics which employed her techniques, she failed to produce a consistent narrative which established the originality of her techniques. The Australian medical profession remained resolute in their assertion that her methods lacked originality and produced effects no better than conventional medical practice. It therefore seems likely that Kenny anticipated that in America she would need a pre-emptive riposte to the criticism she faced in Australia that her techniques were not original. Finally, Kenny may have felt encouraged to give prominence to her personal story because America's most successful medical philanthropic organization was under the control of a lawyer, not a doctor, thereby lessening her need to defer to the collective authority of an empowered medical profession.

The purpose of the discovery story

The analysis presented in the previous chapter shows that the personal experience narrative which Kenny presented to the American public was the embodiment of her claim to be the discoverer of a new and original treatment for polio. This narrative rapidly gained traction with the American public for several reasons. First, and foremost, the narrative resonated with the American myth of the self-made man. The expression *the American dream* , coined by James Truslow Adams in his populist history of America, encapsulates the notion that any American – by default male – can achieve success through individual talent, hard work, and discipline or moral conviction. The proposition that any American can aspire to a better, richer, and happier life, builds on the notion of America being an exceptional society uniquely founded on expressive individualism. Kenny's portrayal of herself as a cultural type forged in a frontier land was readily understood by the American public, as was her claim to have overcome adversity through personal sacrifice.

A further factor contributing to the uncritical acceptance of Kenny's discovery narrative was its correspondence with narratives which appraised the existential threats posed by polio, war, and political ideologies to American values and the American way of life. The metaphorical representation of polio as a shadowy threat to the American dream is discussed in the Introduction chapter. America had been at war with polio for over a decade when Kenny brought her campaign to America. Polio was perceived as a subversive threat which infiltrated families – the foundation of the American dream. As Daniel Wilson observes '*the American dream envisioned only healthy children, not ones wearing braces and using wheelchairs*'.[342] Kenny's narrative opportunistically focusses on the response of an individual pioneer nurse to the terror of stricken children and their helpless families, and characterizes institutional responses as remote, ineffective, and obstructive. It locates the battle with the infiltrator directly in the family home, not in laboratories, hospital wards, or medical clinics. The irony of Kenny's portrayal of her noble endeavors in the Australian outback is that the network of clinics which were established in Australia between 1934 and 1939 were entirely the product of the financial and bureaucratic support provided by her political allies. Notwithstanding these inconsistencies, Kenny's narrative enabled and empowered individuals to actively confront their enemy, whereas the narratives of medicine disempowered the victims of the disease and marginalized their families. Ultimately, Kenny's narrative placed her at the core of recovery; anyone wishing to emulate her success would need to adopt her narrative, not simply mimic her methods.

Whilst the immediate purpose of the discovery story was to bolster Kenny's claim of ownership of a new approach to treating polio, the story had the added benefit of consolidating the episodic nature of her nurse identity and her role in the heterotopia of the clinic. In the 1930s Kenny legitimized her nurse identity by claiming she had developed her concepts and methods during her war time nursing experience. In the 1940s the discovery story confirmed her nurse identity in the pre-WW1 years. Establishing an uninterrupted nursing career over an extended period fulfilled several needs. First, affirming that she was a nurse in a remote area prior to the war helped to explain her marital status, having forsaken personal happiness for her career. Second, affirming she was a nurse prior to WW1 bestowed her life with greater nobility as nursing was more vocation than profession in the pre-war era. Third, aligning her personal identity as a youth with a recognizable historical nursing identity enhanced her credibility as a nurse with an American audience as her behavior and appearance did not match the conventional view of nursing in an advanced industrial economy. Finally, the story provided a narrative glue which gave continuity to the disconnected phases of her habitation of the clinic.

There were clear material benefits to Kenny framing the origin of her nurse identity in this way, but it remains difficult to ascertain the extent to which the story was knowingly shaped by her existential choices. The narrative ends with a call by the narrator for the reader to empathize with the consequences of her fateful encounter, but the reference to the rugged path ahead is superfluous to the core purpose of the story. The addition of these references to the struggles she endured in her quest for recognition reveals more about Kenny than she may have intended. Kenny's words suggest that near the end of her life she may have been struggling with the authenticity of the nurse identity she had constructed throughout her adult life.

Outwardly, Kenny projected the image that she had crafted her authentic identity through choices which were rational and consistent with accepted social roles for women of her generation. These choices included: choosing nursing as a career; acting patriotically in enlisting in the AANS; devoting her energies to the CWA; offering her therapeutic system for no personal reward. In making these choices she gave the impression that she had demonstrated her commitment to live her life in accordance with her freedom to act rather than follow a path which she was expected to pursue; thereby exemplifying Sartre's declaration that *existence precedes essence*. The introduction of elements into the discovery story which imply her destiny had been predetermined by a random event is therefore a contradiction to the narrative which she had disseminated in Australia throughout the 1930s. The conflicting messages in the discovery story suggest that Kenny may have been experiencing angst with respect to the existential choices she had made during her life. It appears that in the final decade of her life Kenny doubted the choices she had made in her attempt to resolve her need for public acceptance and endorsement, and her desire for freedom from societal constraints. Perhaps the leap of faith she displayed when she donned her nurse's cape in 1911 was the ultimate expression of succumbing to the safety of the herd rather than a rejection of it.

Unintended consequences

Despite the instrumentality of the story in demarcating Kenny's ownership of her techniques and defining her identity as a nurse it was a sword with two edges. The story provided a narrative which framed the method as being discovered by an individual rather than being developed through a process. In other words, there was an empirical basis to her discovery which was unadulterated by orthodox beliefs or theories. Unlike medical practitioners, who responded to the known pathology of polio, Kenny treated the observed paralysis regardless of its underlying pathology. This approach shielded her from the criticism she had received when she made her first attempt in 1937 to communicate her treatment regime.

The simplicity of the discovery story undoubtedly enabled its dissemination through the print media, but it may have coincidentally undermined her accompanying objective to maintain control over the use of her techniques by other health care professions. Kenny claimed she developed her method through intuition guided by divine inspiration whilst insisting it could only be properly learned through two years of tuition. The tension between these conflicting positions exposed her to criticism which ultimately was her undoing in America. Kenny claimed that her techniques were difficult to learn yet the definitive summary of her treatment regime, a twenty-nine pages pamphlet published by the NFIP in 1945, *A Guide for Nurses in the Nursing Care of Patients with Infantile Paralysis*, provides a more detailed and useful description of the treatment of spasm than Kenny managed to produce in her twenty years career as a polio therapist.

I believe there could be no better example of the law of unintended consequences than the case of Kenny's invention of her discovery story. The appropriation and adoption of Kenny's ideas and practices by medical practitioners has often been framed as a form of medical plagiarism, but I believe Kenny was responsible for creating the context which allowed this appropriation to occur. In claiming her discovery occurred '*not in the Halls of Science, but in the remote bush land of Australia*' she simultaneously claimed the discovery as her own and trivialized its scientific credibility. Her final memoir, published posthumously, provides no indication she understood that the more convincing the story became the easier it was for the medical profession to adopt her ideas and practices while continuing with their own narrative which prioritized the importance of science in defeating the root cause of the disease.

Rewriting the Kenny legend

For many years I have maintained a deep conviction to rewrite the memorialization of Elizabeth Kenny. As much as I respect her achievements in her lifetime, and her legacy as a pioneer in the field of rehabilitation, I believe her legacy can only truly be understood if she is properly remembered in her entirety as a person, and not as the fictional character which she sought to portray to the world. I sincerely hope that the person who emerges in this book is far more complex and nuanced than the two-dimensional character commonly portrayed in the historical record, or, indeed, fashioned in her own biographical record. Kenny inhabited multiple discontinuous identities throughout her adult life – entrepreneur, nurse, inventor, healer, therapist, and scientist – as she pursued social status and personal autonomy, and as she sought to avoid stigmatization. I offer no apology for demolishing the myth of Kenny as an asexual, quasi-religious, figure who relinquished personal happiness to dedicate her life to the care of children. I believe the real Elizabeth Kenny was a woman who preferred intimacy with women and struggled to conceal discredited characteristics. Whilst there is no direct evidence that Elizabeth Kenny understood or sought to inhabit an idealized lesbian identity, her behavior, previously dismissed as idiosyncratic or defensive, suggests she was aware of the stigma associated with the incongruence between prevailing social norms and her preference for same sex intimacies.

Elizabeth Kenny should properly be remembered as a woman who achieved unprecedented international fame and forged an identity through improvisation, ingenuity, creativity, deception, and concealment, in an era where societal structures subjugated women. Kenny achieved material success and social status without the benefit of financial resources or education but demonstrated none of the altruism or nobility which she sought to portray in later life. Kenny's relegation to the status of an arcane historical curiosity within a decade of her death is testament to the systemic sexism which forgives the frailties of men but demands perfection from women.

Two stories shaped the course of Kenny's life. One acted as the template for the narration of her identity; one became her legacy. This legacy, memorialized in print and film, and venerated until the present day, is a misrepresentation of Kenny's life, but perhaps more importantly, it is a distraction from our proper understanding of the existential foundation of the therapeutic system which bears her name. In this book I have consistently argued that the stories which are synonymous with Kenny's life have universally been interpreted as reports of psychic or experiential reality, whereas they should be understood as personal identity narratives which verify the authenticity of her existential identity. The polio treatment discovery story, one of the great medical legends of the twentieth century, should be understood as a problem resolution personal experience narrative which embodies Kenny's experiences of social stigmatization, her metaphorical understanding of polio, and her quest for a socially sanctioned personal identity.

Notwithstanding my earlier statement of my respect for Kenny's legacy,

I would like to offer my verdict on the legacy for which she should be
remembered and applauded. I believe Kenny should be remembered for
demonstrating that the development of medical knowledge cannot solely be
understood through the examination of a depersonalized scientific method,
it also needs to be understood through an appreciation of the existential
and ethical choices, be they noble or flawed, which shape the individual's
scientific endeavors. I believe Kenny's conceptualization of polio and her
therapeutic system offers a unique insight into the interdigitation between
scientific enquiry and the existential quest of an individual person and
demonstrates the validity of the proposition that the narratives through
which we identify ourselves with others are inextricably linked to public
achievements. Elizabeth Kenny invented her method of treating
poliomyelitis, but more importantly, I would like her to be remembered as
the woman who invented herself.

---

[332] Labov, *Further steps*, p. 397.

[333] McAdams, *Stories we live by*, p. 51

[334] Kenny, *My Battle and Victory*, p. 124.

[335] George C. Rosenwald and Richard L. Ochberg, *Storied Lives*. (New Haven: Yale University Press, 1992), p.8

[336] Rosenwald and Ochberg, *Storied Lives*, p. 265.

[337] Arthur Frank, *Letting stories breather: A socionarratology* (London: The University of Chicago Press, 2010) p. 13.

[338] Susan Latta, personal communication to author, 2 Feb – 4 March 2014.

[339] Frank, *Letting Stories Breathe*, p. 40

[340] Elizabeth Kenny, *The Treatment of Infantile Paralysis in the Acute Stage* (Minneapolis: Bruce Publishing Company, 1941).

[341] Elizabeth Kenny, *Infantile paralysis and cerebral diplegia: methods used for the restoration of function* (Sydney: Angus and Robertson, 1937).

[342] Daniel J. Wilson, Living with Polio: The epidemic and its survivors, (Chicago: University of Chicago Press, 2007), p. 17.

BIBLIOGRAPHY

The following publications have informed my research and thinking over the past twenty years. The grouping does not necessarily represent the intention of the authors.

Biographies and Autobiographies

Alexander, Wade. Sister Elizabeth Kenny. Rockhampton: Central Queensland University Press,

Cohn, Victor. Sister Kenny The Woman Who Challenged The Doctors. Minneapolis: The University of Minneapolis Press, 1975.

Finger, Anne. Elegy for a disease: A personal and cultural history of polio. New York: St Martin's Press, 2006.

Gould, Tony. A Summer Plague. New Haven: Yale University Press, 1995.

Kenny, Elizabeth, and Martha Ostenso. And They Shall Walk. Minneapolis: Dodd, Mead & Company, 1943.

Mee, Charles L. A nearly normal life. Boston: Little, Brown and Company, 1999.

Shell, Marc. Polio and its aftermath. Cambridge: Harvard University Press, 2005.

Wilson, Daniel J. Living with Polio: The epidemic and its survivors. Chicago: University of Chicago Press, 2007.

Wilson, John R. Through Kenny's Eyes: An exploration of Sister Elizabeth Kenny's views about nursing. James Cook University of North Queensland, 1995.

Polio

Cumpston, John Howard Lidgett. "Health and disease in Australia: a history", Milton Lewis (ed.), Canberra: AGPS, 1989.

Highley, Kerry. Dancing in my dreams. Melbourne: Monash University Publishing, 2015.

Patrick, Ross. A history of health and medicine in Queensland 1824-1960.

St Lucia: QUP, 1987.

Paul, John R. A history of poliomyelitis. London: Yale University Press, 1971.

Robbins, Frederick C., and Thomas M Daniel (ed.). Polio. Rochester: University of Rochester Press, 1997.

Rogers, Naomi. Dirt and Disease: polio before FDR. New Brunswick: Rutgers University Press, 1992.

Rogers, Naomi. Polio Wars. New York: Oxford University Press, 2014.

Homosexuality and Homophobia

Doan, Laura. Disturbing Practices: history, sexuality, and women's experience of modern war. Chicago: University of Chicago Press, 2013.

Doan, Laura. Fashioning Sapphism: The Origins of a Modern English Lesbian Culture. New York: Columbia University Press, 2000.

Duberman, George, Martha Vicinus and Martin Chauncey, (ed.) Hidden from History. New York: NAL Books, 1989.

Faderman, Lillian. Odd Girls and Twilight Lovers: A History of Lesbian Life in Twentieth-Century America. Harmondsworth: Penguin Publishers, 1991.

Goffman, Erving. Stigma: notes on the management of spoiled identity. London: Penguin Books, 1963.

Jennings, Rebecca. A Lesbian History of Britain. Oxford: Greenwood World Publishing, 2007.

Marcus, Eric. Making History: The struggle for gay and lesbian equal rights. New York: Harper Collins, 1992.

Miller, Neil. Out of the past. New York: Vintage Books, 1995.

Plummer, David. One of the boys: masculinity, homophobia and modern manhood. Binghamton: Harrington Park Press, 1999.

War Nursing and Nursing History

Burchill, Elizabeth. Australian nurses since Nightingale. Richmond: Spectrum Publications, 1992.

Butler, Arthur G. Official History of the Australian Army Medical Services, 1914–1918 Vol. 1 – Gallipoli, Palestine and New Guinea, 1938.

Butler, Arthur G. Official History of the Australian Army Medical Services,

1914–1918 Volume 3, 1943.

Fell, Alison S. and Christine E. Hallett (ed.). First World War Nursing: New perspectives. Abingdon: Routledge, 2013.

Harris, Kirsty. More Than Bombs and Bandages: Australian Army Nurses at Work in World War 1. Newport: Big Sky Publishing, 2011.

Rae, Ruth. Scarlet Poppies: The army experience of Australian nurses during World War One. Burwood: College of Nursing, 2004.

Schultz, Beverly. A Tapestry of Service: The evolution of nursing in Australia. Melbourne: Churchill Livingstone, 1991.

Storytelling and Narrative analysis

Frank, Arthur W. Letting stories breather: A socionarratology. London: The University of Chicago Press, 2010.

Gubrium, Jaber F., and James A. Holstein. Analyzing narrative reality. Thousand Oaks: Sage Publications, 2009.

Hardcastle, Virginia G. Constructing the Self. Philadelphia: John Benjamins Publishing Company, 2008.

Holstein, James A., and Jaber F. Gubrium (ed.) Varieties of narrative analysis. London: Sage Publications, 2012.

Holstein, James A., and Jaber F. Gubrium. The Self We Live By: Narrative Identity in a Postmodern World. Oxford: Oxford University Press, 2000.

Knowles, Murray, and Rosamund Moon. Introducing metaphor. Milton Park: Routledge, 2006.

Lakoff, George, and Mark Johnson. Metaphors we live by. Chicago: University of Chicago Press, 1980.

McAdams, Dan P. The stories we live by: Personal myths and the making of the self. New York: Willian Morrow, 1993.

Renders, Hans, and Binne de Haan, Jonne Harmsa (ed.). The Biographical Turn: Lives in History. London: Routledge, 2016.

Shenhav, Saul. Analyzing Social Narratives. New York: Routledge, 2015.

ABOUT THE AUTHOR

Allan Hildon was born in Australia. He belongs to the first generation of Australian children to receive the Salk polio vaccine. Allan worked in higher education and health care for close to forty years. For the past twenty years he has lived in the UK. Allan holds a Bachelor's degree in Nursing from the University of New England, a Master's degree in Public Health from the University of Sydney, and a PhD in Sociology from the University of Essex. He lives with his civil partner in a garden in rural Suffolk.

Made in the USA
Monee, IL
07 July 2026